I0128418

State Power and Governance
in Early Imperial China

SUNY series in Chinese Philosophy and Culture
_____
Roger T. Ames, editor

State Power and Governance in Early Imperial China

The Collapse of the Qin Empire, 221–207 BCE

CHUN FUNG TONG

SUNY
PRESS

Cover art: Qin terracotta acrobat. Museum at Qin Shihuang Mausoleum, Lintong District, Xian, China. Photograph by Gary Todd.

Published by State University of New York Press, Albany

© 2024 State University of New York

All rights reserved

Printed in the United States of America

No part of this book may be used or reproduced in any manner whatsoever without written permission. No part of this book may be stored in a retrieval system or transmitted in any form or by any means including electronic, electrostatic, magnetic tape, mechanical, photocopying, recording, or otherwise without the prior permission in writing of the publisher.

Links to third-party websites are provided as a convenience and for informational purposes only. They do not constitute an endorsement or an approval of any of the products, services, or opinions of the organization, companies, or individuals. SUNY Press bears no responsibility for the accuracy, legality, or content of a URL, the external website, or for that of subsequent websites.

For information, contact State University of New York Press, Albany, NY
www.sunypress.edu

Library of Congress Cataloging-in-Publication Data

Name: Tong, Chun Fung, author.
Title: State power and governance in early Imperial China : The collapse of the Qin Empire, 221–207 BCE / Chun Fung Tong
Description: Albany : State University of New York Press, [2024] | Series: SUNY series in Chinese Philosophy and Culture | Includes bibliographical references and index.
Identifiers: ISBN 9781438499376 (hardcover : alk. paper) | ISBN 9781438499390 (ebook) | ISBN 9781438499383 (pbk. : alk. paper)
Further information is available at the Library of Congress.

To my parents

Contents

Illustrations

Figures

Tables

Maps

Acknowledgments

This book is developed from the dissertation—with the title "Fall of an Empire: State Power and Governance of the Qin Empire"—that I submitted to Heidelberg University in September 2020. The idea of writing something on the governance and collapse of the Qin Empire emerged about ten years ago, when I ran into the then newly published volume one of the Liye manuscripts at a reading group organized by Professor Lai Ming Chiu 黎明釗 at the Chinese University of Hong Kong. In it I first realized that the rule of the Qin Empire in the new territories suffered gravely from various challenges and was far from impeccable.

However, it was not until I went to Heidelberg to pursue my doctoral studies that I gradually set this crude idea into motion. At Heidelberg, I enjoy some of the best academic environments imaginable: a picturesque cityscape and warm-hearted colleagues, and in particular Professor Enno Giele, who, with his continued support, encouragement, and guidance, is an ideal doctoral advisor for a young scholar. From him I learned not only the rigorous attitude of traditional Sinology toward primary sources but also the integrity of being a scholar. I will always remember the energized, strenuous discussions we had on sharpening and refining the arguments and structure of this book. A big, sincere thank also goes to Professor Li Feng of Columbia University, who kindly agreed to serve as my dissertation's second adviser. Despite joining this project relatively late, Professor Li meticulously read the whole manuscript and gave numerous incisive remarks on the work's framework, organization, and content. In addition, this book immensely benefits from the many stimulating intellectual exchanges that I have had with Maxim Korolkov, Qu Jian 瞿見, Thies Staack, Sun Hui 孫慧, Paul Nicholas Vogt, and Jeanette Werning during our internal colloquia, lunch breaks, and hallway conversations.

The insights and erudition of all these people helped shape this book into its current form.

Beyond Heidelberg, I would like to express my gratitude to Professor Lai Ming Chiu, who introduced me the way of studying unearthed manuscripts and kept acting as a mentor throughout these years, and to Professors Hsing I-tien 邢義田, Ulrich Lau, and Robin Yates, whose erudition and advice serve as a constant source of inspiration. I am also grateful to Professor Chen Wei 陳偉, who kindly invited me to visit the Center for the Study of Bamboo and Silk Manuscripts at Wuhan University, where I spent a fruitful and memorable three months between September and November 2017.

As someone working on manuscript sources, I am especially indebted to Zhang Chunlong 張春龍 and Yang Xianyun 楊先雲 of the Hunan Institute of Cultural Relics and Archaeology for their hospitality when I came and examined the materials stored in their institution. I must also extend my thanks to Huang Haobo 黃浩波, Li Zhimo 李知默, Ma Tsang Wing 馬增榮, and Song Huaqiang 宋華強 for their tireless help in supplying relevant literature whenever I needed the most, as well as to Kwok Man Tak 郭文德 and Wan Yuk Ping 溫玉冰 for helping me prepare the maps in this book.

The research for this book was financed by the PhD scholarships funded through the Landesgraduiertenförderung (LGF) program, Baden-Württemberg, and the Gerda Henkel Stiftung. Their generous support allowed me to concentrate on my own work, a privilege that should not be taken for granted. I also thank James Peltz and Ryan Morris of SUNY Press, who, among the rest of the production team, have navigated this project through various stages, and the three anonymous readers for their feedback and criticism, which corrected many of my mistakes and prompted me to consider issues that I neglected. James Harbeck, the copyeditor, also deserves praise for acutely pointing out various typos, stylistic inconsistencies, and other language problems in the manuscript. This book would probably never have come out without their help.

A substantial part of this book was finished during the Covid-19 pandemic. For most of that period I was separated from my parents in Hong Kong because of the strict border restrictions instituted by the authorities. My parents always give me their unconditional love and support and no words can adequately express my regret for the times we lost over the past few years. This book is for them.

Conventions

All translations in this book are the author's unless otherwise specified.

The Chinese and Japanese words for "publisher" in literature citations (*chubanshe* 出版社, *shuju* 書局, *shudian* 書店, *shoin* 書院 etc.) are omitted in the bibliography and notes.

A text from standard history (e.g., *Shiji*, *Hanshu*) is cited with its chapter number, together with the name of publisher, the year of publication of the first edition, and the page number. That is, "*Shiji* 史記 (Beijing: Zhonghua, 2014), 48.2371" means page 2371 of chapter 48 of the revised paperback edition of the *Shiji* published by Zhonghua shuju in 2014. The name of the publisher and the year of publication are given only on first citation.

To better represent the material traits of written artifacts, original attention marks (e.g., " · ," " \ ," and "—") are kept in the Chinese transcriptions. Following the present-day editorial convention of early Chinese manuscripts, "☐" indicates an undecipherable character; "☒" indicates a broken piece; "()" indicates a character in modern orthography; "【 】" indicates uncertain but probable transcription; and "……" indicates illegible graphs.

For citations of the Liye manuscripts, their serial numbers always begin with an archaeological stratum of the Liye well no. 1, followed by an individual slip number. For example, "9-1" denotes the first slip of stratum 9. To date, there are two sets of slip numbers for the Liye corpus, namely, the so-called folio number (*zhengli hao* 整理號) and the excavation number (*chutu dengjihao* 出土登記號). I use folio numbers—which are adopted both in the folios published by Wenwu chubanshe and the revised edition prepared by Chen Wei and his team—for manuscripts from strata 5, 6, 8, and 9, whereas pieces from other strata are cited by their excavation numbers.

The alphabetical numbering (e.g., [A]) in the transcription and translation of the Liye material indicates the temporal order according to which a text was written. The spatial setting of the texts written on Qin administrative manuscripts does not necessarily coincide with their temporal order. That is, sometimes an earlier text could be positioned after a later one. If two spatially distanced texts share the same alphabetical number, this means that they were probably written concurrently by the same scribe.

To distinguish historical administrative units from those of present-day ones, the former category is written in lower case, whereas present-day administrative units are capitalized. In this fashion, "Qianling county" refers to a historical unit and "Yongshun County" to a modern one.

For clarity and consistency, all official titles are capitalized as proper nouns.

Introduction

World-shattering events such as the collapse of a state, empire, or civilization never fail to provoke attention. Often such enthusiasm is not
only motivated by scholarly interest but, especially in popular literature,
prompts inquiries into "what went wrong" and how we can learn from the
past. Researchers' explanations for collapses often change concomitantly
with contemporaneous sociopolitical, socioeconomic, or environmental
factors.[1] As a result, discourses generated from collapse studies are constantly reoriented.[2]

One common example to which such ever-changing models are
applied is the collapse of the first Sinitic empire, the Qin 秦 Empire
(221–207 BCE). Despite having fallen apart in less than two decades,
Qin established an imperial framework and government apparatus that
inspired all later Sinitic empires. What it created was instrumental in
shaping "China" as we know it today. Therefore, the imperial Qin period
is widely regarded as an epoch of Chinese history. The attention given
to the Qin collapse is due not only to Qin's historical importance but
also to the seemingly drastic pace of the disintegration of its political
organizations, which happened a mere six years after the empire reached
its greatest territorial size and the pinnacle of its political power in 213
BCE.

The interpretations of the Qin's demise have been under repeated
reconsideration since the succeeding Western Han dynasty (202 BCE–8
CE). The traditional explanations given, however, sometimes become
shackles. Until recently, most scholarly efforts have been hamstrung by
these accounts and the sparse transmitted sources. Remarkably, archaeological discoveries in recent decades have substantially compensated for
such deficiencies and shed light on hidden nuances of the Qin state after
its unification in 221 BCE.[3] Indeed, the rich trove of newly unearthed

Qin manuscripts has contributed unparalleled material regarding the Qin legal and political systems, as well as the intellectual and social lives of people at that time.

Benefiting from these new primary sources, this book provides an empirical historical study that reexamines the Qin's governance, power, and collapse. I will demonstrate that the regime's collapse resulted from the structural limitations of its state power, which could not sustain its expansion and maintain efficient control over its territories. In this respect, the Qin collapse began decades before 207 BCE and was much less dramatic than our modern perception suggests.

But this book is more than a quest to discover clues about the Qin collapse. What I am more interested in is the dynamic process of the collapse rather than the mere reasons for it: the *how* rather than the *why*. Whereas some readers may be disappointed that the explanations I offer are often not far removed from the traditional accounts, studying the "Qin collapse" is merely a means to an end. In the course of this intellectual journey, I aim to dissect and synthesize facets of the complex and often nonlinear sociopolitical and socioeconomic configurations present during the late third century BCE in China.[4] What was the relationship between territorial expansion and the power of a state? How did ideology and social engineering of the state affect people's lives? How did people react to such attempts? How were cultural identities being constructed (and dissolved) in the ancient world? How did interregional networks of communication emerge and function? By addressing these questions—which are in many ways universally faced by civilizations across different spatial and temporal parameters—we can not only gain a more holistic understanding of the formative stage of imperial China but, more fundamentally, know better about the organizational structures and dynamics of human lives, including those of our time. These, I believe, are far more rewarding than a flashy explanation.

The Rise and Fall of the Qin Empire: A Summary

It is difficult to analyze the fall of a state without also knowing the process of its state-building. The major sources on the Qin collapse are the transmitted accounts in standard histories. Since it is pointless to recount the traditional story in detail, here I just provide readers, especially nonspecialists, some relevant background information.[5]

The triumph of the Qin polity in 221 BCE can be traced back to the middle Warring States (Zhanguo 戰國; ca. 453–221 BCE). During the reign of Lord Xiao of Qin (Qin Xiao Gong 秦孝公; r. 361–338 BCE), Shang Yang 商鞅—who was a Wey 衛 native but a Qin statesman—contemplated two large-scale reforms in 356 BCE and 350 BCE. These reforms proved to be remarkably successful and transformed Qin from a peripheral state within the Zhou 周 (1045–256 BCE) cultural proper into one of the major players of the Warring States period.[6]

In the following century, Qin's power continued to grow. During King Huiwen's (Huiwen Wang 惠文王; r. 338–311 BCE) reign, the acquisition of the Sichuan Basin, which was the homeland of two non-Qin groups, the Ba 巴 and the Shu 蜀, in 316 BCE allowed the Qin to occupy territories far beyond their heartland in the Guanzhong Basin. More importantly, the fertile agricultural fields and natural resources of Sichuan granted Qin the economic surplus necessary to further its conquests. Strategically, since Sichuan Basin was upstream from the Chu 楚 territory in Jianghan Plain, the annexation of regional networks in Sichuan thus offered Qin another way to assault its nemeses.[7] After conquering Sichuan, the Qin state already fit the definition of an "empire," that is, a polity controlled by a supreme ruler who can exercise his or her power over originally separate territories comprising diverse ethnic, cultural, and religious groups.[8]

The most significant breakthrough, however, was achieved during the reign of King Zhaoxiang (Zhaoxiang Wang 昭襄王; r. 306–251 BCE), when the triumphant military expeditions against rival states in the east and south resulted in substantial territorial expansion. This progress did not cease until the Battle of Changping 長平 in 262 BCE, which appeared to be a Pyrrhic victory for the Qin side. No consequential military actions were taken until the thirteenth year (234 BCE) of the reign of King Zheng (born Ying Zheng 嬴政 or Zhao Zheng 趙正; later the First Emperor of Qin; Qin Shi Huangdi 秦始皇帝; r. 247–210 BCE), who authorized an incursion into the state of Zhao 趙.[9] Subsequently, Qin dominated its six major rivals, namely, Hann 韓, Zhao, Wei 魏, Yan 燕, Chu, and Qi 齊 in a mere nine years (230–221 BCE), and established, in our conventional understanding, the first unified empire in East Asia, the Qin Empire.[10]

After the Qin conquest, a series of political and social reforms were instigated throughout the empire. According to the *Shiji*, some of the most prominent reforms included the following: (1) a political system centering on the absolute authority of the "August Thearch" (Huangdi

皇帝);[11] (2) the adjustments of customs in accordance with the theory of the five-agent cycle (*wu xing* 五行), in which the Qin Empire, as the successor of the Zhou dynasty, inherited the virtue of water (*shui de* 水德); (3) the universal implementation of a centrally controlled local administrative system featuring the commandery-county and march (*jun xian dao* 郡縣道) hierarchy and the abolition of regional kingdoms; (4) the standardization of measurements, written scripts, currency, and administrative terminologies; and (5) the proscription of unsanctioned learning (*sixue* 私學) and the reformation of social activities. Aside from these relatively intangible reforms, numerous megalomaniacal infrastructure projects, inspection tours, state-organized migrations, and military campaigns were orchestrated to achieve the political, social, and economic unification of the new empire.[12]

The Qin regime is known to have established an intricate, bureaucratic government to govern its territories. In 221 BCE, the empire established approximately thirty-six commanderies, whose number further proliferated with the state's expansion.[13] In the Qin administrative hierarchy, the three levels under the commandery were the county, commune (*xiang* 鄉), and village (*li* 里), although there are no concrete data regarding their numbers during the imperial Qin era.[14] For every commandery there were three major senior officials: the Governor (Shou 守), Commandant (Wei 尉), and Supervisory Prosecutor (Jian Yushi 監御史), all of whom were centrally appointed. Much like their central counterparts, the commandery offices set up various junior officials to handle the paperwork.

While commanderies played a pivotal role in local governance, it was up to counties to implement government policies. Structurally, a county was led by the Prefect (Ling 令), under whom there were one to two Vice-Prefects (Cheng 丞) and Commanders (Wei 尉). The organizations of a county government could be categorized as offices (*guan* 官) and bureaus (*cao* 曹).[15] The heads of offices were the Overseers (Se Fu 嗇夫), whereas bureaus were managed by the Scribe Directors (Ling Shi 令史). A division of labor can be observed between offices and bureaus: Offices were functional organizations that assumed tasks such as compiling accounts and evaluations and monitoring craft production. Bureaus, on the other hand, were complementary organizations auditing statistics and documents submitted by offices.[16] Additionally, bureaus were physically closer to the Prefect and Vice-Prefect than offices were.[17]

Despite the Qin being widely perceived as maintaining a strong control over its lands and people, we should not overestimate the regime's level of territorial control. It is evident that under the Qin rulers' vision, the Metropolitan Area (Nei Shi 內史)—which constituted the imperial capital and the traditional domain of the Qin polity—was the empire's center, whereas the old territories in addition to the Metropolitan Area were the semiperiphery, and the "new territories" (*xindi* 新地) acquired between 230 and 214 BCE were the periphery (map I.1). This internal division of space suggests that despite their indulgence in unity and

Map I.1. Distribution of major administrative units of the Qin Empire. Map based on "Map 1-2" of Zhou Zhenhe, Li Xiaojie, and Zhang Li, *Zhongguo xingzhengquhua tongshi*, vol. 1, 46. Author's own material.

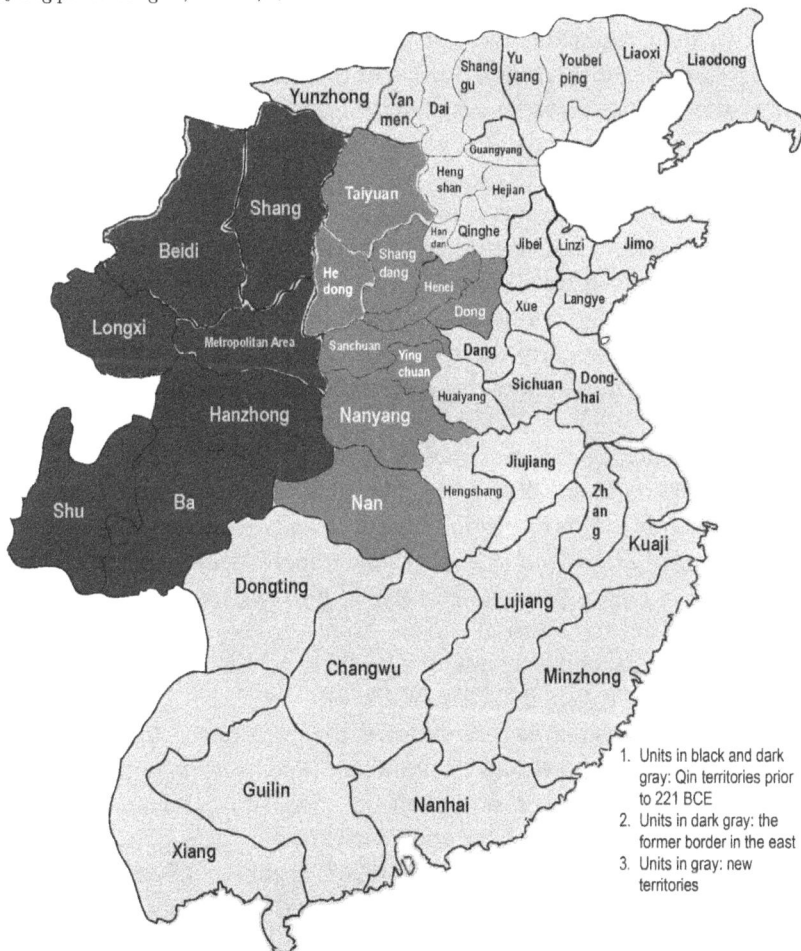

1. Units in black and dark gray: Qin territories prior to 221 BCE
2. Units in dark gray: the former border in the east
3. Units in gray: new territories

standardization, Qin rulers had to concede to the diverse sociopolitical landscape in different parts of this vast empire and admit that their power was not as overarching as their propaganda proclaimed.[18]

Therefore, it may not be so surprising that the collapse of the mighty Qin Empire accelerated as soon as the First Emperor died in 210 BCE. The first domino fell when two low-level military officers named Chen Sheng 陳勝 (also known as Chen She 陳涉) and Wu Guang 吳廣 decided to mutiny against the empire after they were delayed by a heavy rain and thus faced capital punishment because of their failure to reach their assigned garrison post on time. Emboldened by the valor of Chen and Wu, people from the empire's new territories in the east and south who were unsatisfied with the Qin's brutal rule joined in overpowering the Qin authorities. Although most anti-Qin insurgencies came from the east, their instigators did not share a homogeneous social class or background. Historical records document that insurgent groups were often the coalescence of powerful community leaders, Qin officials, and local militias. This guaranteed the diversity of the group members.[19]

Even as the new territories were ablaze, the Qin's local administrative units failed to put the fire out. Many administrators in local governments either fled or chose to stand with the rebels in the wake of the government's dysfunction, which further empowered the insurgents. Some of the rebel groups quickly merged into alliances of powerful warlords who could seriously threaten Qin rule. The poor performance of the Qin Empire in handling this crisis calls into question its governance in the east.

Experiencing what was mostly likely its biggest threat since the last anti-Qin military alliance in 241 BCE, the Qin central government, curiously, did not organize an effective counterattack against the upheaval until Zhou Wen 周文, a general under Chen Sheng, passed the stronghold of Hangu pass 函谷關, camped in Xi 戲 county, and prepared to march toward the imperial capital, Xianyang 咸陽.[20] Appalled by this intrusion, the Second Emperor of Qin (Qin Er Shi Huangdi 秦二世皇帝; born Huhai 胡亥; r. 210–207 BCE), who had been living under the shadow of his revered father, accepted the petition of Zhang Han 章邯, manumitted hundreds of thousands of hard laborers currently constructing the First Emperor's mausoleum, and armed them to suppress the rebellion. While the Qin army succeeded in defeating the Zhang Chu (張楚; literally, "Expanding the Chu") regime of Chen Sheng and Wu Guang, other warlords soon formed another military alliance and continued to threaten the empire. Zhang Han's efforts to extend the empire's life were in vain after the loss of a decisive battle at Julu 鉅鹿, where his troops were annihilated by the Chu army of Xiang Ji 項籍 (also known as Xiang Yu 項羽).

Meanwhile, Xianyang was sacked by Liu Ji 劉季 (who later changed his name to Liu Bang 劉邦). In late 207 BCE, to preserve the city and his people, Ziying 子嬰, the third and last ruler of the Qin Empire, chose to abdicate and surrender himself to Liu, who did leave Xianyang intact so as to gain the trust of people in the Qin core. But the ensuing peace did not last long. When Xiang Ji, accompanied by other former aristocrats from states that the Qin had eliminated, led allied forces to crush Xianyang that same year, the bitter former aristocrats immediately killed Ziying and other imperial kinsmen, ravaged the imperial capital, ruined the magnificent palaces and monuments within, and razed the metropolitan city to the ground. This event marked the termination of the Qin's political organization.

Conceptualizing the "Qin Collapse": What Fell? What Remained?

To avoid any misunderstandings, it seems necessary to conceptualize one of the key terms of this book, the "Qin collapse." In their seminal studies on the theorization of the collapse of ancient empires and civilizations, Norman Yoffee and George Cowgill attempt to differentiate two semantic categories. The first category is the distinction between terms such as *fall*, *collapse*, and *fragmentation* and terms such as *decline*, *decay*, and *decadence*. Yoffee asserts that the first set of terms connotes changes in the quantity or quality of material phenomena, specifically the political aspects of social life, while the second set has moral implications. Therefore, he suggests that researchers employ the former group of terms over the latter, advice that I duly follow.[21]

Another critical categorical differentiation lies between the "collapse of a civilization" and the "collapse of a state." Appropriating the notion of "great tradition" developed by Robert Redfield and Milton Singer, George Cowgill assigns the term *civilization* a more cultural meaning. In this fashion, the collapse of a civilization is the termination of a "great tradition" of the culture of literate social elites. The "collapse of a state," on the other hand, is primarily a political reference and indicates the disintegration of "a large political system into a number of smaller, politically autonomous units." So long as *civilization* is not terminated or drastically transformed, political fragmentation will usually be followed by the reconstitution of empires that adopt the great tradition of their predecessors.[22] Indeed, as noted by various scholars, civilizational collapse is rare if not entirely nonexistent. Usually, kinship structures and belief systems, which are more resilient to change, can find ways to adapt to disturbances in the wake of short-term political events and to retain their basic function and structure. In this light, Patricia McAnany and Norman Yoffee contend that "resilience is a more accurate term to describe the human response to extreme problems" than "collapse."[23]

The insights of these scholars give rise to the following question: What exactly fell, and what remained, after the collapse of the Qin Empire in 207 BCE? This is not an easy question to answer. On the one hand, some parts of the great tradition of the Qin indeed perished along with the collapse of the polity. One of the better examples of this was the destruction of the traditional Qin political center, Xianyang. Serving as the capital of the Qin regime since 350 BCE, the palatial complexes and political center of Xianyang were originally constructed on the north bank of the Wei 渭 River. From the reign of King Huiwen onward, the city of Xianyang had gradually been expanding to the south bank of the Wei River. This trend culminated in the reign of the First Emperor, who created an "uninterrupted chain of palaces stretching on both sides of the river," including the unfinished Epang 阿房 palace.[24]

All these glamorous buildings were destroyed after the sack of Xianyang. After finally overcoming Xiang Ji and enthroning Emperor Gaozu 高祖 of Han (r. 202–195 BCE), Liu Bang chose to construct a new capital by renovating two remaining Qin palaces on the south bank of the Wei River. After their completion, these two palaces were renamed Changle 長樂 and Weiyang 未央, which together constituted the main body of the new imperial city of Chang'an 長安 in its early stage.[25] In contrast, the Qin capital region north of Chang'an was abandoned and never recovered from destruction. Archaeological excavation has revealed that the palatial complexes located in the ancient city of Xianyang were ravaged in conjunction with a sudden breakdown in the number of settlements. During the Western Han period, part of the former palatial complex was used as cemetery.[26] These changes match with the normal patterns following the fragmentation of political regimes.[27]

Another vanquished great tradition of Qin culture was the unique Qin political and cultural identity, which likely emerged in the mid–Warring States period.[28] The ferocious criticisms of the Qin made by Western Han intellectuals have permanently damaged the reputation of the Qin regime. "Qin" acquired a connotation of immoral, oppressive, and uncivilized rule.[29] The ostensible validity of these accusations was strengthened by the brevity of the imperial Qin period and the longevity of the two Han dynasties (202 BCE–220 CE). While the ethnonym *Qin* was still used among peoples in Central Asia and elsewhere to identify inhabitants within the Sinitic proper and might be the etymological origin of the word *China*,[30] in regions under stronger Sinitic cultural influence, *Han* has entirely replaced *Qin* as the byword of cultural identity among the "Chinese" people, even up to the present day.[31]

Subscription to the Qin cultural identity no longer granted the sociopolitical advantages that it once did because of the negative connotation linked to the idea of "Qin." Under such a social change, it is natural that even the people of the traditional Qin heartland stopped identifying themselves as the Qin.[32] Despite the tremendous efforts made by the Qin rulers to publicize and bolster a uniform "Qin" identity, *Qin*, as an ethnonym and self-identification, was almost wiped out concomitantly with the Qin regime in the Sinitic proper.

The fall of the Qin Empire also compelled several instant changes in the statecraft and the political system of the Western Han dynasty, at least at its formative stage. One of the most significant differences was the policy that the Han rulers devised. According to traditional historiography, to mitigate the damaging effect of the "Legalist" (Fajia 法家) ideology adopted by the Qin regime,[33] the early Western Han government subscribed to the principle of "rule by nonactivity" (*wuwei er zhi* 無為而治), which was guided by the "Way of Huang-Lao" (*Huang-Lao dao* 黃老道). This ideology is said to account for the comparatively lenient attitude of the early Han rulers toward their subjects.[34] Although the genuineness of this traditional belief has been under question,[35] extant evidence seems to support the claim that in comparison with the government in the preceding Qin era, the early Western Han government indeed maintained a hands-off attitude toward various social and economic spheres.

For example, the Qin Empire attempted to keep a tight grip on economic activities in both the public sector and the private market despite the swift development of the private market and monetary economy. In contrast, the Western Han Empire was more inclined to embrace this transition.[36] Consider Emperor Wen of Han's (Han Wendi 漢文帝; r. 180–157 BCE) abolition of corporal punishment in 167 BCE. Although standard histories always ascribe the emperor's action to his benevolence, it might also have been done to reduce the number of forced laborers kept by the state, thereby saving state expenditures and releasing the productivity of the unwanted convict laborers.[37] Even if the ideology to which the early Western Han rulers subscribed might not have diverged much from that of the Qin, it did not prevent them from instituting more hands-off policies.

Compared to the political system of the Qin Empire, early Han central government granted greater autonomy to regional governments. Instead of unreservedly continuing the centralized political system of the Qin Empire, early Han rulers chose at first to side with the model set by Xiang Ji, who intended to restore the old multistate system of the Warring States. While Qin's commandery-county system was still implemented within the jurisdiction of the Han central authority, the remaining territories of the Qin Empire were divided into various regional kingdoms (*zhuhou wangguo* 諸侯王國) governed by non-Liu lords, who functioned as essential agents in maintaining local control.[38] Such a blending of political systems is often characterized as the "commandery-regional kingdom" system (*jun-guo zhi* 郡國制). What the Han central authorities controlled was the Metropolitan Area,[39] coupled with two dozen commanderies scattered around the Sichuan, Luoyang, and Nanyang basins and Jianghan Plain.[40]

One of the top agendas of Emperor Gaozu was to replace these non-Liu regional lords with kinsmen of the imperial family. At the end of Emperor Gaozu's reign, the Western Han Empire in fact reinstated a quasi–Western Zhou system of regional kingdoms. It was not until the suppression of the Rebellion of the Seven States in 154 BCE that the Han central government managed to exercise direct control over regional kingdoms. In this regard, the political fragmentation after the Qin collapse lasted decades longer than the ostensible regeneration of the Western Han Empire.[41] This highlights the greatest difference between the political systems of the Qin and early Western Han periods.

On the other hand, the ruins of disintegrated states or civilizations often serve as the foundation of later states. Some of the best evidence for this is the Western Han Empire, which undeniably inherited much of its precursor's legacy. The most apparent inheritance is the title "August Thearch" and the whole set of imperial apparatuses attached to it. Even if regional kingdoms were often regarded as the centrifugal force in dismantling the empire (and indeed, they were), their political system nevertheless mirrored the Qin model. The territory of each of these kingdoms centered on a Metropolitan Area, to which a varying number of commanderies and counties were subordinate. The bureaucratic structure of these regional kingdoms also emulated that of the Han central government and was consonant with the Qin institution.[42] From this perspective, regional kingdoms of the early Western Han era were essentially variants of the Qin administrative system. The impact of the Qin imperial apparatus was so substantial that even those Western Han thinkers and statesmen—who predominantly described the Qin as an evil regime and rarely had any empathy with it—had to admit the unmistakable resemblance of their own political institutions to those of the Qin.[43]

Political system aside, other parts of the Qin great tradition—the culture of its literate social elites—did not fade away after the demise of the polity. The best example of this was perhaps the Qin writing system, which was continually practiced in the Western Han Empire and transformed thereafter. Archaeological findings also reveal that a substantial portion of Qin material cultural elements such as funeral customs, vessel designs, and ritual settings were integrated into other existing regional cultures. The influx of material culture was not one-sided. That is, the material culture of the traditional Qin domain was also influenced by that of other regions.[44] Eventually, the incessant cross-cultural exchanges shaped a new material culture that is usually called Han material culture, which carried unmistakable Qin characteristics. Although regional diversity prevailed in the Western Han Empire, the material culture of this period displayed considerably more homogeneity than in the Warring States period.[45] This cultural integration is exemplified by the development of burial customs around the Western Han capital Chang'an. Huang Yijun points out that tombs within Chang'an "began to exhibit elements drawn from the Six Kingdoms' burial customs" around 100 BCE. Whereas the resulting burial culture—which archaeologists designate as the "Early Western Han" style—still "partly continued the regional Qin style," it "revived key features associated with the Eastern Zhou Six Kingdoms' burials."[46]

Indeed, Qin civilization and its great tradition (political system, statecraft, written script, etc.) not only formed the foundation for later

Chinese dynasties but, to a certain extent, remains influential today. Perhaps one may summarize the resilience of the Qin tradition as follows: The Qin are dead, long live the Qin!

To answer the two questions raised in the heading of this section, what was destroyed after the abdication of Ziying in 207 BCE was not Qin civilization, at least not all of it, but a political entity called "Qin" formed around the early eighth century BCE.[47] Despite the breakdown of the Qin political center and the extinction of the Qin ethnonym and cultural identity, the great tradition of the Qin literate social elites was transformed and remained alive long after the demise of the regime.

Such an understanding delineates the parameters of the present study. This book aims to examine not the fall of Qin civilization (for it only transformed) but rather the breakdown of the Qin political organization. Special attention will be given to the final decades (ca. 234–207 BCE) of the Qin polity, during which it instigated various sociopolitical reforms and new policies to meet the challenges created by the rapid territorial expansion and the complex sociopolitical landscape in the new territories. These actions propelled radical social configurations that profoundly reshaped the lives of the population within the Qin territories, regardless of their level of subjugation to the new political rule. My major focus is discerning how the dynamics between Qin reforms and the concurrent social configurations might have prompted the demise of the Qin regime.

Chapter Summary

This book comprises four chapters. Chapter 1 develops a new theory of the Qin collapse, which suggests that the Qin's rapid expansion caused a large gap between its state power and the territories it occupied. From this perspective, the overexpansion and fragmentation of the Qin regime were a manifestation of its insufficient state power. To gauge the impact of this gap, this model further dissects three dynamics of state power—social tensions stemming from the aggressive social-engineering program, labor shortages in administrative units following the regime's rapid territorial expansion, and inefficient communication logistics—under the framework of state capacity, security, and legitimacy gaps. I will analyze how these three shortcomings made the Qin Empire a fragile state incapable of handling sudden crises long before uprisings started in 209 BCE.

Chapter 2 delves into the lives of the Qin Empire's subjects—especially those of the literate elites—by studying their tensions with the state. It first explores the emergence of a universal ruling class featuring literate administrators, and how this progress temporarily discontinued after the collapse of Qin's political organization. It also examines the negative effects of the Qin's difficult and uncompassionate "moral-legalist supremacism" ideology, which might have discouraged Qin officials from being committed to their duties and counteracted the very purposes of Qin's sociopolitical reforms. These phenomena demonstrate the insufficient infrastructural power of the Qin regime.

Chapter 3 covers institutions and organizations by which different social groups interacted. To this end, it examines labor shortages due to the empire's rapid territorial expansion. The Liye manuscripts reveal that the territorial expansion resulted in severe shortages of officials, convict laborers, and conscripts in the government of Qianling 遷陵 county. These shortages significantly undermined the ability of the local government to handle everyday administrative tasks, conduct economic activities, and ensure security. Although Qin rulers devised institutional reforms to resolve these issues, they hardly improved the paucity of human resources; some of the new measures even precipitated other crises. Existing evidence indicates that the Qin regime might have maintained only a low level of despotic and infrastructural power in the new territories.

Chapter 4 centers on communication among the empire's regional networks. It surveys the state's inefficient logistics of power in its new territories. Statistics derived from Qianling county indicate that its administrative communication was defective. While Qianling maintained relatively efficient internal communication, its external communication was extremely inefficient. The chapter shows that the communication between administrative units in the empire's periphery could hardly have sustained sudden external changes. Overall, the local governments of the Qin Empire were hampered by the inoperability of external administrative communication. Such a deficiency in the communication system was in sharp contrast to the perceived impression of the Qin administration.

The conclusion will assess the three dynamics of state power discussed in previous chapters according to the analytic framework of the legitimacy, capacity, and security gaps mentioned above. Instead of ascribing these gaps to the inaccurate assumption that the Qin rulers were unwilling to adjust their policies, the conclusion focuses on possible repercussions of institutional reforms and new policies that were meant to improve the situation. However, to reach this destination, we must first review our conceptual framework.

Chapter 1

Toward a Theory of the Qin Collapse

The "Qin collapse" has been regarded as emblematic of the dramatic breakdown of a political organization due to poor governance. Traditional political thinkers and their modern followers mostly adopt an "idealist" approach to understanding the demise of the Qin Empire. Whereas their evaluations suggest an array of mental and material factors contributing to this demise, their conclusions invariably relate it to either moral or individual intellectual factors, condemning the cruelty, ambition, and greediness of the Qin emperor as the root cause of the Qin's fall.[1]

Sometimes the purported wrongdoings of the Qin rulers are used merely as a foil for the political agendas of the thinkers. Notably, in the "Bao Fu" 保傅 chapter of the transmitted *Xinshu* 新書, Jia Yi 賈誼, its attributed author, argues that the Qin misdirected the Second Emperor by ordering Zhao Gao 趙高 to teach him the inhumane "Legalist" ideology. This resulted in his lack of awareness and ability to act the correct way, thus causing the Qin's rapid demise. The key to achieving proper statecraft and longevity of polity, Jia suggests, is to rectify the heart-mind of the rulers and make their actions be cultivated in harmony with the Way.[2] The text's emphasis on self-cultivation echoes not only that of the later *daoxue* 道學 followers[3] but also the virtue politics of humanist scholars of the Italian Renaissance.[4]

Despite their political agendas, traditional idealist discourses stem from the logical thinking and keen observations of their advocates and should not be easily dismissed. Without denying the possible connection between the moral character of rulers and state collapse, it is nonetheless difficult to give a clear definition for terms such as *moral* or *intellectual*.

15

Nor can one readily observe the impact of individual traits on the fall of the entire empire. One must therefore be more cautious in discerning possible ideological factors leading to the collapse of enterprises as comprehensive and extensive as states.

Additionally, idealist propositions often assume that the ideology of the Qin Empire was identical with that of the preimperial period. Such a belief is hardly justifiable, as the imperial Qin rulers instituted various social reforms to instill select normative values into the populace through legal and administrative means, thereby softening social tensions and establishing a unitary society. These efforts exemplified a significant transition of state ideology in the imperial Qin era.[5] In this light, Jia Yi's famous assertion in the "On the Fault of Qin" (Guo Qin lun 過秦論) that the collapse of the Qin Empire came about because "benevolence and righteousness were not extended [to its people] and the offensive and defensive conditions differed" (仁義不施而攻守之勢異也) is at best an oversimplified claim.[6]

In contrast to idealist propositions, many modern scholars prefer to interpret this issue in materialist, especially socioeconomic, terms, ascribing the Qin collapse to a failure of the Qin political system, to the regime's rapid territorial expansion, and to the excessive exploitation of labor in building monuments and infrastructure across the Qin territories.[7] Although these attempts indeed shed light on the Qin's collapse and are seemingly more objective than idealist views, most of them assume a linear relationship between one (or several) sociopolitical phenomenon(a) and the demise of the polity. Thus, they often overlook the complexity of state collapse, particularly in terms of the dynamics between differential networks of power relations during the process of political disintegration. One of the main foci of this book is therefore to discern the relations between these factors and the Qin fall.

Measurable systemic models of explanation, on the other hand, have thus far remained hypotheses and require further verification. Gideon Shelach's recent reassessment,[8] for instance, seems to fall into a common trap of system thought.[9] As George Cowgill observes, system theorists often hold the inaccurate assumption that "sociocultural entities are normally highly integrated (highly systemic) with well-developed mechanisms for self-regulation." This notion may nonetheless be a myth of ruling elites.[10] Indeed, the underlying assumption that the bureaucratic system of the newly unified Qin Empire functioned smoothly is another similar illusion, as we will see in the coming chapters.[11] While scholars have now begun to realize the limitations and deficiencies of the state, especially those of government organizations, more work must be done.[12]

Here, I do not aim to refute the potential connection between the deficiencies of government administration after the formation of the Qin Empire in 221 BCE and its seemingly dramatic fall. I only want to stress that we cannot simply assume their causality without a critical discussion. Many problems noted by recent studies, such as the quality of administrators, administrative inefficiency, and labor shortages, probably recurred in government administration throughout history. Often, state collapse is contingent not on what kinds of adversity a state encounters but on *how seriously* it suffers from them, and *how well* a regime can endure and overcome them. The existing literature on the Qin collapse barely explains the latter two points.

The question of how well also calls for a reconsideration of the concept of "overexpansion," which is one of the most popular explanations of the Qin collapse. On the one hand, territorial expansion indeed brought the Qin Empire numerous problems, to the extent that the empire was plagued by serious social unrest and resource shortages; therefore it makes perfect sense that scholars would ascribe the collapse of the Qin polity to factors such as overexpansion or the exhaustion of resources. On the other hand, the essence of "overexpansion" is that it is *over*-expansion: excessive, overreaching expansion. So long as the capacity of a state can sustain its territorial or resource expansion, it is not *overexpansion*. Therefore, the so-called overexpansion of the Qin Empire was only the manifestation of its limited state power, a concept that I will elaborate upon later.

Equally important, the Qin regime was by no means ignorant of or nonchalant about the empire's problems. Reforms and policies were formulated to tackle these challenges. What is more relevant is why the Qin Empire still collapsed despite all the efforts to sustain its rule. Such a concern is one of the features that distinguish the current study from earlier scholarly works.

Going beyond the study of the Qin collapse, the divergence of idealist and materialist interpretations also betrays a pervasive dilemma of collapse studies in general. To paraphrase the words of George Cowgill, how can we as researchers integrate the mental and the material? How can we illustrate the interplay of materialist and idealist concepts? How can we formulate an effective and unified theory that combines both ideas and material circumstances?[13] Regrettably, even after more than thirty years, researchers can hardly meet the challenges voiced by Cowgill. Although theorists of collapse studies have advanced many new models, such as resilience theory,[14] to explain the nonlinear transformation of complex societies, these metaphors are often heavily influenced by natural science theories and consider external crises such as revolts and natural disasters to be catalysts of system destruction. However, in the collapse of political organizations, it is often difficult to determine whether organizational collapses are caused by so-called external disturbances, or whether they are just extensions of internal crises.

In view of these limitations, this chapter seeks a more straightforward model to explain the collapse of the Qin Empire. Rather than developing a lofty, extremely flexible model encompassing almost any type of phenomenon and society, this work aims to construct a simple metaphor tailor-made for the situation of the Qin Empire. As such, it helps to discern the potential correspondence between Qin state power and its territorial expansion, which was the most important variable after the founding of the empire.

Qin State Power and Its Dynamics

Before elaborating the theoretical framework of this book in detail, I want to briefly discuss the notion of state power. In general, researchers working on the collapse of ancient political regimes are more interested in discerning the process of their demise and the subsequent social transformations, thereby patterning the general trends of these phenomena. In contrast, collapse studies often pay little attention to what a "state" was and what types of functions it performed. Nor do they sufficiently elucidate the nuances of social networks, which are pivotal in understanding the sociopolitical configurations that take place during a state's collapse and transformation.

Despite being relatively neglected in collapse studies, notions such as "state power," "state," and "power" are among the most fundamental concepts adopted in the fields of history and sociology. Extensive scholarly works have been devoted to explaining the nuances (nature, ends, means, organization, etc.) of the state and power. While Marxists often reduce the state to an arena where forms of power relations—specifically conflicts between different classes over basic social and economic interests—are embedded,[15] followers of Max Weber tend to view the state as a fusion of institutional functional organizations. In the words of Michael Mann, the

Weberian ideal-type of state is (1) a differentiated set of institutions and personnel embodying (2) centrality, in the sense that political relations radiate outwards from a center to cover (3) a territorially demarcated area over which it exercises (4) a monopoly over authoritative binding rule-making backed by a monopoly of the means of physical violence.[16]

In response to this Marxist functionalist conception of the state, scholars such as Theda Skocpol focus on the autonomy of the state. Skocpol argues that instead of serving merely as an arena for displaying social relations and socioeconomic conflicts or as a vehicle controlled by the dominant class, the state is a potentially autonomous body that may, in pursuit of its own interests (e.g., strengthening its autonomy), act against the interests of the dominant class. State organizations can side with the subordinate class(es) to overthrow the existing dominant class(es) during a revolution and create a new regime. For Skocpol, state power refers to the ability of the state, which comprises a variety of centralized administrative, policing, and military organizations, to design and implement policy and to extract resources from society through administrative and coercive organizations; the resources extracted will in turn be distributed to the administrative and coercive organizations to sustain their existence. Therefore, she believes that administrative and coercive organizations are the basis of state power.[17]

While Michael Mann agrees that the state maintains a certain degree of autonomous power, the "state power" to which he refers differs from that referenced by Skocpol. Mann contends that "societies are constituted of multiple overlapping and intersecting sociospatial networks of power."[18] His conception of state power is part of his IEMP model, which categorizes the networks of interactions of societies into the interrelation of the four sources of social power: Ideological, Economic, Military, and Political relationships.[19] For Mann, all the four sources occupy equal statuses in social developments, although he agrees that they could be developed "at different rhythms," and there could be one dominant power organization that induced bigger developments in social relations than other power sources over a given period of time.[20] The four power sources are never independent of interaction networks, which manifest in the form of organizations. In pursuit of power, human beings always compete to acquire its means (i.e., organizations) rather than to directly accomplish its ends. In this way, social power is organizational.[21]

Regarding state power, Mann's model equates such power with political power, which is derived from the "usefulness of [the] centralized, institutionalized, territorialized regulation of many aspects of social relations."[22] Mann dichotomizes state power into two ideal-types: *despotic* and *infrastructural*. The former denotes the "range of actions which the elite is empowered to undertake without routine, institutionalized negotiation with civil society groups," whereas infrastructural power is the "capacity of the state to actually penetrate civil society, and to implement logistically political decisions throughout the realm."[23] Thus, despotic power is more direct and coercive, whereas infrastructural power is more concerned about the soft power of state—that is, its capacity to influence civil society. That a state maintains adequate physical infrastructure such as roads does not imply that it attains strong infrastructural power.

It must be noted that Mann recognizes that the state is a multifunctional enterprise performing activities such as the maintenance of internal order, military aggression or defense, the maintenance of communications, and economic redistribution. What he argues, however, is that most of these functions are only a combination of the means of power, which are also employed in economic, military, and ideological power relations. As a social organization, the state is distinctive in that it is a place, an arena in which "regulations and coercion are centrally administered and territorially bounded."[24] Such an understanding sets him apart from Skocpol, who recognizes the autonomy of state. Mann's account stresses the eclectic nature of state power. That is, the state always sets up a wide range of institutions to manage social activities in relation to political, economic, military, and ideological matters.

Another of Mann's contributions is his nuanced illustration of the ideal-types of power. He divides organizational power into two general aspects: *collective* and *distributive*. Distributive power references one's mastery over other people, while collective power occurs when people cooperate and strengthen "their joint power over third parties or over nature." These two aspects are not mutually exclusive but often coexist and are intertwined in social relations. Additionally, organizational power can be *intensive* or *extensive*, as well as *authoritative* or *diffused*, embodying both collective and distributive power.

On the one hand, intensivity of power refers to the ability to organize and command a high level of mobilization or commitment from participants regardless of the size of the area covered; extensive power concentrates on the ability to organize large numbers of people over vast territories to participate in "minimally stable cooperation." On the other hand, authoritative power is that wielded by groups and institutions and tends to be inclined to the distributive form of power, whereas diffused power is practiced in a more spontaneous and decentered manner. Those who are under the influence of this type of power usually understand it as "natural or moral or result[ing] from self-evident common interest."[25]

Mann's framework has prompted evaluations and modifications from historians and sociologists. In his bold attempt to discern the pattern of Chinese history, sociologist Dingxin Zhao adds the concept of competition to Mann's framework, arguing that the key engine of historical change is the interaction of competition and the institutionalization of the four power sources rather than interstitial development, as contended by Mann. Since economic and military power relations motivate competitions, they are more "cumulatively developmental" than ideological and political power relations in historical development. Simply put, what Zhao suggests is that the four power sources do not have an equal ability to induce cumulative development.[26]

Another major proposition of Dingxin Zhao relates to the formation of the "Confucian-Legalist state" that merged all four power sources. For Zhao, the "Legalist" ideology and regulations implemented by Qin, despite their instrumental role in strengthening state power, resulted in "an unstable crystallization of the political-ideological power relationship" and ignored state-society cooperation and normative consensus. This led to Qin's rapid collapse. In contrast, the Western Han Empire ingeniously "administered the country using an amalgam of Confucian ethics and Legalist regulations and techniques." This strategy integrated political and ideological powers whose coalesced nature was so resilient that it not only became the paramount political system of Chinese empires, but also to some extent suppressed the development of two other power sources.[27]

Zhao's explanation of the Qin collapse should be closely scrutinized. Qin ideology was far more complicated than the simplistic term *Legalism*. Various scholars have observed that Qin propaganda often promoted social values such as filial piety and reverence, which resembled those advocated by so-called Confucian doctrines.[28] More importantly, as Charles Sanft notes, the Qin strove to motivate compliance among the populace rather than coercing them into obedience. This evidently contradicts Zhao's arguments, as political and ideological power might have merged as early as the Qin dynasty. If the "Confucian-Legalist" crystallization was so stable, why did it fail to contribute to the longevity of the Qin Empire? Zhao's framework does not answer (or realize) this problem.

In addition to Dingxin Zhao, historians of ancient civilizations have also appropriated Michael Mann's framework. One notable effort is the volume *Ancient States and Infrastructural Power* edited by Clifford Ando and Seth Richardson. In contrast to Mann's proposition that ancient states wielded stronger despotic power than infrastructural power, Seth Richardson advocates a "lower-power model" with respect to the situation of early Mesopotamia. Richardson argues that Mesopotamian city states only held presumptive power and devised various infrastructural means to create the illusion of strong states among their populace. The expressions of state power were therefore propaganda in response to the absence thereof.

With this understanding, Seth Richardson reconsiders the relationship between the despotic and infrastructural power of the state. He believes that ancient states often cross-referenced these two types of power, to the extent that "it was very difficult to distinguish clearly whether any particular field of action was ultimately undertaken by the state on the basis of its infrastructural or despotic powers."[29] Moreover, infrastructural power could have been generated through the rhetoric of states. Even if states were not capable of materializing what they claimed to, the masses might still have been convinced and passed down constructed images of strong state power in the form of historical memories, which might in turn have enhanced such presumptions.[30]

Richardson's model unveils important facets of ancient states' power. That said, he does not explain in detail the means by which we can determine if the power of a state was strong or weak. Although Richardson uses evidence such as the Code of Hammurabi to illustrate the limited despotic power of ancient Mesopotamian states, he never explains why the listed phenomena are the manifestation of a lack of despotic power. Rather, he seems to intrinsically compare them with similar practices (e.g., penal proceedings) of modern states and empires and draws the conclusion that ancient states were incapable of coercing the populace into compliance.

Additionally, such a theory seems to reduce the populace living within a state's territory into mindless objects that the state can handily manipulate. In contrast, the penetration of the Qin Empire's infrastructural power into the grassroots communities was heavily contingent on its despotic power to promote its ideology and social values. Once the Qin regime collapsed, the populace quickly renounced Qin ideology and identity (see chapter 2). This indicates the agency of the people, who were not easily deceived by state propaganda once they realized that the state's claims were not backed by any substantial means; that is, when they discovered that disobeying the Qin governance led to no consequences. Therefore, if a state manages to motivate the populace to cooperate through various forms of propaganda, this does not imply that its despotic power was "weak," as this was, at least at the early stage, a prerequisite for its success.

Here, I am not suggesting that the power of ancient states and empires was mostly despotic. Nor do I think that their state power was necessarily strong. What I do believe is that we should not ignore the despotic perspective of state power in premodern contexts.

The above discussion may give the reader the impression that I completely adhere to the tenets of Michael Mann's framework. The biggest difference between our understandings is that I see the state as having more autonomous power than Mann does. In view of the multifunctionality of the state, understanding "state power" as a network of purely political relations may undermine the autonomy of state organizations. In fact, the existence of infrastructural power suggests that the state will try to extend its long arm into the ideological aspects of social power. In this book, I use the term *state power* in a more general sense, denoting the capacity of a regime to exercise influence over not only the political organizational network but also those in ideological, economic, and military spheres.

Evidence from both the transmitted and the newest unearthed sources reveals that the Qin Empire encountered the following challenges: (1) social tensions stemming from the Qin regime's aggressive social-engineering program, (2) labor shortages in administrative units after rapid territorial expansion, and (3) inefficient communication logistics in the new territories.

Let us take a step back and think about the attributes of the above factors. I suggest that they can be understood as the dynamics generated from interactions among actors of differential yet interrelated power networks, especially those between state organizations and the people whom they governed.

Social tensions entailed the discontent of the ruled with the policies that the state forced upon them. Likewise, the failure to create a universal ruling class implied the state's inability to incentivize the compliance of new subjects, especially literate elites of former polities. Both the labor shortages and the inefficient logistics probably emanated from the territorial expansion of the Qin Empire, which was related to the capacity of the state apparatus. Considering that these so-called materialist and idealist factors always encompass interactions derived from intersected networks of social power involving state organizations, I characterize them as the "dynamics of state power"; that is, factors that effect changes in power networks linked with state organizations. Such factors were not merely signs manifesting the insufficient power of the Qin Empire, but were what imposed constraints on its state power. With the heuristic tool developed in this section, I will deconstruct these dynamics. After that, I will further delve into their interaction and interrelation through an integrated framework.

The dynamics of state power listed above suggest that the Qin regime commanded a higher level of infrastructural power in its core than in its periphery, although the overall level of this type of power should have been tenuous. Given that the social tensions of the Qin subjects mostly centered around the coercion of the Qin state and that such discontent likely gave rise to concerns about the legitimacy of the ruling regime, they represented the state's lack of intensive, infrastructural power.

Such an uneven distribution of state power also appeared on the despotic side of the Qin's state power. Although the regime established a centralized and unitary local administrative system, political power and state-controlled military power could not keep up with territorial expansion. The shortages of officials and conscripts—two of the state's most pivotal coercive devices for exercising its political and military powers—in the new territories were also proof of the Qin's insufficient political and military powers. Similarly, the inefficient logistics of state power suggest that the Qin's despotic power was not intensive enough to incorporate new subjects into the empire's chain of command.

Taken together, the state power of the Qin Empire may have been extensive but not intensive, despotic but hardly infrastructural, and more authoritative than diffused. Although the Qin rulers strove to enhance the power of their empire, especially on the infrastructural side, by virtue of various institutional reforms and new policies, these efforts were, in the end, to no avail.

A Theory of the Qin Collapse

Drawing on the above analysis, the dynamics of the Qin Empire's power were often associated with its territorial expansion. This section will develop a theory of the interrelation between the Qin state's power, expansion, and collapse. First, I combine Joyce Marcus's dynamic model and Joseph Tainter's explanatory framework on the cause of the collapse of complex societies, showing that the territorial expansion of the Qin Empire gave rise to a serious gap between its actual state power and the power necessary to sustain the size of its territory. After that, I dissect this gap using the framework of state capacity, security, and legitimacy gaps developed by Charles Call and demonstrate how these gaps made the Qin Empire a fragile state incapable of handling sudden crises even before the uprisings started in 209 BCE.

The dynamic model features repetitive cycles of the consolidation, expansion, and dissolution of ancient political organizations. After summarizing the development and transformation of a number of expansionist states, Joyce Marcus outlines how their territories began to shrink not long after expanding to their maximum size. During this process, some parts of their territories often revolted and sought independence. In the end, some of these newly independent political entities "went on to assemble their own expansionist states, beginning the whole cycle over again."[31] For Marcus, the "peaks of consolidation" were always followed by "valleys of dissolution" potentially because of "the difficulty of maintaining large-scale inegalitarian structures for long periods of time. Large-scale, asymmetrical, and inegalitarian structures were more fragile and unstable than commonly assumed."[32] The potential of the dynamic model hinges on its explicit linkage between territorial expansion and the collapse of political regimes. While this model is not a silver bullet for resolving the mysteries around state collapses, it fits the Qin's situation and therefore deserves our attention.

The dynamic model resembles the framework provided by Joseph Tainter, who applies the law of diminishing marginal returns in the field of economics to theorize about the collapses and transformations of complex societies. Tainter posits that as a society becomes more complex, more investment is needed to subsidize the energy required for its evolution. The investment in complexity will reach a point at which the marginal product (MP) begins to dwindle and a disproportionate amount of resources has to be invested to yield a small growth of total product (TP). Eventually, the total product will become negative.

This trend of diminishing marginal returns causes a complex society to become liable to collapse for two reasons. First, a society experiencing declining marginal returns often needs to use its accumulated surpluses after its excess productive capacity has been exhausted. As a result, society will have "little or no surplus with which to counter major adversities." These problems will ultimately turn into insurmountable calamities that lead to the collapse of a complex society. Second, when marginal returns are decreasing, the attractiveness of maintaining complexity decreases concomitantly. Certain groups in a complex society may choose to deconstruct that society and return to simpler and less costly social forms.[33]

Tainter argues that the usual way for a complex society to eschew or delay declines in marginal returns is to obtain a "new energy subsidy" through territorial expansion or technological innovation (the former means was especially pervasive in premodern societies). However, even these new energy subsidies cannot escape the law of diminishing returns, and they only work in the short run. Regarding territorial expansion, Tainter argues that

> a complex society pursuing the expansion option, if it is successful, ultimately reaches a point where further expansion requires too high a marginal cost. Linear miles of border to be defended, size of area to be administered, size of the required administration, internal pacification costs, travel distance between the capital and the frontier, and the presence of competitors combine to exert a depressing effect on further growth. . . . Growth begins slowly, accelerates as the energy subsidy is partially invested in further expansion, and falls off when the marginal cost of further growth becomes too high.[34]

While Tainter's discourse on the purpose and limitations of territorial expansion is insightful, I hesitate to fully accept his theory regarding the collapse of complex societies. For Tainter, the energy subsidy invested in and benefits generated from the growth of sociopolitical complexity are purely economic and mostly associated with factors such as agricultural and other resource production. This unitary view reduces the multiplicity of a society and, to a lesser extent, a state.

I will make some adjustments to modify Tainter's theory. First, since this book is focused on the collapse of a political organization, the Qin Empire, instead of a complex society in general, I replace "complexity" with "state power" to narrow the scope of examination. As Tainter notes, diminishing marginal returns can be observed in different organizational networks.[35] Given that state power is formed by the intersection and interaction of organizational networks, they are inevitably affected by diminishing marginal returns. Second, since state power is a combination of networks, the fluctuation of state power is rooted not only in economic development, but also in the intensification of all political, economic, ideological, and military power networks associated with state organizations. More importantly, to examine the connection between state power and state expansion, I treat state expansion as a separate variable.

In this model, all other factors are held constant except (1) state power and (2) the expanded territory of the state, both of which succumb to the law of diminishing marginal returns. The level of state power and the size of the expanded territory (total products) initially grow with an increasing ratio, which increasingly narrows as more resources are added as input. After reaching the maximum territory size, resources invested in territorial expansion will lead to a decrease in the size of state territory. Conceivably, the expected territorial expansion should follow the rise of state power. Such desynchronization occurs under the consideration that territorial expansion is an investment that requires a large amount of capital and that has an extremely long payback period. Therefore, a state must accumulate a certain level of surplus state power to afford the cost of expansion.

This assumption is also related to the second assumption, that the growth of state power and the expansion of territory are two interdependent factors. Following Tainter's proposition, I assume that once the investment in territorial expansion pays off, it will generate a positive effect on the growth of state power. At first glance, this seems to contradict Mark Elvin's classic model, which considers the comparative technological advantage(s) (i.e., the organizational, economic and military skills) of a political unit to be the key to successful territorial expansion and its subsequent maintenance.[36] Accordingly, "empires tend to expand to the point at which their technological superiority over their neighbours is approximately counterbalanced by the burdens of size."[37] In other words, territorial size is overall a negative factor for state power in Elvin's framework because of the heavier administrative, coordinating, and military cost in maintenance incurred.

However, Elvin's framework and mine serve entirely different purposes. Whereas Elvin attempts to explain the existence of a recurrent dynastic cycle and long-term political continuity in Chinese history, I focus only on the rise and fall of the Qin Empire between approximately 230 and 211 BCE. In the latter case, the connection between territorial expansion and state power seems much stronger. With an increased territory, the state will have, in theory, a larger market for trade, a larger controllable population, more extractable resources, more disposable income, and stronger economic power.[38] Also, the larger the territory is, the greater the army (military power) and administrators (political power) a state can afford. Lastly, a large population and stronger coercive forces can potentially spread the state ideology. All these effects should lead to stronger state power.

In sum, on the one hand, the expansion of the state always consumes part of its accumulated power surplus, and on the other hand, the potential premium of the economies of scale propelled by territorial expansion may prolong the positive marginal returns of state power. Given such interdependency, and assuming that resources are invested in the growth of state power at a constant pace, although the average growth rate of the marginal returns of state power should be higher than that of expanded territory, when the growth of expansion becomes negative, state power will concomitantly drop more drastically as its once strongest source of support is now a liability.

This model is helpful in explaining why overexpansion occurs. In the declining trend, when the state power is so overstretched and weakened by the costs of expansion, the state apparatus can no longer sustain the existing territories that it occupies. This results in a gap between the actual state power that a regime commands and the level of state power necessary to govern the occupied territories. During the overexpansion stage, the state will encounter acute pressures such as local insurgency to hold on to its territory. In the wake of these challenges, the size of the territory will decrease until it reaches a level that its state power can afford. All other factors being equal, the state power will continue to shrink, and the polity will gradually dissolve. From this perspective, *the overexpansion and fragmentation of state are the consequence of insufficient state power.*

Another important variable in this model, and indeed the most relevant one in relation to the Qin collapse, is the pace of expansion. Sometimes the territorial expansion of a state can be done at lightning speed. The expansion of the Qin regime between 230 and 214 BCE is one of the better examples of such a surge in territory. During this period, the territory of the Qin polity doubled in size. Such a speedy increase in size was quite extraordinary among ancient civilizations. Since the payback time of the investment in territorial expansion often takes decades or centuries, the state power of the Qin Empire should not have seen a substantial growth after its rapid territorial expansion. Consequently, a large gap between the state power of the Qin regime and the territory it occupied emerged. Even if a state can mobilize a gargantuan amount of resources in a short period of time to attain the goal of rapid expansion, such input is unsustainable, and the overdraft of state power may even widen the gap between state power and occupied territory.

Given the unsustainability of expansion, the regime will experience pressure imposed by dynamics of state power to *return* to the territory size at which its state power is effective. If the gap in state power is small, the regime may overcome the pressure through administrative reforms or other means that can boost state power. In contrast, if the gap proves insurmountable, the regime will suffer a significant territorial contraction or, in the worst case, collapse. The fragmentation of the Qin Empire probably indicates that it fell into this worst-case scenario.

Of course, the actual territorial expansion of state is hardly, if ever, as simple as this model depicts. Technological advances, as told earlier, can significantly stimulate the growth of state power and, as such, delay the arrival of diminishing returns. Conversely, external factors such as invasion by foreign enemies, climate change, and sudden natural or environmental hazards will diminish state power even if that power should have been growing. The situation will become even more complicated if we take factors such as geopolitics and diplomacy into account, as the territorial expansion of a state is often constrained by the geopolitical relations between states. For example, after the Battle of Changping, the Zhao state was spared from annihilation only because of the intervention of the Chu and Wei, which were afraid that the annexation of Zhao would make their homelands the next target of the fearsome Qin.[39] Nevertheless, since all these external factors were absent in the collapse of the Qin Empire, this simplified model may still be applicable to the Qin's fall, as well as those of other similar regimes such as the Neo-Assyrian Empire.

Two more questions must be answered before proceeding to the next point: Can a state expand its territory to a size that its state power cannot sustain at the outset? Will it ever do so? The answers to both are "yes."

To begin with, the success of territorial expansion often hinges on the comparative advantage of the conquering regime over its opponent(s), as Mark Elvin says. Even if the state power of the conquering regime cannot sustain its governance or occupation over the new lands, this does not prevent it from eliminating its opponent(s) and thereby ostensibly annexing its (their) territories. In the case of the Qin unification, it is believed that a crucial factor behind the Qin's military successes lay in the advantages of its administrative system, which allowed the regime to produce and organize resources and troops more effectively in military engagements than its opponents.[40]

Equally importantly, the state is sometimes willing to invest a seemingly disproportionate amount of resources in territorial expansion with little or no economic premiums. Ideological and political impulses can also propel expansion. The predominant philosophical discourses in relation to the foundation of a unified and peaceful polity and the ideal of searching for the True Monarch likely contributed to the war launched by the Qin regime from 230 to 221 BCE to eliminate other Warring States polities.[41] The second expansion of the Qin Empire from 219 to 214 BCE may also have resulted from the imperialistic universal mission.[42] This type of ideology-driven territorial expansion cares little about economic returns, or does so only marginally, and will be executed at any cost.

Lastly, state decision-makers can never precisely foresee the point at which their expansion becomes overreaching. The military power of most historic states is not necessarily monopolized by the state. Independent or semi-independent military groups can also undertake military actions and conquests, in addition to the central government doing so. Even if military power is totally under the state's command, military commanders are often granted a certain degree of autonomy to cope with the everchanging conditions during campaigns. Hence, it is not unusual for a state to annex more territory than its governance machine can administer.

The final part of this theoretical section demonstrates the impact of the gap of state power. Whereas Qin rulers might never have consciously held any of the theoretical considerations or terminologies addressed above in their minds, this does not mean that they did not feel the pressure imposed by gaps in state power, which gave them considerable trouble and forced their further territorial expansion to a halt. The dynamics of the state power of the Qin Empire mentioned earlier likely precipitated this gap. Each of these dynamics entailed differential state organizations regulating the state's interactions with various power networks. By examining the detrimental impact of these dynamics on the governance of the Qin Empire, one can discern how the regime was threatened by the gap between its actual state power and the level of state power necessary to govern the territories it occupied.

To facilitate the analysis, I will situate these dynamics within the framework of state capacity, security, and legitimacy gaps, demonstrating how these gaps made the Qin Empire a fragile state that was unable to handle sudden crises even before the uprisings started in 209 BCE.

Here, it seems necessary to explain the rationale behind choosing this framework over others. In the field of international relations, while the concept of "failed states" (or similar expressions such as "failing" or "fragile" states) is ubiquitously used to identify states handicapped by bad governance, scholars have not reached a consensus on what exactly marks a state as "failed" or on how to measure "failure," the definition of which often varies from case to case. In response to the arbitrary usage of these terms, Charles Call offers an alternative analytic framework by synthesizing prevailing tools invented to characterize "failed states." In particular, Call singles out three "gaps," namely, capacity, security, and legitimacy, whose features are as follows:

1. A legitimacy gap is characterized by a significant portion of political elites and society in a state rejecting that state's regulations in exercising its power and in the accumulation and distribution of wealth.[43]

2. A capacity gap refers to a situation in which a state is incapable of ensuring the delivery of its core functions (e.g., the provision of security,[44] rule of law, public finance management, and minimal procurement of public goods such as primary education and primary health care) to the population.[45]

3. A security gap occurs when a state fails to provide minimal levels of security in the face of organized armed groups. In other words, if the state military forces are dissolute or have disappeared in the midst of a military invasion or an uprising, a security gap will form.[46]

This framework can serve as a useful tool to discern how the dynamics of state power impacted the governance of the Qin Empire. As Call points out, the areas of the abovementioned "gaps" overlap, and a state may or may not experience all of them concurrently.[47] These gaps can influence one another, especially the capacity and legitimacy gaps. For example, a state with a serious capacity gap will find itself facing a legitimacy crisis, and vice versa. In the same vein, if a state succumbs to low capacity and/or legitimacy, a security gap will probably follow. Additionally, a legitimacy gap might emerge when a state is unable to protect its people from external invasions.

Call argues that these three categories offer "a useful lens through which to analyze the challenges faced by states, and to formulate policy."[48] As a historical study of the fall of an ancient state, this book does not intend to prescribe any treatment regimen for the Qin Empire. Nevertheless, such an analytic framework does render several notable advantages for the analysis of the Qin collapse.

First, these categories neatly align with the four sources of state power advocated by Michael Mann. While all four sources of power would account for the emergence of each of the three gaps, they have different emphases. The legitimacy gap revolves primarily around ideological and political powers. The capacity gap in this framework, on the other hand, mostly relates to the deficit of political, military, and economic powers. The security gap is obviously associated with military and political powers.

Second, the framework outlines relatively concrete conditions under which a state is regarded as facing each of these three gaps, which is convenient in systematically mapping the deficiencies of the Qin Empire.

Third, these gaps are both comprehensive and easy to understand, to the extent that they can achieve considerable generalization power while at the same time allowing the reader to glimpse their content almost by intuition.

Caveats

Several caveats must be added before we proceed to the empirical analyses. First, while this book explores some of the possible detrimental effects of the sociopolitical and military policies formulated by the Qin Empire, it does not necessarily imply that these measures were useless. That is, the damages could result from either the poor timing or unforeseeable repercussions of these reforms. In this regard, they would be better described as ineffective. That the repercussions of these potentially beneficial measures proved to be unbearable to the Qin Empire evinces its low state power.

Such an understanding leads to the second caveat. It must be noted that the above framework does not tell us about how serious these "gaps" must be to lead to the fall of a state, although it does suggest that when the gap between state power and the expanded territory of the polity is too large, the pressure of returning to the controllable territory size could cause the disintegration of the political organizations that constitute a state. This narrative is, after all, impressionistic and the reader may prefer a quantitative approach to estimate state power.[49]

This omission is nonetheless justifiable. Collapse studies are not hard science. In hindsight, researchers can probe into the possible actors who might have triggered the demise of an organization, but the occurrence of such demise can never be predicted beforehand because collapses are often caused by contingent precipitants and thus vary from case to case. This observation is specifically applicable to the study of ancient history, where primary sources are often so fragmentary that any effort to create quantitative indices may result in superficial generalizations of complex social phenomena. As will be shown in this book, the unanticipated consequences of government policies indeed widened the gaps in the governance of the Qin Empire. The mostly qualitative approach adopted in this book (except in chapter 4) may be a more grounded way to analyze the interrelation of different power relations. In following this approach, we can better discern the fall of the Qin Empire and the sociopolitical configurations emerged during this process.

Lastly, the arguments in this book are mainly derived from the Liye manuscripts, which include the administrative documents of Qianling county (present-day Liye Town, Longshan, Hunan).[50] As a politically peripheral county located deep in the Wuling Mountains, the situation of Qianling likely differed considerably from that of the Qin core in Guanzhong. This calls into question whether the observed dynamics were applicable to other regions of the Qin Empire, or if they were limited to a small fraction of its territories.

While the Liye material is undeniably a somewhat biased source, studying the idiosyncrasies of Qianling county and the empire's periphery is still integral to our understanding of the Qin collapse and Qin history in general. The dynamics of the periphery often function as catalysts stimulating sociopolitical and sociocultural changes in a state. As I will show in chapters 3 and 4, quite a few new policies and reforms that the imperial Qin regime promulgated to tackle emergent crises affected not only the periphery but also the whole empire. That Qianling was a peripheral county is therefore advantageous for deciphering how dynamics of the periphery increased the momentum of the sociopolitical configurations during the imperial Qin period. Furthermore, studying peripheral regions helps uncover the regional diversity hidden beneath the image of a unified empire. By adopting a peripheral perspective, we can better comprehend the interesting and complex cultural diversity, such as the conflict between universal and regional identities.[51]

Admittedly, these two advantages do not solve the issue of representativeness. Hopefully, archaeologists in China will soon discover findings comparable to the magnitude of the Liye cache with which we could obtain more concrete information on the governance and social configurations in other regions—especially the center and the east—of the Qin Empire and, as such, contest the observations made in this book. I will keep my fingers crossed.

Chapter 2

State Ideology and Social Tensions in the Qin Empire

It is not that the Qin did not desire to govern, but its failure was because its actions were too profuse, its use of punishments excessive.

秦非不欲治也，然失之者，乃舉措太眾、刑罰太極故也。

—*Xinyu* 新語 4[1]

The epigraph, attributed to early Western Han thinker Lu Jia 陸賈, is perhaps the most insightful remark on the Qin collapse in the *Xinyu*; it makes a crucial point that is often neglected by later political thinkers. Interestingly, although Lu blamed the Qin for its stern punishments and aggressive policies, he did not think that they emanated from malicious intent.[2] For Lu, the Qin rulers failed not because they were evil in nature, but because they used the wrong methods to do good.

While Lu's comment mainly censured the Qin's large-scale construction projects and expansionist policy, it may well describe the unprecedented social engineering project that the regime formulated. Politically, this project aimed at enlarging the pool of Qin literate elites. Socially, it sought to interfere in social activities and family relations. Intellectually, it tried to exert more direct influence over the minds of the people through the promotion and institutionalization of select social values, such as filial piety (*xiao* 孝), devotion and reverence (*zhongjing* 忠敬), and kindness and love (*ciai* 慈愛). Through punishments and rewards, which were perceived as two quintessential "Legalist" levers, the regime intended to reform undesirable social actions and expand this ideal social order to "all under heaven" through a self-proclaimed "civilizing mission." Eventually, more diffuse, infrastructural state power could be achieved, thereby building a boundless, peaceful, and utopian empire. In view of these traits, I have characterized imperial Qin ideology as the "moral-legalist supremacism" to stress the layered, composite nature of such an ideology.[3]

Despite the Qin rulers' hard work to strengthen the state power and perfect the social order, their oppressive ideology and reckless implementation methods call into question the effectiveness of these measures. This chapter will examine these issues. First, I explore the Qin regime's attempts to construct a new class of ruling elites by promoting Qin literacy, examining how the supremacist tendency of the Qin's ideology prevented the consolidation of this universal ruling class. Second, I discuss how the difficult and uncompassionate "moral-legalist" ideology might have defeated the purposes of the Qin's sociopolitical reforms and engendered tensions between the regime and grassroots communities. These phenomena suggest that the Qin Empire's infrastructural power was not extensive enough to motivate the compliance of its subjects.

Premature Universal Ruling Class and Cultural Identity

The proper governance of states that have developed intricate bureaucracy often relies on agents such as bureaucrats and grassroots leaders. The compliance of such agents is rarely achieved through mere coercion. Instead, a certain degree of ideological integration is needed to motivate and convince the agents to comply with the state, thereby making them part of the "ruling class" of the state, which is defined as an extensive cadre of politically organized, culturally conscious, but economically unequal people. Michael Mann observes that the most vital infrastructure that the Roman Empire used to acculturate local rulers of non-Roman origins was *literacy*. The spread of Latin played an instrumental role in integrating local rulers into the Roman system, turning them into part of a universal ruling class (i.e., the citizens).[4] Despite the nuanced differences between the two ancient empires, the Roman example seemed comparable with the measures of the imperial (or even preimperial) Qin regime. That is, the spread of Qin literacy—the proficiency in understanding and writing the Qin-style scripts—could have helped incorporate new subjects into the government. Consequently, the pool of Qin ruling elites would have expanded, and a more universal Qin identity would be promoted.[5]

Indeed, constructing a universal Qin cultural identity became one of the prominent issues for the newborn Qin Empire. In the wake of persistent institutional consolidation, political division, and military confrontation, the territorial states that survived at the end of the Warring States seemed to have instilled their respective populaces with certain cultural identities. Extant evidence reveals that the preimperial Qin regime had already formed a distinctive Qin identity and developed intricate measures to identify Qin and non-Qin individuals.[6] A lawsuit case in the Yuelu manuscripts centers on the cultural identity of a gang of robbers who resided in Jingzhou 京州 in the Chu state. It is reported that after Jingzhou was surrendered to Qin in 222 BCE, these robbers murdered and injured Qin people and were subsequently arrested by the Qin authorities. The most pressing controversy lay in whether they were to be classified as Qin or Chu, which would affect the bounties rewarded to their captors.[7] This case indicates that cultural identities can serve as an important criterion in deciding legal terms.

The classifications set up by the Qin state were likely not an exception in the Warring States period. Given their relatively stable and direct interactions with state authorities, inhabitants of territorial states might have developed a stronger sense of belonging to the reigning polities. Such nostalgia might have led to resentment toward the Qin conquerors and efforts to restore their own erstwhile political organizations. In view of these possible constraints, we cannot assume that the Qin Empire fully inherited the legacy of these old territorial states and transformed itself into a territorial empire overnight. Quite to the contrary, the Qin regime likely did not (or could not) instantly annihilate the cultural identities of the populace of these former states. New subjects, especially the elites of these former states, likely still subscribed to their old cultural identities and customs.

The universalism displayed in the Qin state ideology and the unification of written scripts and measurement should be placed in this historical context. Whereas these efforts were tools for mediating the differences between the old and new Qin populace and for constructing a new cadre of ruling elites, they did not completely pay off. In reality, old regional identities played a role not only in people's daily lives but also in the administrative practices of the Qin government. More importantly, unlike the succeeding Western Han Empire, the Qin never managed to construct a universal ruling class, despite its desire to do so. From this perspective, the ghost of the Warring States period lingered and haunted the Qin Empire. But before going into detail about Qin's failure, I first address its efforts in consolidating a new "official's identity," which was a pivotal step in forming a new ruling class.

LITERATE ELITES AND THE OFFICIAL'S IDENTITY: WRITING SPECIALISTS IN THE QIN EMPIRE

Recently, scribes (*shī* 史) have been in the limelight of studies on early China. Various scholarly efforts have been devoted to the relationship between literacy and the scribe's identities. Drawing on evidence such as manuscripts and stationary tools (brushes, writing knives, ink stones, etc.) found in Chu (including Zeng 曾) and Qin tombs, scholars even contend that "scribes" as professionals were admired and distinct from other social groups such as the illiterate masses or classically educated *shi* 士. This marked the status of "scribe" as a collective identity.[8]

These arguments, however, do not represent the intricacy of the word *shī*, which was deeply entangled with *li* 吏 (official) as late as the Warring States period. To distinguish the nuances of 史, below I use the capital *Scribe* for 史 as an official title, whereas the lowercase *scribe* is for writing specialists in the general sense, including groups such as Scribes, Assistants (Zuo 佐), Diviners (Bu 卜), Invocators (Zhu 祝), and the like. I use the romanized *shī* for a social group whose members might have identified themselves as 史.

While the *shī* undoubtedly formed a distinct identity, the representativeness of this social identity among writing specialists serving in the Qin and Han governments seemed questionable. Extant Qin sources give little direct evidence that scribes identified themselves or were being seen collectively as *shī*. In other words, *shī*, as a collective identity, might not be as prominent as we thought in the late Warring States and imperial Qin government. As I will demonstrate below, "official" seemed to be the identity that Qin administrators more commonly used to think about themselves, and that was used by Qin rulers to collectively address them. In view of the predominance of the "official's identity," it may be a more fitting term to characterize the collective identity of Qin administrators than *shī*.

By the late Warring States and early imperial period, the *shī* had lost much of their former prestige despite retaining their hereditary status.[9] Consider the Prefect of Grand Scribe (Taishi Ling 太史令), who,[10] unlike his prominent Western Zhou counterpart, was only a middle-level officer in the early Western Han (and presumably Qin) government.[11] The depiction of the prominence of *shī* in various Warring States historical and quasi-historical texts is but a fiction invented to address contemporaneous questions through the *shī*'s mouths.[12] In reality, the vast majority of *shī* worked as low-level administrators using their writing skills, which were obtained through years of family education, at official scribal schools, and/or through primers.[13]

More importantly, the *shī* were not the only group of administrators in the late Warring States Qin government. The incessant bureaucratization and militarization of the Qin government led to the inclusion of nonhereditary writing specialists such as Assistants, as well as military officers who climbed the ladder of success through their martial achievements and thus probably acquired limited literacy.[14] These groups usurped the hegemony of the *shī* in government administration and subsequently gave rise to a new cadre of professional bureaucrats permanently in charge of certain offices: the *li* officials. Indeed, evidence suggests that the late Warring States and imperial Qin regime preferred to identify this new cadre of clerical staff as *li* rather than *shī*. Paleographical analysis reveals that the character *li* stemmed from *shì* 事 ("to serve for," "task," "affair") in the Qin writing system around the late Warring States period.[15] Considering its proximity to *shì*, the notion of *li* seems to focus on the task to which a person is assigned and the affair that he serves. This contrasts with *shī*, which denotes the ability of a person rather than the task. To some extent, the word *li* manifests the impersonal nature of bureaucrats.

Bureaucratization also had profound impacts on the *shī* community. As early as the Western Zhou period, the *shī* were somewhat bureaucratized and became the linchpin of the government.[16] But the level of bureaucratization in the middle Warring States Qin was beyond compare. By that time, *shī* received a fixed salary from the regime according to their individual status in the bureaucratic hierarchy and had to be selected and promoted along a regular path.[17] In other words, *shī* became a type of officials serving in the government. It is therefore not a coincidence that the *shī* were often associated with administrative tasks such as the inspection of other offices and law enforcement in the Warring States "Legalist" texts.[18]

That the position of *shī* was still hereditary seems incompatible with the bureaucratization progress, as it probably restrained the expansion of the bureaucracy. This may be understood as a tactic to protect the interest of the *shī* community on the one hand and to maintain better quality control over administrators on the other.[19] The emergence of state-organized scribal schools (*xueshi* 學室) and a central qualifying exam designed exclusively for the descendants of *shī* might have been the compromises made to preserve the traditional privilege of the *shī* community and satisfy the need for training qualified bureaucrats en masse.

According to the "Statutes on Scribes" (Shi lü 史律) of the *Statutes and Ordinances of the Second Year* (*Ernian lüling* 二年律令), to qualify as Scribes, scribal trainees needed to receive three years of formal training, after which they would be tested by the Grand Scribe at the capital and by Commandery Governors at the local level. The content of the examination constituted tests of both the oral and writing abilities of the examinees, who had to recite and write out more than 5,000 characters, and be able to handle eight different calligraphic styles. However, it is unclear if non-Scribes also had to reach this high standard to be classified as "literate."[20]

Despite all these efforts, *shī* as a social identity was sidelined by the dominance of the official's identity. Specifically, *official* became a generic term that was frequently used in Qin emperors' decrees and legal enactments to address the state's administrators. One notable example was the decree on the banning of unsanctioned learning in 213 BCE, by which officials were designated to serve as instructors carefully transmitting the state's ideology and values to the masses. In contrast, the term *shī* was only used as a nomenclature of social identity in texts pertinent to scribal training such as writing primers and the "Statutes on Scribes." Outside this context, the word 史 predominantly denoted the ability to read and write or served as an official title.[21] A Qin ordinance even lists "*shī* of writing" (*shu shī* 書史) alongside servants (*pu* 僕) and errand runners (*zou* 走).[22] The context in which the term *shu shī* is embedded indicates that literacy was no longer a guarantee of high social status.

The *shī*'s decline was epitomized in the Qin "Ordinance pertaining to the scribal trainees who committed fraud to not enter the examination" (史學童詐不入試令) dated to 218 BCE. Given its importance, a full quotation is warranted:

> For those officials who commit fraud to be dismissed and leave [their position] as officials: for [positions from] Accessory Scribe, Vice-Prefect, and Commander on up, submit [the report with respect to their crime] to the Chief Prosecutor;

for [positions from] subordinates, Assistant of Commander, and [any official whose salary grade] entitles him to a carriage on down, submit [the report with respect to their crime] to the Chancellor. The Chancellor and Chief Prosecutor have to first provide commanderies in the new territories which are distanced and perilous [with the dismissed officials], and [when their demands] are met, further dispatch [the dismissed officials] to [other commanderies] according to their priority, and in every case, order [the dismissed officials] to carry out their official duties in the new territories for four years; only after their days of service are completed [can they be] released. If their days of service are not completed but [they] fraudulently and intentionally commit other [crimes that match the punishments of] fining or expulsion so as to be dismissed from [their positions] as officials, add one degree to [their] punishments.

Now the Grand Scribe . . . scribal trainees from counties of the central region (the Metropolitan Area) who have assembled and been tested now altogether [amounted to] 841, 111 of whom did not enter [the position of] scribe.

Your servant heard that for those who did not enter [the position of scribe], it was mostly [because] they are loath to become officials, and thus joined with their . . . (employ?) statutory labor as a pretext for committing fraud and for refusing to enter [the position of] scribe, thereby escaping from being an official. [When scribal trainees] commit fraud like this but receive no punishment, it causes disadvantages.

Your servant petitions: Order the Grand Scribe to send [those scribal trainees who had committed fraud to circumvent government services] to be the Assistants of the counties of Liaodong [commandery] for four years; [only] after their days of service are completed can they be dismissed. [Should their] days of service not be completed but [they] commit [crimes that match] the punishment of banishment, keep them placed in Liaodong [commandery]. [Should] they commit [crimes that match] the punishment of shaving their beard, also transfer [their residence] to Liaodong [commandery], and in every case, order their parents, wives, children, and coresidents [appearing on the same] household register to follow them. [Adopting the abovementioned measures to] punish them for committing fraud is advantageous. Your servant braves death to petition this. The imperial decision says: Approved.

In the twenty-ninth year, on the *jiaxu* (eleventh) day of the fourth month, [this imperial decision] arrived at Huyang county.

The "Ordinance pertaining to the scribal trainees who committed fraud to not enter the examination." Taken from C27 of the ("Ordinances on) the Court."

諸吏為詐（詐）以免去吏者，卒史、丞、尉以上上御史ㄴ，屬、尉佐及乘車以下上丞相。丞相、御史先予新地遠、轚害郡，備，【以】次予之，皆令從其吏事新地四歲，日備免之，日未備而詐（詐）故為它貲、廢，以免去吏，駕（加）皋一等。

　　·【今泰】史□☑ 23 中縣史學童今茲會試者凡八百卅一人ㄴ，其不入史者百一十一人。

　　·臣聞其不入者泰抵惡為吏，而與其

　　(missing slips?)

　　□繇（徭）故為詐（詐），不肎（肯）入史，以避為吏ㄴ。為詐（詐）如此而毋罰，不便。

　　·臣請：今泰史遣以為潦東縣官佐四歲，日備免之。日未備而有罨（遷）皋，因處之潦東ㄴ。其有耐皋，亦徒之潦東而皆令其父母、妻、子與同居數者從之，以罰其為詐（詐），便。·臣眛（昧）死請。制曰：可

　　·廿九年四月甲戌到胡陽。

　　·史學童詐（詐）不入試令；·出廷丙廿七。 24

The ordinance comprises two parts. The first part is a citation of an existing ordinance on the punishment of officials and scribal trainees who defrauded their way out of their jobs. Accordingly, such an act was equivalent to committing fraud, and offenders had to serve as "officials in the new territories" (*xindi li* 新地吏) for four years. This ordinance also prioritized the undesirable new territories over regions with less urgent needs. The second part revolves around an incident reported by the Grand Scribe in 218 BCE, three years after the epochal unification. It is reported that over 13 percent of the scribal trainees from counties of the Metropolitan Area failed their examinations and could not become qualified Scribes. Apparently, such a low pass rate was uncommon and thus instantly drew the attention of the Grand Scribe. After an investigation, it was discovered that this was because the scribal trainees were "loath to become officials" (*wu wei li* 惡為吏). Given that no existing legislation could have punished their crime, the petitioner(s) suggested appointing these deceiving trainees as the Assistants of the counties of Liaodong commandery in the remote northeastern frontier for four years.

Two points are worth noting here. First, the reluctant attitude of the trainees should be partly attributed to the precarious conditions of their future service locations. Regardless of the underlying reasons, however, that a substantial proportion of scribal trainees refused to serve in the government indicates the regime's incapacity to command the compliance of their functionaries. In this fashion, this incident bespeaks the regime's low infrastructural power. Second, Qin administrative documents from Liye mention the title "Junior Scribes" (Xiao Shi 小史), which was usually given only to newly qualified, gradeless Scribes prior to completing their probationary period.[25] The "officials" mentioned in the 218 BCE ordinance are likely these Junior Scribes. This indicates that for the Qin policy-makers, these "Junior Scribes," notwithstanding their greenness, were still *li* officials. For them, *shī* as a social identity was inseparable from and subordinate to the position of officials.[26]

More importantly, Qin administrators often positioned themselves as "officials." The most direct evidence of these writing specialists' self-identification is a few synonymous handbooks concerning the conduct of government officials. In addition to the manuscript found in Shuihudi tomb no. 11, the collections of the Yuelu Academy and Peking University house two other such handbooks, both of which are unprovenanced,[27] although researchers generally believe that they were looted from tombs in Jianghan Plain.[28] Since the occupant of Shuihudi tomb no. 11, Xi 喜, was a Scribe serving in Anlu 安陸 county at the turn of the Qin unification, this type of handbook was presumably popular reading or teaching material in the Qin scribal communities during the late Warring States period.

In the Shuihudi tomb no. 11 version, the text begins with the line "Taken together, the way of making a good official" 凡為吏之道, which the editors excerpted as its title. Textually, *The Way of Making a Good Official* lists, in columns, manifold maxims by which an "official" should abide.[29] While the text is basically a patchwork of didactic items assembled over different times,[30] its target audience was undoubtedly officials, and, on top of that, its focus was primarily on transforming an individual into an exemplary "official" rather than a *shī*.

Similarly, the Yuelu Academy handbook also targeted officials. The Yuelu textual witness by itself carries a title, *On Being an Official Who Managed Offices and Black-headed Ones* (*Wei li zhi guan ji qianshou* 為吏治官及黔首),[31] which was inscribed on the verso of slip 87. The opening statement summarizes the main theme of the whole text and is particularly notable:

> Here is the essence of managing offices, black-headed ones, and [an official's] own self! Other official evaluations have models and ordinances [to follow], [but even if an official] can earn the first place [in the evaluation by abiding these regulations], when he wants to avoid coming in last place or being incriminated, in every case, he cannot attain [these objectives]. The way of reaching first place is to hold this [handbook] and look at it on a daily basis, be respectful and not give it up, and recite, chant, and make it your primary agenda.

> 此治官、黔首及身之要也與（歟）！它官課有式令，能最，欲毋殿，欲毋罪，皆不可得。欲最之道，把此日視之，簍（僂）勿舍，風（諷）庸（誦）為首。[32]

The fact that the above passage stresses that the only way to attain excellence in official evaluations was to thoroughly study the handbook rather than government models and ordinances alludes to the text's unofficial nature.[33] One of its conceivable producers was a low-level administrator, who may have compiled the work as a reference and/or teaching material for officials.[34] Of course, this does not imply that this type of handbook had nothing to do with the Qin regime. Given that the layout of the abovementioned passage differs from other sections of the text, it may be a paratext prepared by the compiler(s), who attached it to the source material disseminated by the authorities.[35] If this was the case, handbooks such as *On Being an Official Who Managed Offices and Black-Headed Ones* manifested both the self-identification of "officials," that is, their users, and the Qin regime's recognition of such a collective identity for officials.

This self-identification can also be observed through the selection of manuscripts for burials. Aside from handbooks of officials' conduct, other quintessential manuscripts found in the tombs of Qin functionaries included statutes and ordinances, model forms (*shi* 式), chronicles (*yeshu* 葉書), and event calendars (*zhiri* 質日) recording official and personal activities, as well as divination, medical, and mathematical manuals. In addition to legal and administrative texts, mathematical, hemerological, and medical knowledge and skills were also integral to a Qin official's everyday administrative tasks.[36] Hence, the genres of manuscripts listed above might have been deliberately chosen to present the deceased's identity as an official, even if some of the tomb occupants (e.g., Xi) were clearly Scribes.

Additionally, the relationship between the inclusion of writing utensils in Scribes' tombs and their identity is not self-evident. As a highly bureaucratized regime relied on written communication, writing undoubtedly played a pivotal role in everyday administration. It is therefore with good reason that Western Han government administrators earned the title "writing-knife-and-brush officials" (*daobi li* 刀筆吏) rather than "writing-knife-and-brush *shī*." Although this somewhat dismissive title postdates the Qin period, it demonstrates that writing instruments were a crucial component of the *li*'s image.[37] In fact, most epithets of Western Han administrators—"harsh officials" (*kuli* 酷吏), "exemplary officials" (*xunli* 循吏), and "refined officials" (*wenli* 文吏)—invariably designated them as officials (*li*) rather than *shī*.[38] This may be another instantiation of the preponderance of the "official's identity."

Of course, the predominance of the official's identity does not imply the extinction of the *shī* identity. After all, identities are fluid and layered and one can subscribe to multiple identities at once. Therefore, a writing specialist working in the Qin government could simultaneously self-identify as a *shī* and as an official. What I argue is that both the Qin regime and its writing specialists *preferred* the identity of an official to that of the *shī* at the end of the Warring States period.

One of the reasons behind such a preference may be that government administrators were no longer limited to Scribes. As noted earlier, the Qin regime introduced another group of clerical staff called the Assistants to meet the increasing demand for literate administrators. In contrast to hereditary Scribes, the Assistants acquired literacy more through long-term practical experiences inside the administrative system. As a result, the Assistants usually began their service when they reached maturity (*zhuang* 壯)—that is, at around thirty years old or older.[39] Given that Assistants lacked the formal training and shared knowledge of Scribes, they were rather marginalized within the government and could only fill vacancies left by Scribes if there was a shortage of the latter.[40]

Nonetheless, this situation started to change in the imperial Qin period. A "Statute on the Establishment of Officials" from the Yuelu manuscripts reveals that the age restriction on the Assistants began to be loosened:

> For counties that appoint Junior Assistants who have no salary grade, each of these counties can only appoint [candidates] within their own purview, and in every case, can only select and appoint holders of *bugeng* (the fourth rank) on down to [rankless] *shiwu* who are literate to be Assistants; when [eligible candidates] are insufficient, further appoint sons of *junzi*[41] and *dafu* (the fifth rank), minor rank-holders, as well as sons of *gongzu* and *shiwu* who are eighteen years old on up to meet the staff quota. Do not force new black-headed ones to [be Assistants]. Do not let those who are over sixty years old be Assistants.

> 縣除小佐毋（無）秩者，各除其縣中，皆擇除不更以下到士五（伍）史者為佐；不足，益除君子子、大夫子、小爵及公卒、士五（伍）子年十八歲以上備員。其新黔首勿強。年過六十者勿以為佐∟。[42]

The title "Junior Assistant" (Xiao Zuo 小佐) parallels the "Junior Scribe" mentioned earlier. Here the word *xiao* does not refer to the actual age of the Assistant but serves as a denomination for his credentials. That persons who had just reached adulthood could only serve as backups indicates that the Qin regime still preferred mature candidates (but not those older than sixty) in selecting Assistants. Nevertheless, this prescription shows that the "maturity principle" was no longer strictly enforced. This contrasts with a preimperial stipulation in the Shuihudi tomb no. 11 legal texts that proscribed newly registered persons (*xin fu* 新傅) from serving as Assistants.[43] One underlying reason behind this change was the desire to maximize the talent pool of potential writing specialists, thereby curbing the severe shortage of administrators in the empire's new territories caused by the empire's rapid territorial expansion (see the first section of chapter 3 for details).

The second-to-last sentence of the above statute underlines that counties could not force new subjects to be Assistants. In other words, the long list of eligible groups enumerated in the preceding parts likely included new subjects who met these criteria. This implies that the Qin government was recruiting the indigenous population in the new territories to be Assistants. Such a choice is understandable, as Scribes were hereditary and the position was not open to older candidates. In contrast, once equipped with Qin literacy skills, writing experts of former polities could have been handily channeled into the Qin government as nonhereditary Assistants. Conceivably, this policy was already in place during the preimperial period, but the severe shortage of administrators in the wake of the empire's rapid expansion probably caused a surge in demand for additional literate personnel. This resulted in an unprecedented influx of Assistants during the imperial Qin era, to the extent that they started to outnumber Scribes in certain regions.

One such place was Qianling county. According to the "Report on the Officials of Qianling" (Qianling li zhi 遷陵吏志), Assistants occupied 53 of the 101 staff quotas in Qianling. Administrative records from Qianling also reveal manifold new Assistant titles, many of which had direct parallels to the position of Scribes.[44] One salient example is the Scribe Director (Ling Shi 令史) and Assistant Director (Ling Zuo 令佐).[45] These pieces of evidence suggest that Assistants seemed to have emerged as the majority of administrative personnel in the Qianling government.

Qianling county was likely not an isolated case. The policy of training and recruiting local writing specialists is also evident in the early activities of Xiao He 蕭何 and Cao Can 曹參, both of whom were from Pei 沛 county and later founded the Western Han Empire. Accounts in standard histories record that Xiao and Cao established themselves as Pei's Head of Officials (Zhu Li Yuan 主吏掾) and Head of Prisons (Yu Yuan 獄掾), respectively.[46] As both positions played prominent roles in county administration and involved substantial amounts of mundane paperwork, Xiao and Cao must have mastered the Qin-style script at an advanced level. Considering their local background and ages,[47] Xiao and Cao likely started their careers as Assistants. These examples suggest that Assistants became preponderant in peripheral counties such as Qianling and Pei.

More importantly, the influx of Assistants blurred the distinction between Scribes and Assistants. The Liye manuscripts document a Qianling local named Hun 圂, who first appeared as an Assistant of the Warehouse (Ku Zuo 庫佐),[48] and was likely promoted to Assistant Director not later than the thirty-first year of the First Emperor (216 BCE). Given his background, and the fact that he started his official career as an Assistant, he probably learned the Qin writing system as an adult. Around 214 BCE, Hun was transferred to the position of Scribe Director.[49] On the one hand, this indicates that Assistant was still below Scribe in the bureaucratic hierarchy and the differences between Scribes and Assistants did not disappear during the Qin dynasty. On the other hand, that Hun was eventually promoted from Assistant Director to Scribe Director evidences a gradual assimilation of Scribes and Assistants.[50]

The spread of Qin literacy and the introduction of indigenous literate personnel propelled the expansion of the Qin official's identity. While the intricacy of identity transformation is hardly tractable in written records, the peculiar "Chu-style" manuscripts that appeared at the Tuzishan 兔子山 site may help us glimpse this phenomenon. Serving as the seat of ancient Yiyang 益陽 county, the site was built around the fourth century BCE and was not abandoned until the fourth century CE. Manuscripts have been found in eleven wells and, remarkably, consist of specimens from almost every polity that had existed at that site. In this fashion, the Tuzishan manuscripts comprise by far the most complete continuum of wooden and bamboo manuscripts in China.

Manuscripts found in well no. 9 are especially worth noting. The archaeological report divides the well into nine strata. Since fragments of the same piece of tile were scattered in different strata, the report contends that the sediment in the well accumulated over a short period of time.[51] Regarding the distribution of manuscripts, the seventh stratum included 567 pieces of inscribed bamboo slips, whereas the third and eighth strata respectively yielded only two and ten pieces of manuscripts, along with earth, building debris, and other wastes. Given this lopsided distribution, archaeologists infer that the manuscripts in stratum seven were discarded concurrently.[52]

The archaeological report discloses two manuscript specimens from stratum three, 151 from stratum seven, and one from stratum eight. The two specimens from stratum three are wooden tablets written in the Qin clerical script, including the accession edict of the Second Emperor of Qin datable to 209 BCE. The remaining manuscripts are all fragments of personnel registers inscribed on bamboo slips, whose writing style and formulaic language are characteristic of those from the Chu state.[53] Given this distinctive feature, the report proposes that they were Chu administrative documents produced during the late Warring States period, although slip 7.151 carries Chu-style script on one side and Qin-style script on the other.[54]

The report's view has been challenged by paleographers, who have pointed out that the graphs on these slips are in fact a blending of the Chu- and Qin-style scripts. The interpretations of this intriguing phenomenon are divided. Some surmise that these peculiar manuscripts evince efforts to revive the Chu writing system among former Chu scribes who, after years of practicing the Qin writing style, were no longer accustomed to the earlier script with which they had once been familiar.[55] An alternative view nonetheless argues that this peculiar mixture of different styles results from those subjugated Chu scribes now serving in the conquerors' regime. Having just learned the Qin script, they reflexively blended elements of the Chu script into their writings.[56]

Considering the archaeological context and materiality of these bamboo slips, they were more likely written by former Chu scribes who were new to the Qin script. These hybrid-style slips were buried beneath two Qin wooden tablets and are thus likely earlier than the latter. This fact is also supported by the distribution of hollow bricks found in well no. 9. These bricks were spread between strata three and six. Since their design is consonant with those used in the Qin palaces in Guanzhong,[57] they were most likely building blocks of Qin-era edifices.[58] In other words, artifacts in these strata might have accumulated when the Qin local government in Yiyang was overrun and the county seat was destroyed in the anti-Qin movement. This also coincides with the fact that most building debris featuring strong Qin cultural traits was discovered in strata three to six, whose soils are described as having a much darker color than those of the bottom strata.[59] If this is so, the bamboo slips found in the seventh and eighth strata likely date to the Qin and/or earlier times.[60]

This phenomenon bespeaks the nuances of the spread of Qin literacy and the emergence of a more universal identity among officials. Although the extant evidence makes no mention of the identities of those who produced these hybrid-style slips, they were presumably former Chu scribes working as Assistants in the Yiyang county seat. Possibly, these "Chu administrative documents" might have served as writing practices for these surrendering former Chu scribes, who attempted to familiarize themselves with the newly learned Qin-style script by copying Chu administrative texts. This might explain why distinctly Chu- and Qin-style scripts appear on both sides of slip 7.151. In short, these "Qin-Chu-style" slips signify the Qin regime's efforts to turn writing experts of former polities into its own functionaries.

The development of Assistants signals an increase of administrators. From the imperial Qin period onward, Assistants were no longer inferior substitutes for privileged Scribes in the Qin bureaucracy. Rather, the merging of Scribes and Assistants suggests that the latter group became accepted members of the administrator communities. This phenomenon further substantiates my proposition that the official's identity may more closely approximate the way the Qin conceptualized the identity of their administrators, who were no longer only Scribes.

The expansion of Qin literacy heralded an emerging, more extensive ruling class. The identity of Qin officials was bound by a similar bundle of ideological beliefs. Officials shared a body of knowledge of Qin literacy, experiences (including misfortunes) in the Qin bureaucracy,[61] and common habits and interests, all of which likely cultivated their collective identity as Qin officials. Although officials were not aristocrats and were not necessarily high in meritorious rank (*jue* 爵), they could potentially be promoted to high-level officials such as ministers or governors through their performance in the government. Even if such prospects were only achieved by a small cohort of high-flyers, with their literacy skills and official background, local administrators likely acted as key influencers in their communities.[62] In view of these features, Qin officials, regardless of their salary grades, should be considered literate elites and members of the empire's ruling class (which was not confined to officials, of course).[63]

By acquiring Qin literacy skills and serving as administrators of the Qin regime, new subjects were given the chance to become rulers in the empire. Consider again the examples of Xiao He, Cao Can, and Hun, all of whom were entrusted with prominent positions in their respective administrative units. Xiao He's story is especially worth recounting. We observe that Xiao worked under Supervisory Prosecutor of Sichuan 四川 commandery,[64] who was impressed by Xiao's competence and let him act as the commandery's Accessory Scribe (Zu Shi 卒史). Xiao once again performed so well that he placed first in an evaluation and received the Supervisory Prosecutor's recommendation to serve in the central government. Xiao He, nonetheless, refused this generous offer.[65]

The implications of Xiao He's anecdote are twofold. On the one hand, Xiao was granted the chance to work in the central government, proving the openness of the Qin regime to their new subjects. Xiao's example suggests that new subjects could be accepted as members of the ruling class insofar as they attained Qin literacy skills and embraced the identity of official. From this perspective, subscription to such an identity performed a function comparable to that of Roman citizenship in the formation of a universal ruling class, even though the notion of citizenship probably did not exist in imperial China.[66]

On the other hand, Xiao He's reluctance to serve in the central government hints at the strong bond between these new administrators and their domiciles. Despite the addition of a more extensive official's identity in company with existing regional cultural identities, the infrastructural power of the Qin regime was not sufficient to incentivize the total compliance of these indigenous administrators. When the Qin's despotic power dwindled and officials needed to take side between the regime and their locality, they often chose the latter. Hence, this universal ruling class was a work-in-progress.

DISCONTINUATION OF AN EMERGING UNIVERSAL RULING CLASS

The formation of a universal ruling class was not a linear process. The adaptation of Qin literacy and the expansion of the official's identity discontinued after the Qin Empire's collapse and only resumed later in the Western Han dynasty. In sum, the emergence of a community of officials that was heavily influenced by the Qin bureaucratic tradition in the Han dynasty was not teleological but contingent.

Several unearthed manuscripts produced during the Qin–Han transition capture the identity shifts of officials serving in the new territories of the Qin Empire. For instance, in stratum five of Liye well no. 1, there are a handful of bamboo slips whose graphs are reminiscent of the Chu writing style (fig. 2.1).[67] Since the fifth stratum was the top layer that yielded manuscripts and thus likely contained the latest written artifacts, Zheng Wei 鄭威 relates the "Chu" slips therein to the Zhang Chu regime and infers that they were likely the product of local Chu insurgencies, which tried to revive the once-abandoned Chu calligraphy after the collapse of the Qin Empire.[68]

While Zheng's proposition is apt to explain the existence of Chu slips in stratum 5, it does not accord with the recently surfaced slip 9-2330 from the Liye corpus (Fig. 2.1c).[69] The slip is a long wooden tally whose formulaic language is quintessentially Chu in style. Consider the term "the month of offering horses" (*xianma zhi yue* 獻馬之月) in slip 9-2330. It was one of the names of months in the Chu calendar and corresponded to the ninth month in the Qin calendar.[70] Although the text is composed in the Chu-style formulaic language, it was written in Qin script and lacked the characteristics of Chu writing.

At least two speculations can be made regarding its production. First, this slip could have been made by a native Qin scribe or someone otherwise familiar with Qin administrative practice who served under

Figure 2.1a. Specimen of Chu-style slips after the collapse of the Qin Empire, Liye slip 5-7. Photo courtesy of Wan Yuk Ping.

Figure 2.1b. Specimen of Chu-style slips after the collapse of the Qin Empire, Liye slip 5-9. Photo courtesy of Wan Yuk Ping.

Figure 2.1c. Specimen of Chu-style slips after the collapse of the Qin Empire, segment "the month of offering horses" (獻馬之月) excerpted from Liye slip 9-2330, which was written in a Qin-style script but carries a Chu calendar name and administrative language. Photo courtesy of Wan Yuk Ping.

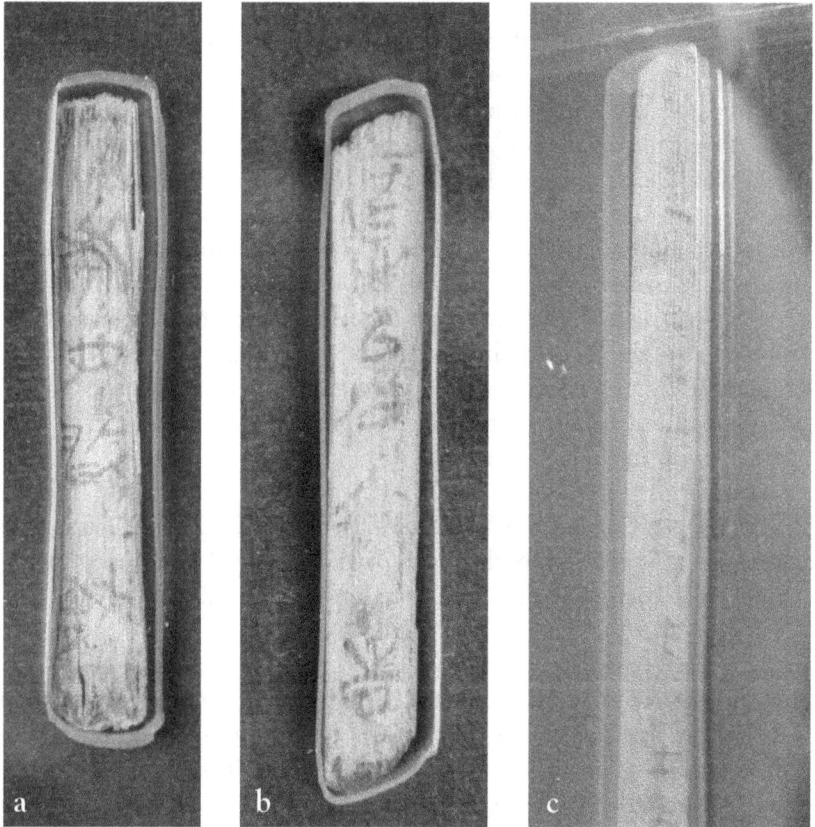

the Zhang Chu or other neo-Chu regimes and mimicked the Chu writing style for the new ruler. Second, it could have been written by a former Chu scribe who had served in the Qianling government and was unable to write in a genuine Chu style after years of practicing the Qin writing system. Either way, these so-called Chu slips bespeak the complexity involved in adapting the writing system, which is one of the best indicators of the adaptations of culture and identity.

This phenomenon shows that the choice of writing in the Qin or Chu script, as well as the subscription to the cultural tradition that the writing system represented, was subject to the despotic power of the Qin state. Any sudden situational changes could result in the interruption of this transformation. This point is especially valid in the case of Assistants, who did not receive the formal Qin scribal education and were likely less influenced by the Qin value system. This may partly explain indigenous officials' frequent participation in the anti-Qin movement, as most of them should have been Assistants given their backgrounds and ages. That said, even if the transformation ended abruptly, fingerprints of Qin culture were likely left on the lives of these scribes who went halfway through the "Qinification" process.

In addition to time, another obstacle to the emergence of a universal ruling class was the condescension expressed by the "old" Qin people. A Qin ordinance reveals that some new subjects were inexperienced in performing government tasks and "the governance of officials might have been too harsh" (吏治或泰嚴), to the extent that they often "gave vicious remarks as well as cursed and insulted such new subjects" (惡與言及詈辱之) or even physically abused them. Since senior officials often appeared indifferent to their subordinates' misbehavior, the ordinance aims to deter these phenomena by imposing punishments on unbenevolent officials.[71] Nevertheless, we cannot overestimate the impact of this regulation, as transmitted literature reports that acute regional confrontations prevailed even at the end of the Qin Empire. A typical example embodying this resentment comes from the "Basic Annals of Xiang Yu" (Xiang Yu Benji 項羽本紀) of the *Shiji*:

> When the officials and soldiers of the regional lords, in former time, had been levied to perform statutory labor or been conscripted for garrison duty in the Qin heartland,[72] the officials and soldiers therein often treated them improperly. Now the Qin army has surrendered to the regional lords, and many of their officials and soldiers have availed themselves of their victory to use the Qin surrenderers as servants and slaves, holding them in contempt, tormenting and insulting them.

> 諸侯吏卒異時故繇使屯戍過秦中，秦中吏卒遇之多無狀。及秦軍降諸侯，諸侯吏卒乘勝多奴虜使之，輕折辱秦吏卒。[73]

This concise passage epitomizes the conflict between the old and new subjects of the Qin Empire. The old Qin, as conquerors, believed that they were socially superior to the people from the former independent states. The arrogant attitude described in the passage was apparently not an isolated case and, quite understandably, stirred up resentment among the new subjects, whose discontent eventually allegedly prompted a horrendous massacre of some two hundred thousand surrendered Qin soldiers in 207 BCE.[74] Inasmuch as the development of ethnic consciousness often results from the existence of an external coercive and oppressive force, the ideology and policy of encouraging a belief in Qin cultural superiority might have induced or strengthened the awareness of the people living in the periphery toward their old cultural identities, which were used as a pivotal marker in differentiating themselves from the center.[75]

With respect to this issue, Qin administrative practices might also have solidified existing regional identities. Administrative records unearthed from Liye unveiled that regional social identities were duly recorded and recognized by Qin authorities. Documenting the rank of householders, the registers would specify their social identities if they were of non-Qin origin. For example, several holders were listed as the "*bugeng* (the fourth rank) of the Jing (Chu) region" (荊不更).[76] Although the nature of "*bugeng*" is still debated, the word "Jing" in these registers unequivocally indicates that these householders were Chu inhabitants who lived under Qin rule.[77] Additionally, a fragmentary official letter reads, "two persons, one of whom is a Qin, whereas another person is a Jing; all of them are soldiers" (☑二人，其一秦、一人荊，皆卒☑).[78] By the same token, it is conceivable that the designation of social identities of other erstwhile polities, if applicable, would also be notated in the household registers of those new subjects.

Such a differentiation was primarily administrative in purpose. Since the Qin government designated specialized policies for its new subjects, it was necessary to record the former identities of new subjects in their registers to implement these policies. However, the documentation of these identities might inadvertently evoke or enhance existing cultural identities in the minds of new subjects. This was not in line with the goal of establishing a common identity.

The collective effects of the aforementioned factors likely led to serious confrontations between the Qin and non-Qin. An anecdote of Guan Ying 灌嬰 vividly depicts this sentiment. The story says that when Liu Bang decided to select commanders to lead a new cavalry contingent against the onslaught of his nemesis Xiang Ji, his military officers recommended two elite riders named Li Bi 李必 and Luo Jia 駱甲, both of whom came from Zhongquan 重泉 county in the Metropolitan Area,[79] the center of the Qin Empire. Li and Luo nonetheless declined Liu's offer lest their Qin origin provoked outcry from a cohort of soldiers mainly from the eastern regions. Instead, they suggested acting as the deputies of one of Liu Bang's trusted generals. In the end, Guan Ying was appointed to the position.[80]

This anecdote not only exemplifies the consciousness of peoples from different regions about their respective cultural identities, but also demonstrates that "Qin" as a social identity completely lost its social advantages after the collapse of the Qin Empire.[81] Of course, issues such as identities and ethnic consciousness are always fluid. Li Bi and Luo Jia seemed to have no qualms about jumping on the Han bandwagon. But one must not assume that every transformation of social identity went so smoothly.

A similar pattern can be detected with identity transformations that took place during the imperial Qin period. Different regions, groups, and individuals likely reacted differently to the Qin identity. Inhabitants in the former territory of the Hann state, on the whole, showed little interest in rebelling against the Qin's authority during the anti-Qin movement,[82] despite the active participation in that movement of former aristocrats such as Zhang Liang 張良, who was the scion of a prominent Hann aristocratic family and conspired to assassinate the First Emperor during one of his inspection tours.[83] On the contrary, the Chu people were well known for their strong anti-Qin sentiment, which was epitomized in a famous quote: "Even if only three Chu households remain, they will destroy the Qin!" (楚雖三戶，亡秦必楚！)[84]

Still, it is quite unlikely that every person residing in the Chu territory shared such unambiguous hatred for the Qin conquerors. After all, prior to the emergence of the notion of the "nation state," people might not have been as resistant to foreign rulers as they are today. An individual's level of anti-Qin sentiment was likely predicated upon his or her social class, background, and personal experience.[85] That said, the strong anti-Qin sentiment present at the end of the Qin dynasty indicates that the regime failed to instill the "immanent morale" into social elites and the general populace alike, who lacked commitment to the Qin identity.[86]

To conclude, the materiality of the discussed manuscripts embodies the complex social configurations taken place during and immediately after the Qin dynasty. If the Qin Empire had continued to rule, the spread of Qin literacy might have finally forged a universal ruling-class identity marked by a more homogenous culture and ideology. The ephemeral rule of the Qin Empire and the mutual hatred between the old and new Qin people, however, prevented this from happening. Although the Qin's efforts paved the way for the Western Han Empire, which took up and eventually completed such a construction process, this result was largely a historical contingency.

State Ideology and Disobedience of Officials

The Qin's lack of infrastructural power manifested not only in its failure to consolidate a universal identity for officials, but also in the disobedience of these literate elites. Shang Yang and his followers posited that an effective legal system marked by draconian laws and punishments was a vital means to prevent subjects from damaging the social order.[87] The Qin government was substantially influenced by Shang Yang's ideology, though it probably did not unequivocally implement all his advocacies. This dogma inevitably had a strong impact on Qin policy-making, even though scholars often dispute the existence of a draconian Qin legal culture since the discovery of the Shuihudi Qin manuscripts, suggesting that it was not as harsh and uncompromising as traditional sources portray.[88] These revisionist accounts are undoubtedly beneficial for removing Qin history from the allegedly prejudiced Western Han narratives.

As I have pointed out elsewhere, however, such revisionist accounts have their limitations. First, they are often based on sources such as stele inscriptions and handbooks for officials' conduct, which do not necessarily represent the Qin's political ideology and legal culture in practice. Consequently, they may ignore the more coercive, draconian aspect of Qin statecraft. Second, they tend to assume a static legal practice between the preimperial and imperial Qin period, during which the regime was more aggressive to intervene in social lives at the grassroots level.[89] In this section, I first unveil how the social engineering project that stemmed from the moral-legalist ideology might have generated social tensions and eventually eroded the legitimacy of the Qin regime. Then I illustrate how the traditional practices of the Qin government apparatus might have negated the positive impacts of new policies that the Qin instigated during the imperial era.

SOCIAL ENGINEERING AND SOCIAL TENSIONS

The Qin contemplated various measures to institutionalize social values. While their intention was possibly perfecting the social order, the strong "Legalist" atmosphere in the government may have twisted these policies from their initial spirit. The following stipulations from the Yuelu manuscripts are worth noting:

> The statute states: black-headed ones who do not cultivate fields or trade at the market, who do not exit or enter the village according to the [official] schedule, and who disobey their parents or speak to them carelessly and rudely,[90] when the parents, [village] chief, or the leader of the mutually accountable group of five cannot bear to denounce their misbehavior, order the Commune Overseer to swiftly investigate and interrogate them, arresting, detaining, and presenting the offender to the [county] court. Should the crime of the offender match being left intact and made a wall-builder or above, if his parents, [village] chiefs or the leader of the mutually accountable group of five do not denounce the offender in advance, fine his father or mother two sets of armor, and each of the [village] chiefs and leaders of the mutually accountable group of five one set of armor; if the Commune Overseer did not arrest the offender, fine him one set of armor, and the [county] Prefect and Vice-Prefect one shield.
>
> For those who have violated this statute, immediately sentence them in accordance with the statute. For those who should be liable for the offender's crime, if the Commune Overseer did not arrest [the liable persons], sentence him in accordance with this statute. In addition, the [County] Prefect and Vice-Prefect to whom [the Commune Overseer who failed to arrest those liable persons] is subordinate should dismiss the Commune Overseer. A1.11 of the [Ordinances on] the Court.

> 律曰: 黔首不田作、市販，出入不時，不聽父母，笱（苟）若與父母言，父母、典、伍弗忍告乚，令鄉嗇夫數謙（廉）問，捕毄（繫）【獻廷】。其辠當完城旦以上，其父母、典、伍弗先告，貲其父若母二甲，典、伍各一甲。鄉嗇夫弗得，貲一甲，令、丞一盾。

有【犯律者】，輒以律論。及其當坐者，鄉嗇夫弗得，以
律論。及其令、丞有（又）免鄉嗇夫。 ‧廷甲 十一。[91]

This text can be divided into two parts. The first part is the citation
of an unnamed statute, whereas the section starting with the line "for
those who have violated the statute" (有犯律者) is its specification.[92] The
statute prescribes the arrest of community members who diverge from the
sanctioned social norms. Aside from everyday activities, it gives special
attention to persons who act with filial impiety (*buxiao* 不孝), which
was considered a heinous crime that warranted capital punishment.[93]
Specifically, if a person acts unfilially toward his or her parents, and the
parents, the village chief, or the leader of the mutually accountable group
of five do not report him or her, the Commune Overseer administering
the village should step in and arrest the offender.

Despite being undated, the use of the term "black-headed ones"
(*qianshou* 黔首) suggests that both the cited statute and its supplementary
ordinance were copied or revised after 221 BCE. The content of the
earlier Shuihudi tomb no. 11 and the later Zhangjiashan tomb no. 247
legal corpora indicate that acts of filial impiety were always reported
by someone's parents, thus making it strongly resemble the present-day
Antragsdelikt, which refers to a type of offense that can only be prosecuted
with the complaint of the victim.[94] The underlying reason probably lies
in the fact that the determination of "filial impiety" was predominantly
dependent upon the subjective feeling of the parents.[95] Due to the private
nature of the offense, it was difficult for authorities to interfere. This
statute nonetheless bespeaks that at one point, agents of the Qin regime
were also given the power to prosecute the unfilial children. This reflects
the state's direct intervention in internal family affairs, which was part
of the social engineering program of the Qin Empire.

The statute is followed by an "Ordinance on the Court" (*ting
ling* 廷令). It states that if an offender's crime warrants the punishment
of being "left intact and made a wall-builder" or above but his or her
parents do not denounce the misbehavior in advance out of leniency,
the parents should be fined two sets of armor, which is even heavier
than state agents who failed to report the offender. This treatment was
probably under the consideration that parents should naturally know
more about the details of the unfilial actions of their children than
outsiders do. Since the offense of filial impiety warranted capital punishment, this regulation implies that if parents did not want to turn

their children in to the authorities and let them be executed because of their unfilial behavior (or be punished and made a wall-builder because of other offenses), they themselves would be punished. Needless to say, this stipulation encouraged parents to denounce their unfilial children on their own initiative.

The spirit of this regulation went against Ruist principles, which acknowledge the mutual concealment of misconduct between family members. The transmitted *Lun yu* 論語, for example, includes a quote ascribed to Kong Zi (Confucius): "When a father conceals [the misconduct of] his child, and a child conceals [the misconduct of] the father, the uprightness is in their action" (父為子隱，子為父隱，直在其中矣). While this anecdote possibly derives from Warring States accounts such as those found in the *Master Lü's Spring and Autumn Annals* (*Lü shi Chunqiu* 呂氏春秋) rather than from the historical Kong Zi, its rationale is of a typical Ruist character and differs substantially from a similar anecdote appearing in *Master Han Fei* (*Han Feizi* 韓非子), in which the narrator approves the son's reporting of his father.[96] This again attests that although the social values that the Qin regime intended to disseminate aligned with those of Ruist thinkers, the method with which they implemented these values departed considerably from the Ruist way.

The state's direct intervention in family relationships might have jeopardized family harmony. The new regulation transformed the right of the parents to denounce the filial impiety of their children into an obligation they had to uphold. More importantly, it invited the state apparatus to interfere in family affairs. Note that, unlike modern totalitarian regimes such as those formed by fascist or communist parties, this new regulation did not encourage the mutual denunciation of family members (e.g., a son reporting his father). In the end, this prescription aimed not at revolutionizing but at further consolidating the patrilineal hierarchy. That said, one can imagine that under this new arrangement there would be parents unwilling to hand over their children to the authorities, and tensions among family members might have emerged.

For leaders of grassroots communities, perhaps the more worrisome change was the potential infringement on their autonomy because of the active intervention of government agents in communal affairs. Although grassroots communities in the Qin state were bureaucratized through the household registration system and mutually accountable groups of five (*wu* 伍) during the preimperial period, communal and lineage organizations were still influential in the everyday lives of the populace. An anecdote pertinent to Liu Ji reveals that after he was approached at his hometown Pei county and asked to rebel against the Qin government, he first sought the assistance of local elders (*fulao* 父老), who eventually led their clansmen to kill the County Prefect and opened the town gate for Liu. The support of community leaders was no less decisive in the center of the Qin Empire. It is said that when Liu Ji seized Xianyang, he immediately summoned the elders and leaders (*haojie* 豪桀) of the adjacent counties and made an agreement with them, thereby comforting the Qin people.[97]

Unearthed sources also reveal the existence of various communal organizations in the preimperial Qin state. A legal case from the Yuelu manuscripts confirms that the quasi-cooperative *dan* 僤 organization already emerged at the dawn of the Qin unification.[98] These strands of evidence point to the conclusion that communal organizations were important in the fabrics of communal livings. Given the damaging effect of this new stipulation on their autonomy,[99] we can imagine that there was strong resistance to the Qin's long arm, especially from people in the new territories. This could be the reason that the Qin regime promulgated a supplementary ordinance to reaffirm the enforcement of the earlier policy by increasing the punishment of incompetent (or unwilling) Commune Overseers, who were now punished with dismissal rather than merely fines.

The worries of those community leaders might not have ended there. A Qin "Statute on the Accessory Scribes of the Commandant" (Weizu lü 尉卒律) prescribes the criteria for the selection and appointment of village chiefs and village elders, which were titles of officially appointed community leaders. Accordingly, these two positions had to be chosen by villagers and the results would be reported to the Commune Overseer, who would forward them to the county headquarters for approval. It is stipulated that only people who were old and had no rank were eligible for these positions.[100]

Regarding these criteria, Chen Kanli 陳侃理 notices that unlike the selection of officials, this prescription does not establish a minimum requirement for the amount of property owned by potential candidates for the two positions. He infers that the spirit behind the policy design was that the Qin regime did not want these positions to fall into the hands of existing community leaders, who were likely rich and relatively higher in rank. Rather than letting potential troublemakers dominate village elections, this statute ensures that those chosen would be individuals who were absolutely dependent on the regime. In other words, the main objective of this measure was to replace existing community leaders with another group of more controllable communal elites, thereby undermining the influence of existing clans and communal organizations. This policy radically differs from the relevant regulations in the preimperial legal texts from Shuihudi tomb no. 11,[101] and should thus be regarded as one of the social reforms instituted by the Qin Empire.[102]

To sum up, previously, individuals were appointed to posts such as village chief and village elder because they were grassroots leaders, while in the imperial period, people became leaders because of their allegiance to the state. Again, such an intervention in communal autonomy would probably upset existing powerful leaders and intensify the tensions between the state and grassroots communities.[103] This may account for the strong resentment of community leaders toward the Qin regime and its rule during the anti-Qin movement, as noted in the introduction.

The social reforms of the Qin regime embodied the contrast between ideals and reality. While the policy was probably well intended, it might have created tensions within families, backlash from communal societies, and, if it succeeded, an unraveling of the old social fabric. Such a contrast could be caused by two somewhat conflicting guiding principles. On the one hand, ever since Shang Yang's reforms, the Qin bureaucratic culture had always emphasized stern punishment and the mutual surveillance of individuals. On the other hand, the new policy of the Qin Empire required administrators to actively disseminate social values to its subjects. Under these two principles, any policy designed to soften social tensions and enhance the Qin's legitimacy might have overreached and been enforced in a relentless manner that backfired on the regime. In particular, since the people in the new territories did not experience Qin-style statecraft and presumably retained stronger community autonomy than those in the old Qin territory, the oppressive direct rule imposed on these people must have spurred the general resentment of the new subjects in the east and south, who eventually rebelled against Qin rule once they had the chance.[104]

FAILURE OF POLICY ENFORCEMENT

The Qin state was known for its highly sophisticated bureaucracy following Shang Yang's reforms. While the Qin's bureaucratic tradition partly accounted for its success, it was not always advantageous to the development of infrastructural power. Existing evidence suggests that such a tradition often negated the positive impact of the new policies initiated by the Qin regime.

Extant Qin and early Western Han legal materials reveal that the Qin legal system developed what one might call a "draconian principle." Characterized by a preference for heavy-handed punishments, this principle dictated that a judicial officer, when deciding a lawsuit, had to choose the most severe punishment if there were multiple options available. Prescribing the punishments for corrupt judicial officers, an unnamed Qin ordinance specifies that if a judicial officer intentionally acted not uprightly (*buzhi* 不直) when sentencing an offender and if the punishment that he warranted because of such actions was heavier than the one that corresponded to receiving illicit profit (*zang* 贓), or vice versa, he had to be sentenced to the heavier punishment.[105]

To discern the context of the above stipulation, one must understand the sentencing principle in deciding the punishments for "acting not uprightly" and "receiving illicit profit." The second category is straightforward. A "Statute on Robbery" (Dao lü 盜律) from the *Statutes and Ordinances of the Second Year* prescribes that the punishment of committing thievish offenses depended on the amount of illicit profit that an offender gained:

> The illicit profit from a robbery valued in excess of 660 cash: tattoo [the criminal] and make [him or her] a wall-builder or grain-pounder; from 660 to 220 cash: leave [the criminal] intact and make [him or her] a wall-builder or grain-pounder; not a full 220 to 110 cash: shave [the criminal] and make [him or her] a bondservant or bondwoman; not a full 110 to 22 cash: fine four *liang* (approx. 62 g) of gold; not a full 22 to 1 cash: fine one *liang* (approx. 15.5 g) of gold.

> 盜臧 (贓) 直 (值) 過六百六十錢，黥為城旦舂。六百六十到二百廿錢，完為城旦舂。不盈二百廿到百一十錢，耐為隸臣妾。不盈百一十到廿二錢，罰金四兩。不盈廿二錢到一錢，罰金一兩。[106]

Accordingly, an offender would already become "tattooed and made a wall-builder or grain-pounder"—the heaviest punishment after the death penalty—if his or her amount of illicit profit exceeded 660 cash (*qian* 錢). While this statute is from an early Western Han corpus, the legal material of Shuihudi tomb no. 11 indicates that similar standards already existed in the preimperial Qin era.[107]

In reference to the first category, another "Statute on Robbery" from *Statutes and Ordinances of the Second Year* states that the punishments for corrupt judicial officers were contingent on the severity of their punishments for offenders. For a case where the offender's crimes warrant the capital punishment, the unjust judicial officer should be sentenced to have "the left foot severed and be made a wall-builder" (*zhan zuozhi wei chengdan* 斬左趾為城旦); for an offender whose crime warrants a punishment below the death penalty, the judicial officer would be sentenced to the same punishment to which the criminal would rightly have been sentenced.[108] Taking these two sentencing principles into account, if a judicial officer intentionally spared a culprit who matched the punishment of being "tattooed and made a wall-builder or grain-pounder" after taking a bribe of 120 cash, he should be sentenced to being "tattooed and made a wall-builder" rather than the lighter punishment of being "left intact and made a wall-builder." In contrast, if the judicial officer advertently released a culprit who should have been fined four *liang* 兩 of gold by receiving 500 cash from him, he should be "tattooed and made a wall-builder" but not be fined.[109]

The "draconian principle" was also applicable to similar offenses such as "distorting the facts" (*wangshi* 枉事) or "distorting the law" (*wangfa* 枉法), either because they took bribes from others, or because they were persuaded to commit such a crime through a third party.[110] Aside from written legal enactments, the penal decisions of judicial officers also reflect this principle. Given that the key criterion in determining if a judicial officer intentionally did not act uprightly or distorted the facts or the law was predicated on whether they had "exhaustively interrogated" (*qiongxun* 窮訊) an offender beforehand or "exhaustively verified" (*qiongshen* 窮審) his or her crime afterward, it was natural that officers would choose the most drastic punishment against offenders.

Such a preference for heavy punishments is captured in an instruction from 227 BCE issued by a Governor of Nan 南 commandery whose given name was Teng 騰:

Now the law, statutes, and ordinances have been disseminated and made known, but officials and commoners who violate the law and act on behalf of their private interests do not stop, and their hearts [yearning for] private preferences and local customs do not change. When [officials] from Prefects and Vice-Prefects on down know but do not report and sentence [the offenders], it means that they flagrantly violate the Ruler's luminous laws and hide evil and wicked people. If this is so, it is also disloyalty in being a subject. Or if [officials] do not know [these situations], this means that they are incompetent and unwise; if they know but do not venture to sentence [the crimes], this means that they are corrupt. All these are serious crimes and the fact that Prefects and Vice-Prefects do not clearly understand [their seriousness] is extremely disadvantageous. Now I am going to order personnel to investigate and inspect [the hidden crimes in your purview], raising accusations against those who do not follow the ordinances and prosecuting [these offenders] in accordance with the statutes; sentencing will reach up to [the level of] Prefects and Vice-Prefects. Additionally, [these inspectors] are going to evaluate government offices exceptionally filled with people breaking ordinances but whose Prefects and Vice-Prefects do not arrest [the offenders], and report these Prefects and Vice-Prefects, making them known to me.[111]

今瀍（法）律令已布聞，吏【民】犯瀍（法）為閒私者不止，私好、鄉俗之心不變。自從令、丞以下智（知）而弗舉論，是即明避主之明瀍（法）殹，而養匿邪避（僻）之民。如此，則為人臣亦不忠矣。若弗智（知），是即不勝任、不智殹（也）；智（知）而弗敢論，是即不廉殹。此皆大辠（罪）殹，而令、丞弗明智(知)，甚不便。今且令人案行之，舉劾不從令者，致以律；論及令、丞。有（又）且課縣官獨多犯令而令、丞弗得者，以令、丞聞。[112]

This letter was found in the tomb of abovementioned Xi. The recipients of Teng's instruction were magistrates of counties and marches subordinate to Nan commandery. There are two things that should draw our attention here. First, Teng's attitude on adjudication was absolute and relentless. His message was clear: Officials had no excuse for tolerating law breakers who placed their own interests over that of the state, and whose customs deviated from the state values. Every sort of concealment by officials warranted serious punishment. Second, that Teng so strongly articulated law enforcement indicates that officials in Nan commandery had taken a relatively soft stance toward local customs and interest groups.[113] The *Way of Making a Good Official* even lists "to change the people's customs" (變民習俗) alongside other misbehavior such as "being irreverent when undertaking affairs" (臨事不敬). This suggests that the Qin regime, or at least the Nan commandery authorities, once encouraged a flexible governing strategy.[114] This accounts for Teng's sending of inspectors to investigate not only those hidden lawbreakers but also senior officials such as County Prefects and Vice-Prefects. In this respect, what Teng intended to rectify was not only the "evil" Chu local customs but also the governing strategy of previous Nan commandery officials.

Teng's discontent notwithstanding, the flexible (and, to some extent, nonactive) approach adopted by his precursors seemed effective. Archaeological evidence reveals that by the time Teng issued his instruction, Anlu county where Xi served was inhabited by cultural groups such as Chu natives, Qin migrants, and other minorities. Despite its diversity, the region was neatly consolidated under Qin governance, and Qin material culture gradually came to dominate indigenous Chu practices.[115] Moreover, transmitted records make no mention of anti-Qin insurgencies in Nan commandery after the empire's collapse.[116] Rather, despite occasional deviance, at least a portion of the residents of Nan commandery identified themselves as the old subjects (*gumin* 故民) of the Qin Empire.[117] These findings indicate the solidity of Qin rule over Nan commandery at the dawn of the Qin imperial period.

Why did Governor Teng give such an ostensibly unnecessary instruction? Keum Jaewon 琴載元 relates this action to the upcoming military campaign against the Chu, which highlighted the need to strengthen state control over Nan commandery.[118] Keum's proposition corresponds with the content of a *gu* 觚 polyhedron (M247:1) recently discovered in tomb no. 247 of the Zhengjiahu 鄭家湖 cemetery in Yunmeng County, Hubei. Based on the typology of the grave goods and the orthography of the polyhedron's writing, archaeologists theorize that the tomb occupant might have been a low-level Qin official living in the late Warring States Anlu county like Xi.[119]

The polyhedron's text is mainly about the remonstrance of an orator called Tu 筡. In it Tu criticizes the expansionist policy of a Qin king, claiming that the Qin people were suffering because they "unanimously loathe the use of troops" (壹惡用兵). To remedy this mistake, Tu exhorts the Qin king to "halt his troops and stop issuing mobilization orders" (止兵、毋興令) and concentrate on maintaining the well-being of his people.[120] The strong anti-war sentiment displayed in Tu's speech runs contrary to King Zheng's expansionist policy after he fully seized power. Although we do not know if the tomb occupant held his office during Governor Teng's term, the circulation of such writings was likely not an exception in the late Warring States Nan commandery, which served as the bridgehead for Qin's campaigns against Chu and might have been particularly affected by the regime's increasingly aggressive military operations. Considering the remonstrance's acute criticism of the government policy, it may be among the "private preferences" that prompted Teng to issue his instruction, or the "discussions on the streets" (*xiangyi* 巷議) that Li Si 李斯 proposed to ban in his memorial to the First Emperor in 213 BCE.[121] Even this was not so, the existence of such "treacherous" writings may explain why Teng felt the need to tighten his grip on the governance of Nan commandery.

Moreover, Teng's zero-tolerance policy may have stemmed from the culture shock of an official from the central region of the Qin state. Prior to his appointment as the Governor of Nan commandery, Teng served as the Metropolitan Scribe (Nei Shi 內史) and Temporary Governor (Jia Shou 叚守) of Nanyang 南陽 commandery, and led the Hann campaign in 230 BCE. Given his credentials, Teng was likely a trusted minister of King Zheng and grew up with the draconian legal culture of the Qin regime.[122] It is conceivable that he would have regarded his precursors' appeasement policies as unacceptable and demanded a stricter adherence to Qin central government standards. Teng's instruction, therefore, embodies the conflict between Qin's draconian legal tradition and the smooth-things-over governing strategy of previous Nan Governors and local officials.

Under the draconian principle, sentencing convicts to a harsher punishment became the politically correct way for Qin officials to act. A judicial case file dated to 217 BCE documents the verdict given by the Governor of Nan commandery on a case pertaining to the crime of document forgery (*wei weishu* 為偽書). The only remark that the Governor handed down was to "carefully and exhaustively sentence the offender in accordance with the law" (謹窮以法論之).[123] From this perspective, Qin legal culture played a vital role in encouraging judicial officials to apply the most draconian laws to the populace.

Even if the central authorities promulgated a more lenient policy to alleviate existing harsh punishments, officials might have been reluctant to deliver it in order to protect themselves from potential personal liability. The tragedy of magistrate Tui 庫 readily illustrates such a contradiction. His case is presented as the eighteenth case in the *Book of Submitted Doubtful Cases* (*Zouyan shu* 奏讞書) from the Zhangjiazhan tomb no. 247.[124] Tui, who served as Prefect of You 攸 county (present-day Zhuzhou 株洲 City, Hunan) in Cangwu 蒼梧 commandery, proposed a lighter punishment for new subjects who fled and hid in the mountains after being defeated by Chu insurgents. The exact punishment that Tui suggested in his proposal was the "removal of rank and serving in frontier garrison" (*duojue ling shu* 奪爵令戍).[125]

The first test of this punishment was a legal case that arose in the ninth month of the twenty-sixth year of the First Emperor (221 BCE). The case was referred to in an imperial decision, in which the emperor authorized that if a group of soldiers flees from battle and thereby commits the crime of cowardice (*weiruan* 畏偄), those least severe ones have to be removed from their rank and serve in the garrison on the frontier for fixed terms according to their former rank. Obviously, this punishment was the "removal of rank and serving in a frontier garrison," which Tui proposed.[126]

Given that Tui's report was likely submitted between 222 and 220 BCE,[127] the punishment of "removal of rank and serving in a frontier garrison" was likely already in place by the time. Curiously, Tui's suggestion was rejected by the Accessory Scribe of Lawsuit Reinvestigation (Fuyu Zushi 覆獄卒史), who was sent (once again) from Nan commandery and claimed that "there are no formal categorical principles or ordinances for this" (*wu faling* 毋法令). Eventually, the new subjects who had fled were executed. Due to his leniency, Tui was charged with "releasing and letting guilty persons go" (*shi zong zuiren* 釋縱罪人) and sentenced to be a hard laborer for life.[128]

The reason for this contradictory outcome may lie in the mentality of Qin officials. Since the draconian principle demanded that officials sentence offenders to the heaviest possible punishment (otherwise they might be charged with "releasing and letting guilty persons go," as was Tui), it is not surprising that judicial officials would develop a harsh and uncompromising mentality in the sentencing of lawsuits. In the end, officials might not have been accustomed to the more lenient policy that the central government issued because it was more politically correct and thus safer to abide by the old, severe punishments that had been practiced for generations. In this regard, Tui's case embodies the tension between the issuance of new policies and local enforcement. The resulting discrepancies reflect the miscommunication between central and regional administrations in the broad sense. Additionally, the ostensible contradiction might also be predicated on the miscommunication and carelessness between different local administrations. That is, although the new prescription had already been officially promulgated before Tui's case, the Accessory Scribes did not receive the news, thereby falsely accusing him of releasing guilty persons. Either way, Tui's example demonstrates that there was a serious dislocation of administrative communication or the whole decision-making process.

CONCEALMENT BY LOCAL OFFICIALS

The Qin's oppressive ideology might also have dissuaded candid communication between the state and its administrators. Among the published Liye manuscripts, there are several fragments of wooden slips that revolve around the landscape of Qianling county (fig. 2.2). Since these manuscripts were drafted by Qianling officials, they allow us a glimpse into the official image that these Qin administrators tried to portray. Below are the texts of six relatively complete slips:

> The black-headed ones of Capital commune are not those who feel unfair and unpleasant.
>
> 都鄉黔首毋不平苦者。 (8-1796[129])
>
> The black-headed ones of Capital commune are not those who have efficacious medicines, fragrant herbs, and other marvels.
>
> 都鄉黔首毋良藥、芳草及它奇物者。 —(9-1305+9-1739[130])
>
> The black-headed ones of Capital commune are not those who absconded and not reside in Qianling.
>
> 都鄉黔首毋亡不居遷陵者。 \ □☑ (9-2279[131])
>
> The black-headed ones of Capital commune are not people of the Pu, Yang, and Yu tribes.
>
> 都鄉黔首毋濮人、楊人、與人。 (9-2300[132])

The black-headed ones of Erchun commune are not those who are sentenced because of being held liable for [crimes pertinent to] illicit sex.

貳春鄉黔首毋坐奸以論者。 (9-1614+8-1675[133])

The custom of black-headed ones . . . favors the fundamental occupation (agricultural activity) and dislikes worthless production (commerce). Their custom is to [create] swidden fields and shift the cultivation once a year, [and such a practice] differs from counties within the central region.

☑ 黔首習俗好本事，不好末作。其習俗槎田歲更，以異中縣。—(8-355[134])

With regard to the materiality of these slips, the complete slips reach about 23 cm length, which is equal to one foot in the Qin-Han measurement system. All six slips bear similar handwriting and were likely prepared by the same scribe. At the upper end of slip 9-2279, there is a notch, which is often observed in multi-piece manuscripts, that helps in tightening the binding strings. Additionally, the content of the first five slips is expressed in the form of negation and is organized according to the communes of Qianling county. While the formulaic language of slip 8-355 differs from that of the other five slips, the congruous material attributes among them suggest that it might be a different section of the same document. Even if the six listed slips did not belong to the same multi-piece manuscript, their materiality and formulaic language suggest that their texts were closely related.

Since these slips bear similar handwriting but their contents cover multiple communes, they were probably compiled based on the primary sources submitted by the scribe's colleagues. Notably, two other fragments also carry the same text as slip 8-355,[135] though the three slips appear to have been written by different hands. The overarching contents and the existence of multiple versions of the text of slip 8-355 hint that the listed slips may be part of a draft of an official report and were discarded after the completion of the final version. This can explain why fragments of this report, which was supposedly sent to other administrative unit(s), appeared in the county seat of Qianling. Another possibility is that these fragments belonged to a kind of internal annual

Figure 2.2a. Manuscripts recording the populace of Qianling county, Liye slip 8-1796. Photo courtesy of Wan Yuk Ping.

Figure 2.2b. Manuscripts recording the populace of Qianling county, Liye slip 9-1305 and 9-1739. Photo courtesy of Wan Yuk Ping.

Figure 2.2c. Manuscripts recording the populace of Qianling county, Liye slip 9-2279. Photo courtesy of Wan Yuk Ping.

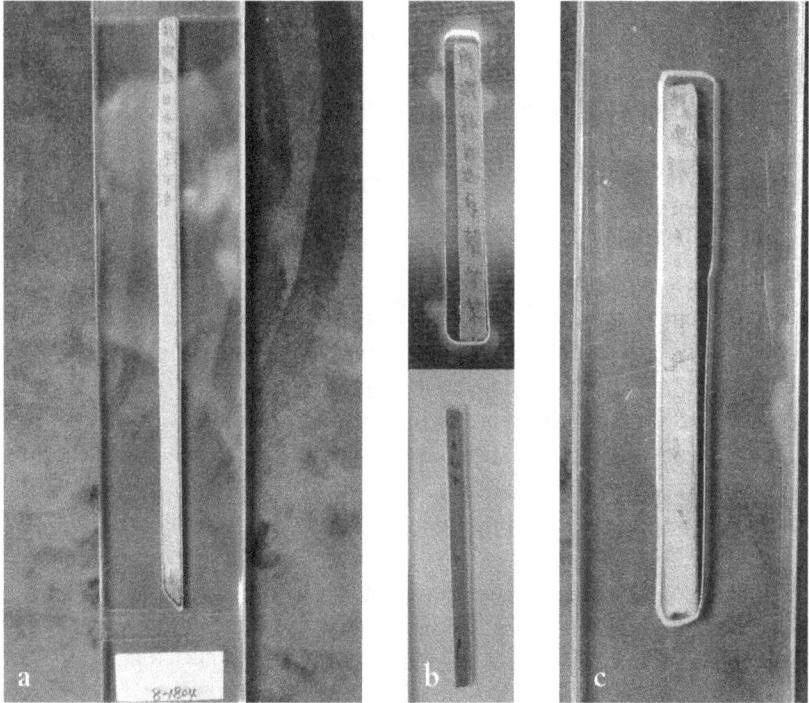

report. Since such reports were compiled every year, the county seat held multiple versions of them.

The first option seems to be more probable. It is worth noting that in Han and later sources, subordinate counties often collected data pertaining to the landscape of their jurisdictions and presented a report alongside annual accounts to the Commandery Governors.[136] The report discussed here may be the precursor to such a genre. If this is so, this report might have targeted Dongting 洞庭 commandery, Qianling's direct superior.[137]

Figure 2.2d. Manuscripts recording the populace of Qianling county, Liye slip 8-1675. Photo courtesy of Wan Yuk Ping.

Figure 2.2e. Manuscripts recording the populace of Qianling county, Liye slip 8-355. Photo courtesy of Wan Yuk Ping.

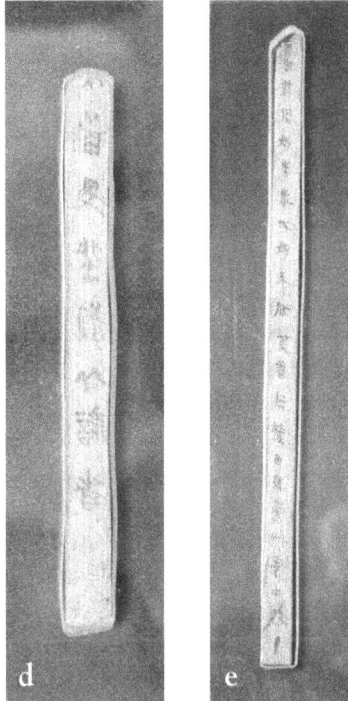

The report focuses on the natural and social landscape of Qianling county. It encompasses multifaceted themes such as the livelihood of residents dwelling in subordinate communes, the local customs of these residents, their level of life satisfaction, the possession of valuable resources, public security, and the distribution of non-Qin tribes. The tone of this report is incredibly positive. Of the six statements, none is depicting something negative about Qianling; and only slips 9-1305+9-1739 and 9-2300 are neutral in their narration.

Notably, slip 8-355 even openly praises the virtue of Qianling's populace, despite the disparity between their customs and the traditional practices of the Qin central region. The inclusion of such an entry was likely a calculated move, as the strong physiocratic tendency of Shang Yang's ideology was staunchly against commercial activities and encouraged the populace to devote themselves to agricultural production. The Mount Langye stele inscription even considers "diligently labors on the fundamentals and exalts agriculture, eliminates worthless occupations" (勤勞本事，上農除末) as one of the emperor's merits.[138] In this fashion, noting that Qianling's populace prioritized the fundamental occupation over worthless production was a way to advertise the local government's success in transforming "barbarians" into "civilized" subjects who upheld Qin social values.

In this official report, Qianling county almost became a "utopia" in the periphery. It was a place where residents had consummate lives, the behaviors of residents aligned with state-sanctioned social values, social stability was maintained, there was no threat of "barbarians," and, as a whole, the ideal social order had been attained. This was exactly the goal pursued by the Qin regime through social reforms. By any means, the content of this report was provided in response to the state ideology encouraged by the central government. Based on this report, the Qin Empire seemingly achieved an extraordinary level of territorial control over Qianling county despite the area's politically peripheral status.

In contrast to the peaceful image portrayed in local officials' reports, more unbiased sources such as private letters and administrative records reveal that the sociopolitical landscape of Qianling county was, to say the least, chaotic. The dynamics between the indigenous population and the empire turned the Qin Qianling region into a politically unstable area where the Qin had extremely limited territorial control.[139] In this light, the purpose of drafting such a positive report is obvious. By deliberately stressing that Qianling was governed in accordance with the state's prescribed ideology, the reporter might have intended to ingratiate himself with his superior and thereby receive rewards or compliments or at least to protect himself from the harsh punishments that would result from incompetence. Simply put, the appropriation of state ideology was likely motivated by the self-interest of administrators.

The contradiction between the officials' report and the local reality throws the former's integrity and competence into question. Bureaucrats are notorious for their reluctance to provide timely responses and for their conservatism in adjusting to new situations.[140] Being confronted with several options for resolving one particular issue, instead of picking the one that can most possibly solve the problem, bureaucrats often inherently choose the "safest" option, the one that accords the best with their ideology, bureaucratic culture (customs, precedents, formality, etc.), and individual interests. While such behavior may seem inefficient or even ridiculous for outsiders, it often embodies rational attempts to "maximize their own well-being in the face of incentive and constraints."[141] One of the possible consequences of such a self-benefiting action is the deviation from the original spirit of government policies.

For premodern bureaucracy, which was often embedded in autocracies that had little external monitoring across the whole decision-making process, extra problems might have evolved. One of the most recurrent patterns in the bureaucracy of autocratic or totalitarian regimes is the mis- and disinformation spread from bottom to top, and vice versa. Since these types of regimes often keep a tight grip and exercise harsh punishments over their administrators, to protect themselves from getting into trouble or, conversely, to receive compliments from their superiors and to pursue their personal welfare, administrators tend to either downplay serious matters and/or exaggerate minor issues at the expenses of state interests, insofar as they are able to continue their prevarication without being caught by their superiors. Such bureaucratic behavior should be prevalent among governments across different times and spaces, and imperial China was no exception.[142] Likewise, superiors might also prefer to cover up urgent matters to save face and protect their career, and maintain the legitimacy of their regimes. In short, although bureaucracy as a whole may be the rational, impersonal, and impartial institution that accords with the Weberian model, functionaries working within such institutions are always biased by their surroundings and their own agendas.

In autocratic regimes such as the Qin Empire, the performance of bureaucracy could be undermined by its suffocating ideology, which could often encourage administrators to prevaricate and procrastinate amid sociopolitical crises. The previous section has shown that Qin administrators were sometimes blinded by the regime's strong draconian traditions. The significant discrepancy between the official reports and actual situation of Qianling county was likely another example of Qin officials' pursuit of their personal utilities. This unfaithful behavior may have led to miscommunication in the government, endangered the enforcement of government policies, and delayed appropriate actions. The consequences of such concealment could be devastating in the sense that it might turn a small unrest into a crisis and turn controllable crises into disasters.

Another potential problem for officials lay in their conduct. One of the major sources of officials serving in the new territories were those functionaries who had engaged in misconduct or crime. While this does not necessarily imply that these officials had integrity issues, their competence was in doubt. To deter officials serving in the new territories and their affiliates from accepting bribes or taking advantage of people, Qin subjected them to stricter conduct requirements.[143] The punishment of such crimes followed the same principles as the punishment of robbery. In other words, if the illicit profit generated from these activities was equal to or above 660 cash, an offender already warranted the harsh punishment of being "tattooed and made a wall-builder," as discussed earlier.[144]

Moreover, government personnel were not only held accountable for their own crimes but were also liable for the offenses of their peers. This probably increased the prevalence of convicted officials. A statement datable to 216 BCE records that sixteen officials of Qianling were found to deserve the punishment of being fined.[145] Given that the average number of staffed positions in Qianling was approximately eighty, this number implies that 16 to 30 percent of administrators were liable to the government for offenses.[146] While fines were a relatively minor punishment, a convicted person would be assigned years of hard labor if he or she could not repay the debt.[147] Also note that a large portion of officials serving in the new territories were convicted former officials who were reshuffled from the old territories. Since these "officials in the new territories" were only required to serve a fixed term before returning home, their interest lay in completing their terms rather than in fulfilling their duties as competent administrators. Thus, they might have lacked incentives to deal with urgent matters.

Concealment by bureaucrats was a probable reason behind the production of the abovementioned unfaithful report. Given its level of congruence with the state ideology, it should be understood as a piece of deliberately drafted misinformation. Although the *truth* narrated in the report might not have been fake, the point of view that it represented was unilateral and did not sufficiently depict the reality of Qianling county. As Ernest Caldwell points out, the crux of the Qin's dominance was their ability to address sociopolitical problems through legal reforms.[148] One of the prerequisites of this mechanism hinged on smooth and candid communication among different levels and sectors of government, which ensured the timely transmission of unbiased information. Obviously, the report discussed in this section failed to fulfill this function due to its unfaithful, or at best incomplete, descriptions of the locality. The consequences of this alleged deceitful behavior might have been devastating.

While we may never know how often officials in the new territories compiled such problematic reports, it is by no means unusual for government personnel serving in a totalitarian or autocratic regime to draft deceitful reports in order to avoid punishment and/or to enrich themselves.[149] Hence, one can imagine that this type of practice was pervasive across the Qin Empire, especially in the new territories. This problem severely damaged the political power of the Qin regime.

Qin Infrastructural Power: Unfinished Business

This chapter has scrutinized the limit of the Qin Empire's infrastructural power, especially in the political periphery, through the lens of a Qin county called Qianling. I center on the Qin's failure to construct a universal ruling class, and the negative impacts of the state's oppressive ideology on the incentives for its officials.

The case of Qianling county demonstrates that the process of building a new ruling class was precarious. While traits of several peculiar administrative manuscripts written in a mixture of the Qin and Chu styles indicate the local Chu scribes' gradual adoption of Qin literary habits and the absorption of literate local elites into the Qin establishment, this process was nonetheless interrupted because of the empire's disintegration, during which some former Chu scribes seemed to decide to resume their Chu identity as the Qin state dissolved. Additionally, the hostile attitude of the old Qin people hampered the emergence of a universal ruling class that shared a homogenous culture and ideology.

Extant evidence from the Qin era also reveals that the "moral-legalist" ideology might have had negative impacts on the policy design and enforcement of the Qin's social engineering project. Some of the social reforms pertaining to the institutionalization of state-encouraged social values not only entailed direct interference in the daily lives of communities, but also damaged the interests of local leaders. These reforms probably induced social tension, especially in the new territories in the east and south, and damaged the legitimacy of the Qin regime.

The pervasive draconian principle in the legal system of the Qin government apparatus also undermined the effects of lenient policies that the regime promoted. Judicial officers adjudicating lawsuits would try to bypass the more lenient new punishments and abide by the existing, harsh punishments to better adhere to the draconian legal tradition. In doing so, they may have been trying to protect themselves from potential personal legal liability. In the end, the dream of utopia of the First Emperor and his ministers remained, to a large extent, only a dream.

In a nutshell, although the Qin regime destroyed all other major players of the Warring States, governed its lands through the universal installment of the commandery-county system, and launched a series of social engineering schemes to transform the diverse local societies into one unitary society, these efforts still fell short of building a genuine, consolidated territorial empire. The Qin regime's dream did not materialize until the mid-first century BCE under the Western Han Empire, which finally succeeded in diffusing its power universally and intensively, maintained a high level of territorialization, and created a universal ruling class through the emergence of scholar-officials bound by their common devotion to Ruist doctrines. In this way, the situation in the Qin Empire resembled that in the late Roman Republic, which, after substantial territorial expansion following the Second Punic War (218–201 BCE), faced difficulties consolidating its new provinces and did not manage to form a territorial empire until from around 100 BCE onward.[150]

The Qin example informs us that the establishment of territorial control was often a long process full of setbacks, especially when the conqueror and conquered once underwent endemic military confrontations and persistent violence. The surreal speed of the Qin regime in swallowing the vast territories of other Warring States polities likely presented immense challenges to its ability to transform these new lands into centralized local administrative units, let alone to turn the conquered into the empire's devoted subjects. Perhaps one can sum up the Qin Empire with the following paraphrased quip from Michael Mann: The First Emperor's empire was a territorial empire not in *extent*, but in *intent*.[151]

Whereas this chapter focuses on the infrastructural side of the Qin's state power, the next two chapters will examine the empire's limited despotic power. Again, my focus will be on Qianling county, which demonstrates that administrative units in the new territories seemed to be deeply embroiled in problems arising from the empire's expansion. While reforms to deal with these challenges were contemplated, they were either impractical or thwarted by the incapability of the administrative system and thus failed to achieve their initial objectives.

Chapter 3

Territorial Expansion and Personnel Shortages in Local Governments

The Qin Empire's territorial control in politically peripheral regions was weak. While revolts among the people were indeed the final nail in the empire's coffin, one wonders why the Qin bureaucracy, which was long believed to have maintained an administrative efficiency and military prowess far superior to those of other major powers in the Warring States period, failed to subdue the small-scale unrest led by Chen Sheng and Wu Guang before that unrest had a snowball effect that encouraged more and more people to step up and overthrow the Qin regime. Traditional accounts attribute such a slow response to Zhao Gao's deceit of the Second Emperor of Qin, who, as a result, did not realize the seriousness of the upheaval in the east until it was too late.[1] While this narrative is both dramatic and intriguing, quite a few early Western Han accounts hardly mention such an event.[2] This reminds us not to unequivocally accept the story told by the *Shiji*.

More importantly, the military failure of the Qin regime started more at the local than at the central level. In the face of revolts, local administrative units in the new territories were in disarray and failed to organize a systematic defense or offense against the insurgency. The frequent betrayals of Qin officials not only proved the empire's failure to build up a universal ruling-class identity among its administrators, but also called into question the capacity and functionality of local governments in the new territories.

The low capacity of Qin local governments becomes even clearer through the lens of unearthed material. Administrative reports from

Liye indicates that the meager revenue and tax income collected from state-run fields and households probably never sufficed to support the military force stationed in the Qianling region,[3] and the government had to rely on external food supply.[4] A fragmentary administrative letter reveals that Yuanling 沅陵 county once transferred 2,000 bushels (shi 石) of grain to the Qianling region. This echoes the record stating that other counties of Dongting commandery were asked to deliver grain to Qianling.[5] Moreover, Qianling requested Dongting commandery to transfer 80,000 cash for the procurement of clothing for convicts.[6] These records suggest that Qianling county seemed to occasionally face various shortages of everyday necessities.

The shortage of personnel—the linchpin of government organizations—was especially alarming. Extant Qin textual evidence reveals that the empire encountered a severe and persistent paucity of government personnel such as officials, convict laborers, and conscripts. While scholars have already examined the relationship between personnel scarcity and the collapse of the Qin Empire,[7] most of them seem to take this connection for granted. Moreover, secondary literature rarely discusses the reaction of Qin policy-makers to the shortage problem, which was by no means unknown to them. Did the Qin regime initiate any measure or institutional reform to alleviate such scarcity? Did the reforms succeed or merely generate even more problems?

Additionally, shortages are ubiquitous among government organizations. Since resources are always scarce, it is normal for government administrations in different periods and regions and at different levels to be affected by certain degrees of scarcity. However, not every shortage is serious enough to change the long-term behavior of decision-makers or to stimulate institutional reforms to reallocate resource distribution. To give a present-day example, as of 2018, every judge serving in the prefecture-level court of Suqian City in Jiangsu, China, had on average almost 200 cases in his or her docket. This ratio far exceeded the prescribed standard, and the paucity of personnel indeed prolonged the waiting period for legal proceedings. It did not, nonetheless, affect—at least visibly—the decision-making of these judges. Nor did it compel any immediate institutional reforms or changes in labor allocation to increase the number of judges in Suqian.[8] Hence, the major issue with resource paucity is not merely the absolute number of missing resources. Rather, what matters most is the extent to which such paucity impacts the decision-making and resource allocation of an administrative unit and stimulates institutional changes and shifts in government policy.

Bearing these concerns in mind, the term "shortage" in this chapter refers to a status in which the amount of a particular resource is insufficient to fulfill its instrumental function within the government. Along this line, the major focus of this chapter is to examine (1) the way that these shortages compelled the Qin administration to deviate from its protocols to conform with the real conditions it faced, (2) the policies and institutional reforms that the Qin authorities devised to tackle the scarcity problem, and (3) the effectiveness of these measures. While I mainly focus on the situation after unification due to the dating of sources at hand, some of the phenomena discussed in this chapter emerged prior to 221 BCE.

Overall, the Qin's personnel shortages should be placed within the context of its territorial expansion, which greatly crippled the power of the regime. These shortages most affected the political, economic, and military power networks affiliated with the Qin regime. Politically, the Qianling government malfunctioned due to having insufficient administrators. Economically, the shortage of convict laborers interfered with the normal production activities of government organizations. Militarily, the paucity of conscripts put the state security at risk. Simply put, given the rapid expansion of the Qin Empire, the amount of resources invested in the new territories hardly met the huge demands of these new lands. Rather than being an efficient vehicle as we believed, the governmental organizations of Qianling county—and those in the empire's new territories in general—were in peril.

Officials

Having a highly bureaucratized government, the Qin regime counted on its administrators to enforce its policies. Training an adequate official was a time-consuming task in the Qin period. The acquisition of literacy was usually confined to specialists like Scribes and Assistants, who handled most of the paperwork of daily administrative activities. In addition to these two groups, social groups such as soldiers and craftsmen might also gain a limited level of literacy for their professions, although it was often inadequate to meet the more intricate paperwork demands of the government administration.[9]

Shortage of Officials and Misfunctions in Government Administration

The rapid expansion of the Qin state likely incurred an incessant demand for officials. The regime doubled its territories within nine years, and since the founding of the empire, it continually marched through regions farther north and south. Considering this historical background, it is not surprising that the Qin Empire faced a shortage of officials despite the inclusion of non-Scribes in the government. Consider the figures recorded in the "Report on the Officials of Qianling" (table 3.1).

Table 3.1. Staff and vacancy numbers in Qianling county

Title of officials	No. of staff	No. of vacancies	No. of officials undertaking government service and assignments elsewhere	No. available for service	% of vacancies	% of vacancies + government service and assignments elsewhere
Senior Official	3	2	0	1	67.67	67.67
Scribe Director	28	0	10	18	0	35.71
Overseer of the Office	10	2	3	5	20	50
Constable	6	4	0	2	67.67	67.67
Assistant of the Office	53	7	22	24	13.21	54.72
Supervisor of the Prison	1	0	0	1	0	0
Total	101	15	35	51	14.85	49.5

Author's own material.

The report indicates that almost half of the officials in Qianling either were undertaking statutory labor service elsewhere or were vacant positions. This includes two-thirds of senior officials and over 50 percent of Assistants; only 51 officials were on duty. Another fragment of a similar nature also reveals that only 50 of the 104 functionaries were on duty, and the percentage of vacancies reached 33.65 percent (35 of 104 posts), which is even higher than the number in the "Report on the Officials of Qianling."[10] These figures demonstrate that personnel shortages in Qianling county were not uncommon.

The dearth of officials was not confined to Qianling county. The Liye manuscripts reveal that when Li 禮 served as the Governor of Dongting commandery from 220 to 212 BCE, there were at least four different Temporary Governors.[11] Additionally, all documented Commandery Commandant positions of Dongting[12] and a majority of the governorships of other commanderies were held temporarily.[13] The preponderance of Temporary Governors suggests that senior officials at the commandery level were often absent from their duties. This phenomenon is also found in transmitted sources. The *Shiji* records that when Chen Sheng attacked Chen 陳 county, the incumbent magistrate was not in office and the defense was led solely by an Acting Vice-Prefect (Shou Cheng 守丞), who died in the ensuing combat.[14] Likewise, when Xiang Liang 項梁 plotted his rebellion with his nephew in Kuaiji 會稽 commandery, it only had a Temporary Governor, who chose to side with the Xiangs to overthrow the Qin Empire.[15]

These sources, albeit fragmentary, give us a glimpse into the shortage of administrators in new territories outside Qianling county. Legal stipulations enacted during the same period also suggest that the shortage of officials was universal among the empire's new territories. As a result, the Qin central authorities instigated various new policies to increase the number of administrators serving in these regions. In the next section I provide a comprehensive analysis of these measures.

Measures to Reduce the Shortage of Officials in the New Territories

As the last chapter has discussed, one of the policies that the Qin regime deployed to mitigate the shortage of officials was the introduction of indigenous writing experts. New subjects in the new territories were taught the Qin scripts and worked as Assistants in local governments. Additionally, scribal schools were set up to train new Scribes. For example, a scribal school was established in Qianling county as early as 221 BCE.[16] As there were several Junior Scribes working at the Qianling county court,[17] they were possibly graduates of that school.

In addition to training specialists such as Scribes and Assistants, the Qin regime also prepared other less literate locals to fill low-profile administrative staffs in the government. Two good examples were Liu Ji and Lu Wan 盧綰. According to the biographical chapter on Lu Wan in both the *Shiji* and *Hanshu*, it was not until he and Liu Ji reached the age of maturity that they learned to write.[18] Regarding Liu's age, a third-century commentary records that he was sixty-two when he passed away in 195 BCE.[19] Thus, Liu Ji was likely in his mid-thirties around the founding of the Qin Empire. Such an age met the "maturity" criterion for becoming a nonhereditary Assistant. Therefore, the scripts that Liu Ji and Lu Wan learned were probably in Qin style. While it is impossible to give a precise assessment to the level of Qin literacy that Liu Ji achieved, that he filled only the modest post of the Constable of Sishang 泗上亭長 suggests that he did not gain an outstanding skill at writing.[20] The stories of Liu and his comrade, however, evince that the training and employment of locals was not limited to filling the positions of Scribes and Assistants.

Training locals with Qin literacy skills might have been a sustainable long-term move to solve personnel shortages, but it could not immediately mitigate the looming crisis. Therefore, Qin initiated a more immediately impactful measure. Aside from officials who were transferred to the new territories through formal procedures, Qin authorities decided to allow corrupt officials who should have been dismissed from office to repent their crime or mistake by working as "officials in the new territories."[21] By deploying these unfaithful officials to the newly conquered areas, the Qin authorities not only punished the deceptive behavior of their officials but also prevented the brain drain of valuable literate personnel. From this perspective serving in new territories was not far removed from exile despite the fixed term of such posts.

The policy of reshuffling former officials to the periphery was applied in a plethora of conditions. One Qin ordinance records a petition from Dingyin 定陰, saying that the Major (Si Ma 司馬) of Nan commandery faked an evaluation in his previous tenure as the Prefect of Yuanju 冤句

county. Under the new regulations, the Major had to work in the new territories for four years, comparable to the punishment of the above-mentioned unfaithful officials.[22] Another ordinance stipulates that if an official is sick and cannot fulfill his duties for more than three months in one year, he should be expelled from his office. When this official recovered, however, he would automatically become an "official in the new territories" and be treated like those officials who make mistakes warranting the punishment of exile and are thus expelled or dismissed from their original positions.[23] Other possible conditions prompting tenure in the unfavorable new territories include if a judicial officer obtains last place in the evaluation of the number of aptly tried criminals,[24] if a Scribe does not levy judicial functionaries in accordance with the ordinance,[25] or if officials cannot meet certain standards.[26] Aside from the sporadic amnesties (*she* 赦) granted by the Qin emperors,[27] the only way that such officials could be exempt from serving in the new territories was to compensate for their crimes by delivering 1,000 bushels of grain to the government or by giving up one level of rank.[28]

Sometimes the destinations are more specific. One ordinance prescribes that these delinquent officials should serve in commanderies in the Jiangdong 江東 or Jiangnan 江南 regions, the latter of which included new commanderies such as Dongting and Cangwu.[29] The implementation of these new policies resulted in the reallocation of an ample number of existing officials from the old territories to the peripheral regions.

MALFUNCTIONING OF GOVERNMENT AND MEAGER POLITICAL POWER

The previous section discusses some of the reforms that the Qin authority contemplated to solve the shortage of administrators. However, even a policy with the best of intentions may precipitate terrible outcomes if policy-makers cannot envisage the risks and costs that it will incur. Also, even if a policy per se could be effective, a failure to enforce that policy may further exacerbate existing problems. Instead of taking such stipulations for granted, I provide an evaluation of the effectiveness of these measures. Drawing on evidence from the Liye and Yuelu manuscripts, I argue that these reforms generally failed to resolve the shortage of officials.

Administrative records from Qianling county indicate that the scarcity of officials persisted until the end of the Qin Empire. What follows is a complaint letter that can shed additional light on this issue.

In the thirty-fourth year (213 BCE), the first month, which began on a day *dingmao*, on the *xinwei* (fifth) day, Acting Vice-Prefect of Qianling Yi presumes to report: Qianling's black-head ones . . . [since] Assistants, Reassigned Scribes, and Assistants whose days of service are mostly completed and [they have] returned, officials still working in the office are filled with statutory labor and assignments, and . . . documents [concerning this matter] had been repeatedly sent, but until now, we still have not received their replacements. The officials still working in the office are few and insufficient to handle the government duties . . . of officials. I call upon your (the commandery office's) reply. [To reply to this letter,] inscribe "to let the Bureau of Officials open" [on the postal label]. This I presume to report.

卅四年正月丁卯朔辛未，遷陵守丞巸敢言之: 遷陵黔首☑佐，均史、佐日有泰抵已備，歸。居吏被徭使，及☑前後書，至今未得其代，居吏少，不足以給事☑吏。謁報。署主吏發。敢言之☑³⁰

The letter was composed by Yi, then Acting Vice-Prefect of Qianling, who urged his superior, probably the Governor of Dongting commandery, to fill the administrative vacancies. This letter was not the only one that had been sent. Having received no response or replacements, Yi reissued this document to the commandery and complained that "the officials still working in the office are few and insufficient to handle government duties." The anxiety of the remaining officials was so strong that their grievances are almost audible.

This document highlights three vital aspects of the shortage of officials. First, it shows that the shortage persisted as late as 213 BCE, only four years before the empire collapsed. Second, it demonstrates that the insufficient number of officials negatively affected the performance of everyday administrative tasks and the empire's inability to dispatch the necessary number of new personnel. Last and most importantly, it tells us that the Qianling government failed to produce sufficient numbers of local writing specialists. In the end, they likely still needed to rely on the central government and other local administrative units in the old territories to transfer them experienced administrators.

The significant numbers of "acting" (*shou* 守) and "temporary" (*jia* 假) officials in the Qianling government further confirms the persistent scarcity of officials. Acting officials were only temporary positions that would have been discontinued upon the return of "incumbent officials" (*zhen guan* 真官). While it was normal for an administrator to momentarily hold a colleague's position while the latter was absent, the percentage of acting officials in Qianling seems exceptionally high. As shown in table 1 in appendix 1, although the service terms of real and acting officials overlapped, of the 232 valid examples that clearly record the name and title of an Overseer of an office, 151 were acting officials, who outnumbered "real" officials by almost 50 percent.[31]

Figure 3.1 indicates that the number of real Overseers exceeded, per year, the acting Overseers only two times in a decade. Within the cases pertinent to acting officials, more than 100 cases are concentrated between 217 and 212 BCE. These numbers reflect a greater reliance on acting officials during the latter half of the Qin occupation. Of course, given the incomplete sampling, these figures could be misleading, especially when most discovered material has not yet been published.

To better analyze the predominance of acting officials in the Qianling administration, perhaps it is better to look at more complete records. The transitions among Overseers of the Office of Granary (Cang Guan 倉官) in the thirty-first year of the First Emperor (216 BCE) are noteworthy. Table 1 in appendix 1 lists twenty-five examples from that year. Most of them are drawn from the transaction tallies of grain rations.

Figure 3.1. Distribution of Overseer and Acting Overseer of offices of Qianling from 221 to 209 BCE. Author's own material.

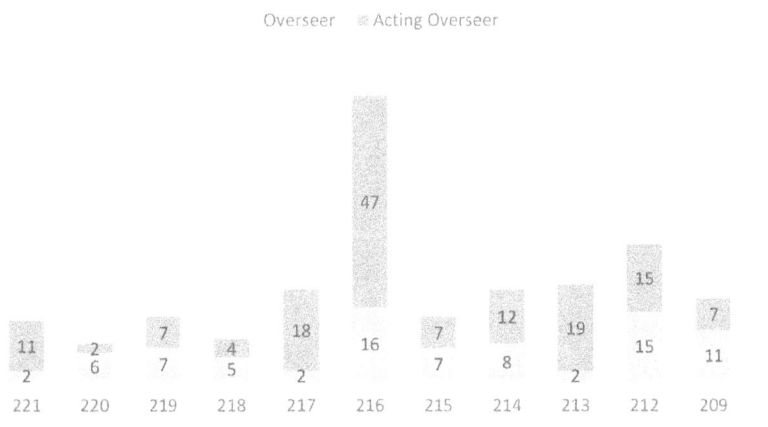

Overseer   Acting Overseer

These examples are distributed quite evenly, comprising records for every month except the sixth month, thereby giving us a relatively reliable picture of the transitions between real and acting Overseers. Among these entries, those from the first day of the tenth month—the beginning of the official calendar year—to the first day of the third month are worth noting. Two acting officials, namely, Fei 妃 and Wu 武, served during this timespan, even though other records suggest that Shi 是 was the real Overseer of the Office of Granary. This demonstrates the rapidity of transitions between real and acting officials.

In terms of the appointment of acting officials, certain Vice-Prefects are equally interesting. While the Vice-Prefect was one of the most vital decision-makers in the county government, forty-six of the seventy-three records pertaining to Vice-Prefects in extant sources relate to acting or temporary posts. Intriguingly, the distribution of exemplars was also polarized (fig. 3.2). Most extant examples of acting officials are dated either to the formative years of the empire (221–219 BCE) or after the fourth month of the thirty-second year of the First Emperor (215 BCE). In fact, from 214 BCE onward, all but one extant example are Acting or Temporary Vice-Prefects. This trend also matches that seen in the earlier discussion of Acting Overseers.

Several preliminary observations can be made on the basis of figures 3.1 and 3.2. First, the absence of officials seems to have accelerated

Figure 3.2. Distribution of Vice-Prefect and Acting Vice-Prefect of Qianling from 221 to 209 BCE. Author's own material.

after 216 BCE, when the Qianling government increasingly counted on acting officials to fill the vacancies left by real officials. Second, table 2 in appendix 1 reveals that Chang 昌 held the position of Vice-Prefect from 218 to 215 BCE, a tenure of approximately three years, which is congruent with the service term of "officials in the new territories." In this light, Chang was likely one of the "officials in the new territories" sent from the old territories who returned home after completing his term in office. That there were no Vice-Prefects on record until 212 BCE seems to imply that the authorities did not send Chang's replacement until that year, which matches the account of the abovementioned Liye tablet 8-197. Perhaps due to the repeated requests from Qianling, the regime finally appointed a new Vice-Prefect, Qian 遷, who lived in the city of Luoyang and became an "official in the new territories" because he was indebted to the regime.[32]

While most existing material centers on Qianling county, the official letter below reveals that it was not the only place in the Dongting region stricken by a scarcity of officials:

> In the thirty-second year [of the First Emperor] (215 BCE), Acting Overseer of Qiling commune Fu should be held liable for a crime. Fu ranks as a *shangzuo* and resides in Wuchang [county] of Zitong [commandery]. Now, he is transferred to be the Overseer of Convict Labor of Linyuan [county], where there are no officials at this time.

> 卅二年啓陵鄉守夫當坐。上造，居梓潼武昌，今徙為臨沅司空嗇夫，時毋吏。[33]

Linyuan was a county southeast of Qianling and likely served as the seat of Dongting commandery between 216 and 214 BCE.[34] Although the letter does not detail the crime for which Fu was liable, its context strongly implies that the reason that he managed to continue his official career was because Linyuan county had "no officials" in 215 BCE.

Drawing on existing evidence, the Qin's measures made little headway in improving the shortage of officials in Qianling or the Dongting region. Because of this failure, local officials had to take on the extra workload. This brought intense pressure on the remaining officials, resulting in the situation described in tablet 8-197.[35]

What were the reasons behind the failure of these policies? First, the failure may be predicated on Qianling's inability to train qualified indigenous officials to undertake daily administrative tasks. Although multiple sources suggest that the Qianling government trained and employed former Chu scribes in the Qin establishment, the latest studies indicate that the overwhelming majority of literate officials working there came from the central and semiperipheral regions of the empire. Local personnel mostly filled low-profile positions such as Postman (Youren 郵人), Sailor (Chuanren 船人) or Thief Catcher (Qiudao 求盜),[36] all of which required only limited proficiency in writing.

The Qin Empire's expansion also provoked a failure of administrative reforms. After seizing land in Luliang 陸梁 and driving out the Xiongnu 匈奴 in 215 BCE, the Qin delivered convicts being punished with exile to guard these new territories, constructing fortresses and watchtowers therein.[37] In the following year, they again exiled judicial officers who did not justly try lawsuits to "build the Great Wall or send them to the territories of Nan Yue."[38]

New evidence from Liye confirms the pivotal position of Dongting commandery in the Yue campaign. An administrative letter dated to 214 BCE mentions that Xincheng 鐔成 county was responsible for disseminating a letter from the Governor of Dongting commandery to the "new counties."[39] This suggests that Xincheng was under the jurisdiction of Dongting commandery.[40] According to the *Huainanzi*, Xincheng was one of the five strongholds at which the Qin Empire stationed troops before sending them to battle the Yue tribes.[41] Given the strategic position of Xincheng, it is natural for officials in that locale to dispatch administrative documents to the newly established counties in the Yue region. In short, the 214 BCE letter provides strong support for the connection between Dongting commandery and Qin's Yue campaign.

It is worth mentioning that the Yue campaign basically overlapped with Qianling's shortage of administrators. Since service in the new territories had much in common with the punishment of exile, the exiles mentioned in the *Shiji* would likely have become officials in regions such as Dongting commandery had they not been engaged in the southern campaign. Given that such workers were mobilized in other areas and the number of corrupt officials did not suddenly increase, the second expansion of the Qin Empire likely offset the effect of these administrative reforms.

The quality of officials in the new territories was also worrisome. Throughout history, newly conquered areas have often presented complicated landscapes, ethnicities, and cultural differences. Maintaining strong governance requires careful guidance by administrators with excellent credentials. Contrary to this ideal situation, officials serving in the Qin Empire's new territories were inferior administrators with doubtful integrity and competence.[42] Again, the anecdote of Liu Ji warrants our attention. Records in standard histories describe that after Liu was appointed the Constable of Sishang, "there was not a single officer in the county seat that he had not insulted" and that he was "fond of wine and women" and "regularly bought wine on credit" but never actually repaid the debt.[43] He also continually failed to fulfill his official duties.[44] Needless to say, Liu Ji openly violated the regulations about the conduct of officials in the new territories.

A fragment from the Liye corpus also mentions that "Overseers and officials are befuddled and harmful [to government matters] and are not capable of taking up their responsibilities" (是嗇夫、吏秏亂毋益，不勝任).[45] All these examples explain why multiple accounts in transmitted texts claimed that the people in the eastern region were "sickened at the atrocity of Qin officials" (苦秦吏暴).[46] The discontent induced by the poor quality of administrators inevitably undermined the legitimacy of the empire.

Convict Laborers

The second type of shortage pertains to convict laborers, the pivotal labor force for the state economy of the Qin Empire. As Maxim Korolkov illustrates, the state played a crucial role in Qin's economic development in the Warring States period. It was the ultimate distributor of the fiscal revenue (both monetary and in-kind) collected through a rather narrow tax base (land tax, household tax, etc.) and the products generated from state-controlled economic activities (e.g., field cultivation, iron and salt industries, handicraft workshops).[47] Additionally, state agents were actively engaged in market transactions and often appeared to be the largest group of consumers of and investors in labor service and infrastructure. The major goal of the whole fiscal model was to finance wars and resulted in a fiscal regime that always prioritized the center over the rest of the polity in the distribution of the economic surplus. This state-dominant fiscal model was nonetheless forced to change because of the much higher transportation cost of transferring revenue collected locally to the center. Consequently, the regional administrative units were granted greater freedom in using extracted monetized income so as to satisfy their demand for more monetary liquidity.[48]

That said, the changes in the Qin's fiscal model did not reduce the government's demand for laborers. By contrast, the establishment of new administrative units during the territorial expansion, coupled with the large-scale infrastructure construction projects, created an upsurge in the demand for laborers, especially coerced and convicted government slaves. Indeed, in the design of the Qin rulers, convict laborers were one of the groups that took priority over commoners in terms of labor service.[49] Given their instrumental position in state-controlled production and construction projects, the demand for such laborers likely skyrocketed after the establishment of the Qin Empire.

The Qin penal system demarcated convict laborers into two major categories. The first group consisted of "wall-builders or grain-pounders" and "gatherers of fuel for the spirits or white-rice sorters" (guixin baican 鬼薪白粲), who were managed by the Office of Convict Labor (Sikong Guan 司空官). The second group were "bondservants or bondwomen" (lichenqie 隸臣妾) supervised by the Office of Granary.[50] All three types of convict laborers experienced a derogation of their social status.[51] Because of this social damage, such punishments were lifelong and often hereditary.

As a punishment, the "wall-builder or grain-pounder" was one degree more severe than the "bondservants or bondwomen." In addition to these lifelong slaves, commoners who "worked off fines, redemption fees, or debts" (juzi shu zhai 居貲贖債) or were "detained with wall-builders or grain-pounders" (xi chengdanchong 繫城旦舂) would also work alongside convict laborers. For the former category, their service periods were determined by the amount they owed, whereas the latter group usually served fixed terms.[52] These unfree laborers were required to undertake a wide spectrum of tasks such as field cultivation, handicraft production, tribute collection, document dispatchment, service as cooks or servants of functionaries, and other miscellaneous duties.[53]

The prevalence of using convict laborers in production activities conducted by the government apparatus is evidenced in the administrative records of Qianling county. The Liye manuscripts reveal that the county employed a great number of convict laborers in manual production activities and routine administrative tasks. "Registers of Convict Laborers" (zuotu bu 作徒簿) of the county reveal that as of 213 BCE, the Office of Granary employed about 146 convict laborers per day,[54] whereas the Office of Convict Labor managed 226 convict laborers in 215 BCE.[55] Considering that Qianling was only a small county with fewer than two hundred registered households,[56] the number of convict laborers working at the same time (about 372) probably exceeded one-third of the total controllable population.

Shortage of Convict Laborers and Disturbances to the State Economy

In the wake of the enormous demand, material from Liye indicates that despite having a strikingly high convict-laborer-to-household ratio, Qianling county still experienced a shortage of convict laborers. A slip from Liye reads, "The staff number of bondservants in Qianling is not fully equipped by fifteen" (遷陵隸臣員不備十五人).[57] According to the abovementioned 213 BCE Register of Convict Laborers, the average number of bondservants, including both adults and minors, used per day was approximately fifty. Therefore, a shortage of fifteen bondservants was already a substantial issue that should not be underestimated.[58] Another fragment also documents that convict laborers in an unknown office were in short supply because of the mining of tin.[59] These citations suggest that the insufficient number of laborers imperiled the production activities of the Qianling government.

A key factor causing the shortage of convict laborers may be their high turnover rate. An evaluation dated to 219 BCE reveals the condition of bondservants, bondwomen, and commoners working off fines in Qianling's offices. It records that 18.5 percent (28 out of 151) of bondservants and bondwomen had either died or absconded, whereas only 2.6 percent of commoners (1 in 38) working off fines encountered similar issues.[60] Such a significant divergence can be attributed to the austere working conditions of convict laborers, who were responsible for the most laborious and unfavorable tasks.

On the one hand, given that the responsible officials were either charged with or held liable for punishments because of this evaluation, such a high turnover rate seems to be unacceptable by official standards.[61] On the other hand, it reflects the nonchalant attitude of some, if not most, of the Qin officials about the lives of convict laborers. As will be discussed later, convict laborers working in Qianling included retainers or relatives of aristocrats of states that had been wiped out by the empire as well as members of non-Qin local populations. This composition might also let the Qin officials, who were mostly imported from the old Qin regions, belittle the value of convict laborers' lives and regard them not as human but as disposable goods.

The shortage of convict laborers in Qianling county affected the government's ability to extract and produce resources. A report from the Acting Overseer of Erchun commune reads:

(A) In the twenty-eighth year (219 BCE), the second month, which began on a day *xinwei*, on the *gengyin* (twentieth) day, Xing, the Acting Overseer of Erchun commune, presumes to report: the annual tribute tax as of the twenty-eighth year consists of two yellow pheasants, two white pheasants, two black pheasants, two *mingqu* birds, and four golden pheasants. The Prefect ordered communes to hunt [those tributary animals] prior to the end of the third month. Since Erchun commune has no officials and laborers[62] and I am stationed here alone, I did not hunt [those tributary birds]. [Besides,] given that catching apes requires ample officials and laborers, I call upon offices with [sufficient] officials and laborers to lead [a mission of ape] hunting comparable to that in the twenty-seventh year, so that we can seize apes. This I presume to report.

(C) [Overseer of] Granary Wu has given . . . (convict laborers to Erchun?)

(B) On the twenty-eighth day of the second month . . . Chengren, who holds the *shiwu* status, arrived [with this document]. Chu opened it. (A) Xing handles [this document].

(A) 廿八年二月辛未朔庚寅，貳春鄉守行敢言之：廿八年歲賦獻黃二乚、白翰二乚、黑翰二、明 (明) 渠鳥二、鷩鳥四。今令鄉求捕，毋出三月乚。鄉毋吏徒，行獨居，莫求捕。捕爰用吏徒多，謁令官有吏徒者將求捕如廿七年捕爰，乃可以得爰。敢言之。

(C) 倉武[63]已付 . . . . . .

(B) 二月戊戌□□□□□□□□士五 (伍) 程人以來/ 除半。 (A) 行手。[64]

This report concerns the insufficiency of convict laborers for catching tributary animals such as exotic birds and apes. Xing, then the Acting Overseer of Erchun commune, claimed that the office had no one but him working; thus, he requested that the county delegate the ape-hunting mission to an office with sufficient officials and laborers. While we cannot completely deny the possibility that it was just mere bureaucratic rhetoric espoused to evade a difficult task assigned by a superior, this letter was copied by Xing himself instead of the usual Commune Assistant (Xiang Zuo 鄉佐), which aligns with the labor shortages he describes. Furthermore, other evidence in Liye does record that an ape-hunting mission employed at least 150 units of labor force[65] and could have taken as long as three months.[66] While catching birds required far less labor, it was still not something that could be done alone.[67] These pieces of evidence confirm the validity of Xing's report.

It is worth noting that at the end of the main text, the line "[Overseer of] Granary Wu has given . . ." was inscribed. Since its handwriting evidently differs from the preceding text, it was probably appended by the responsible functionary after the letter was delivered to the county seat. It seems that the county government rejected Xing's request and decided to send him reinforcement laborers instead. This indicates both the scarcity of laborers in Erchun commune and the uneven distribution of laborers across different organizations within Qianling government, which in turn hints at the low logistical efficiency of its management.

Sometimes the shortage was in terms of not only quantity but also quality. A report from Office of Warehouse reads,

> In the twenty-seventh year (220 BCE), the eleventh month, which began on a day *wushen*, on the *jiaxu* (twenty-seventh) day, Zhong, the Acting Overseer of the Warehouse, presumes to report: Formerly I reported to order the [Office of] Convict Labor to make assembled [crossbow] triggers, and the [Overseer of the Office of] Convict Labor said that there were no convict laborers who could assemble a trigger. Now it is the year-end, and [the production of] triggers cannot be completed. I call upon the Office of Granary to send . . . convict laborers. I beg you to copy this letter to the [County] Commander and call upon your reply. This I presume to report.

> 廿七年十一月戊申朔甲戌，庫守衷敢言之: 前言組用幾令司空為，
> 司空言徒毋能為組幾者。今歲莫（暮），幾不成。謁令倉為□□
> 徒。騰尉。謁報。敢言之。[68]

Since assembling crossbow triggers is a sophisticated task that requires skilled laborers, what bothered Zhong the most was the lack of qualified labor force. The phenomena described in this section indicate short-comings in both the quantity and the quality of convict laborers, which considerably hindered the efficient exploitation of resources.

REFORMS AND MEASURES TO INCREASE THE NUMBER OF CONVICT LABORERS IN THE NEW TERRITORIES

Qin rulers were well aware of the shortage of adequate convict laborers. Prior to the unification war between 230 and 221 BCE, they already envisaged such a potential problem. The "Statutes on Abscondence" (Wang lü 亡律) housed in the Yuelu Academy include the ordinance below:

> From the *xinchou* (thirteen) day of the seventh month of the fourteenth year [of King Zheng] (233 BCE) onward, for those who commit abscondence before completely working off their fines, redemption fees, or debts, they shall be held liable for their unpaid amount of [fines, redemption fees, or debts] in cash; [the punishments of their crimes] share the same categorical principle with robbers.

> 十四年七月辛丑以來，諸居貲贖責（債）未備而去亡者，坐其未備錢數，與盜同灋。[69]

This ordinance targeted absconders who were working off their fines, redemption fees, or debts. Previously, these people would have been sentenced in accordance with prescriptions imposed on normal absconders, who suffered the punishment of having their beard shaved (usually coupled with the hard labor punishment of "bondservants and bondwomen") after they had worked for one full year or should be "detained with wall-builders or grain-pounders" if their period of abscondence occurred within less than a year.[70]

The punishments of the targeted group became much harsher under the new regulations, whereby punishments for the absconders were dependent not on the duration of their abscondence but on the amount of their unpaid fines, redemption fees, or debts. Accordingly, their punishments were to share the same "categorical principle with robbers," which is detailed in the "Statute on Robbery" cited in chapter 2. Under this principle, if a person absconded when his or her unpaid amount was more than 220 cash, the person would become a wall-builder or grain-pounder, and if the amount was more than 109 cash, he or she would become a bondservant or bondwoman (table 3.2). One of the possible consequences of this new policy was that there would be more commoners who were degraded to wall-builders or grain-pounders.

The promulgation of this new prescription was likely part of the institutional reforms enacted to increase the number of available convict laborers in preparation for a long-term war. Notably, this new ordinance was enacted in 233 BCE, the year before the first "massive mobilization of troops." As Miyake Kiyoshi points out, the phrase "massive mobiliza-

Table 3.2. Correlation and conversion of the unpaid fines, redemption fees, or debts of absconders and their punishments

Amounts of unpaid fines, redemption fees or debts of absconders (in cash)	Punishments of offenders in the Qin period	Days of abscondence after conversion
> 660	Tattoo and make wall-builders or grain-pounders	≥ 111
220–660	Leave intact and make wall-builders or grain-pounders	37–110
110–219	Shave beard and make bondservants or bondwomen/detain with wall-builders or grain-pounders[1]	19–36
22–109	Fine two sets of armor[2]	4–18
1–21	Fine one set of armor	1–3

1. According to the abovementioned "Statutes on Robbery" in the *Statutes and Ordinances of the Second Year*, offenders who stole 110–219 cash warranted the punishment of "shaving beard and making bondservants or bondwomen." For existing bondservants and bondwomen, it was possible that they would be detained along with wall-builders or grain-pounders (like the preimperial legal case cited above) or be further degraded to wall-builders or grain-pounders.

2. The Western Han government transformed the punishment of fines to complete monetary terms (although it is evident that the punishment was monetized as late as the imperial Qin period). Here, I reconstruct this punishment according to the Qin penal system.

tion of troops" appears only three times in the *Shiji*, all of which appear in the content covering the reign of King Zheng, and likely denoted mobilization on an unprecedented scale that exceeded even that in the Battle of Changping.[71] Given that the actual mobilization had to be planned beforehand, by the time the abovementioned ordinance was enacted, the Qin regime probably knew that massive mobilization, or even the unification war, was on its way.

In the Qin military system, the major suppliers of military force were peasant-soldiers, who were conscripted from each household and are believed to have served full-time in the army for about one year during the late Warring States period.[72] The mobilization of large groups of peasants likely resulted in a reduction in the overall productivity of the state, especially in terms of agricultural production, which provided the most important strategic resources during times of war. To compensate for such a loss, Qin rulers probably felt the need to increase the supply of convict laborers such as wall-builders or grain-pounders, who provided lifelong and by far the most intensive labor services for the state.

Similar changes can be found in the punishments for other types of absconders. The abscondence of convicts who would become bond-servants or bondwomen is one such change. A Qin lawsuit case datable to 246 BCE from the Yuelu manuscripts indicates that the punishment for an absconded bondservant was to be "detained with wall-builders or grain-pounders" for a fixed term.[73] A "Statute on Abscondence" from the same corpus nonetheless stipulates much harsher punishments:

> And for the abscondence of those who match the punishment of shaving beard and making bondservants or bondwomen, calculate [the amount that they owe to the state under the standard of] six cash per day. And for the abscondence of those robber-guards serving long-term in offices and those who should perform periodic service, in every case, calculate [the amount that they owe to the state] by using the days that they should have served long-term and should have performed periodic service [under the standard of] six cash per day; [the punishments of] every [aforementioned offender] should share the same categorical principle with robbers. For those [whose debt amounted to] less than 22 cash, fine one set of armor. Should [offenders] appear voluntarily, reduce their punishments by one degree.

及諸當隸臣妾者亡，以日六錢計之；及司寇冗作及當踐更者亡，
皆以其當冗作及當踐更日，日六錢計之，皆與盜同灋。不盈廿二
錢者，貲一甲。其自出殹，減罪一等L。[74]

Again, the categorical principle of robbers was applied to determine the punishments of absconded bondservants and bondwomen, as well as robber-guards and commoners who should have served in government organizations but escaped. As listed in table 3.2, if a bondservant absconded for thirty-seven days, he would be demoted to a wall-builder. This new sentencing principle was evidently harsher than that in 246 BCE and might have increased the number of convict laborers. Like the above ordinance, this new measure likely aimed at compensating for the potential loss of productivity due to the large-scale and protracted mobilization of peasant-soldiers.

The application of the categorical principle of robbers was not limited to the above two cases. Legal manuscripts from the imperial Qin period reveal the pervasiveness of such a practice. According to my own counting, the preimperial Shuihudi tomb no. 11 Qin legal corpus mentions the phrase only three times, and the early Western Han *Statutes and Ordinances of the Second Year* contain eight such references.[75] In contrast, the imperial Qin Yuelu Academy corpus alone includes thirty-one specimens after excluding repetitive contents.[76] Even in the Longgang corpus, with its small sample size and fragmentary status, this phrase appears five times.[77] Most of these stipulations entail infringements on private or government property, which indicates that the term *robbery* was being used in a broad sense.

The wide application of the categorical principle of robbers in legal corpora from the imperial Qin period seems to be indicative of the times. Although we cannot assert that all these regulations related to the Qin ruler's desire to increase the supply of convict laborers, it is conceivable that a commoner could easily have been degraded to a wall-builder or a grain-pounder in the imperial period. In this fashion, the share of convict laborers among the overall labor force of the Qin government should have been proportionally higher than most of the preimperial period. This also conforms with the records of the standard histories, where hundreds of thousands of convict laborers were said to be employed by the state to undertake laborious construction projects.

Aside from the above reforms, special policies were also generated to target the shortage of labor force in the new territories. Notably, commanderies in the periphery became the usual destinations for the placement of convict laborers.[78] Sending convicts to administrative units on the fringes of the state was already a common practice in the Warring States period, especially to southwestern areas such as Ba and Shu commanderies, in which both the "offices of salt in Ba commandery" (*Ba xian yan* 巴縣鹽) and the "border counties of Shu commandery" (*Shu bianxian* 蜀邊縣) were designated as workplaces for convict laborers.[79]

To usher in the imperial era, a new placement policy for convict laborers was designed. An unspecified ordinance in the Yuelu collection stipulates the treatment of followers (*zongren* 從人) of the states eliminated by the Qin. Originally, these people and their affiliates were sentenced to being "left intact and made a wall-builder or a grain-pounder" (*wan chengdanchong* 完城旦舂) and worked in the offices of salt in Ba commandery.[80] However, the Chief Prosecutor (Yushi dafu 御史大夫) decided to review this policy, suggesting that they instead be transferred to Dongting and Cangwu commanderies in the southern periphery. The ostensible reason for this arrangement was that "the offices of salt in Ba commandery were full of people" and thus did not need further reinforcement.[81] That said, given the severe shortage of convict laborers in Dongting and Cangwu, this policy was likely also aimed at increasing the number of convict laborers therein.

Dongting commandery also appears in another Qin ordinance pertaining to the punishments of rumor-mongers:

> Henceforth, should someone conspire[82] or spread rumors [accusing] innocent people of being insurgents, immediately sentence him or her to statutes pertaining to "forwarding sacrileges"; should there be discontented(?) persons [incited by rumor-mongers], transfer them to Dongting [commandery], whose [Governor should] locate them in areas that have ample fields. [Ordinance number] thirteen.

> 【●】自今以來，有誨、傳言以不反為反者，輒以行訛律論之。其有不□[83]者，徙洞庭，洞庭處多田所。　・十三。[84]

The ordinance details that the incited people should be delivered to Dongting commandery, where they would be responsible for field cultivation. In all likelihood, the Dongting region was a popular destination for the placement of convict laborers.

MEASURES TO FACILITATE THE LOGISTICAL EFFICIENCY OF CONVICT LABORERS IN NEW TERRITORIES

The Qianling government was also plagued by low logistical efficiency in transferring convict laborers. This problem was a direct result of the shortage of convict laborers on the one hand, and the high information cost caused by the complicated topography of the region on the other. While one cannot definitively say whether this problem was pervasive across all administrative units of the empire, it likely existed in regions that had a similar landscape to that of Qianling.

The Qin regime enacted at least two measures to improve its logistical efficiency. One of them was to simplify the administrative procedures pertinent to the distribution of convict laborers:

> In the twenty-seventh year (220 BCE), which began on a day *wushen*, on the *guihai* (sixteenth) day of the eleventh month, Chang, the Temporary Governor of Dongting, informs the Vice-Prefect of Qianling: Qianling has submitted the names of sixty-six convicts who are liable for the crime of escaping from exile and thus should be reassigned and delivered to the commandery. Now all [sixty-six convicts] are to be delivered to Qianling, which should listen to this document and carry out the affairs. The remaining [procedures should be carried out] according to statutes and ordinances. [The document was] carried forward through the seal of [County Prefect] of Xinwuling.

> 廿七年十一月戊申朔癸亥，洞庭叚守昌謂遷陵丞：遷陵上坐反
> （返）適（謫）皋當均輸郡中者六十六人。今皆輸遷陵，其聽書從
> 事，它如律令。‧以新武陵印行事。[85]

This letter is a reply from Dongting commandery to Qianling regarding the arrangement of sixty-six convicts who apparently needed to be transferred to the commandery for reallocation. Interestingly, the Temporary Governor designated Qianling as the destination of the group. Conceivably, these convict laborers might never have left Qianling's purview, and the earlier report was sent only as a formality. Such a treatment could significantly reduce both transportation and time costs, thereby improving the efficiency of transferring laborers.

The Qin regime also created new organizations to facilitate logistical efficiency in delivering convict laborers. One Qin ordinance stipulates that if convict laborers cannot cultivate fields because of other miscella-neous tasks, the county seat should provide the subordinate offices that engage in field cultivation with convict laborers at a ratio of six unable convict laborers to four field laborers (*tiantu* 田徒). The ordinance later prescribes that if a county is short of convicts, it must compile a register and submit it to the "Prosecutor of the Management of Captives" (Zhilu Yushi 治虜御史) and ask him to allocate the necessary labor force.[86]

Here, the title Prosecutor of the Management of Captives is par-ticularly intriguing. In Qin administrative and legal documents, the term *lu* 虜 usually denotes captives or prisoners of war.[87] Therefore, it is likely that this office managed followers of former states, who were a crucial component of convict labor in the new territories. Despite not being explicitly stated, it is plausible that there were multiple Prosecutors of the Management of Captives whose major task was to allocate convict laborers upon the request of counties within their respective jurisdictions. The major purpose of setting up such a highly specialized office was likely to enable more timely responses to the demand for field laborers. This ordinance shows that the Qin rulers felt an urgent need to effectuate the logistics of using convict laborers.

Insubstantiality of the Convict Labor System and Insufficient Economic Power

Existing evidence suggests that the policies promulgated by the Qin authorities gave little help in solving Qianling county's shortage of con-vict laborers or improving the logistical efficiency of the labor force. The demand for convict laborers was not met and the gap in economic power controlled by the state organizations was as wide as it had been before.

Earlier in this chapter, I cited a report from an Acting Overseer of Erchun commune who complained of a shortage of convict laborers in 219 BCE. Seven years later, Erchun's situation had not changed much:

(A) In the thirty-fifth year (212 BCE), the seventh month, which began on a day *wuzi*, on the *renchen* (fifth) day, Zi?, the [Overseer of] Erchun, presumes to report: While there is a document [asking for] feather tax, I have no laborers to collect feathers. I call upon the office to immediately [send laborers?] to collect feathers, thereby fulfilling the tax. This I presume to report.

(C) In the seventh month, which began on a day *wuzi*, on the *bingshen* (ninth) day, Jian, the Acting Prefect of Qianling, hands down [the document] to the Offices of Granary and Convict Labor, saying that: immediately deliver [the requested laborers?], reply [to the Erchun commune], and transfer a document [there]. Zu handles [this document].

(D) In the morning of the *bingshen* (ninth) day of the seventh month, bondwoman Sun forwards [this document].

(B) In the seventh month, in the afternoon of the *yiwei* (eighth) day, a minor who holds the *shangzao* (the second) rank from the Dongcheng village arrived [with this document]. (A) Ruyi handles [this document].

(A) 卅五年七月【戊子】朔壬辰，貳【春茲（？）】敢言之: 賦羽有書，毋徒捕羽。謁令官巫□捕羽，給賦。敢言之。/ (C) 七月戊子朔丙申，遷陵守建下倉、司空: 巫遣報之，傳書。/歜手 / (D) 丙申旦，隷妾孫行。

(B) 七月乙未日失（昳）【時，東】成小上造以來。　　(A) 如意手。[88]

The "feather tax" in the letter refers to an in-kind tax that was to be paid in the form of feather, which appears to be one of Qianling's specialties.[89] The purpose of charging such a tax might have been motivated by the need to manufacture arrow fletching,[90] or by the imperial court's desire for luxury goods, which feathers could be used to decorate.[91] The demand for feathers was immense. A slip from Liye records that the feather tax as of 220 BCE amounted to 2,500 *hou* (鍭; a measurement unit for feathers).[92] Another report even documents that the imperial workshop of the Lesser Treasury (Shaofu Gong Shi 少府工室) alone received 3,500 *hou* of feathers,[93] and at least 1,000 feathers were collected and given to Qianling at once.[94]

The Qianling government invested a large number of laborers in the collection of feathers. One Register of Convict Labor reveals that feather collection alone accounted for about 6.6 percent of all convict labor, making it second only to field cultivation.[95] Multiple sources even indicate that the government was purchasing feathers from the private market.[96] While Zi's report makes no mention of whether the Offices of Granary and Convict Labor had enough convict laborers at their disposal, it unveils that the logistical efficiency of labor allocation did not improve much even when the downfall of the Qin Empire was almost assured.

Qianling's situation suggests that the Qin's reforms and measures to mitigate the shortage of convict laborers were to no avail. One of the fundamental reasons behind this failure was the incessant territorial expansion and building projects of the empire, which kept causing surges in the state's demand for convict laborers. Indeed, there was a strong correlation between military campaigns and the concentration of convict laborers. According to transmitted accounts, the Qin Empire launched a massive southward campaign that can be divided into two stages. The first phase started in 217 BCE. Led by Cangwu Commandant Tuwei 徒唯 (Tusui 屠睢 in the transmitted *Huainanzi*), 500,000 soldiers were split into five groups and marched to the Yue territories.[97] It is worth noting that over 50 percent of the extant Registers of Convict Laborers from Qianling county date to between 217 and 216 BCE.[98] This probably indicates a concentration of convict laborers related to the preparations for the empire's Yue campaign.

Most of such hard laborers were called upon to facilitate the logistics of the 214 BCE campaign. In military campaigns, logistics greatly impact success. Given that the southern territory of the Dongting commandery was one of the military bases for the empire's southern campaign, the region might have functioned as a conduit for military reinforcement and supplies from the north.

Two of the preparatory actions that Qianling county undertook were the "paving of roads" (*chudao* 除道) and the "transfer of food" (*tongshi* 通食). A report states that in 215 BCE, Fu 福, then Acting Overseer of Erchun commune, was held liable for his crimes. In lieu of receiving a punishment, he was sent to "construct roads and transfer food."[99] Additionally, an undated fragment seems to request that all available personnel in Qianling had to perform the two abovementioned tasks.[100]

Road construction and food exchange remained two of the most urgent duties for Qianling county's personnel after the completion of major battles in the Yue lands. A letter dated to 213 BCE documents a new title called "Commandant of the Road Construction of Dongting Commandery" (Dongting Chudao Wei 洞庭除道尉).[101] Another fragmentary letter reveals the existence of the "Temporary Vice-Prefect of Dongting Governor for Swiftly Urging and Transferring Food" (Qu Quan Tongshi Dongting Shou Jia Cheng 趣勸通食洞庭守叚丞), who was forwarding this document to Xincheng and possibly also to Yuanyang 沅陽.[102] Based on their titles, these two positions seemed to be set up exclusively to facilitate military logistics. Contemporaneous records also indicate that the Qin Empire devoted a substantial share of its labor force to supporting the logistics of its new southern territories, and the Dongting region was one of the conduits for channeling resources to the south.[103]

The above discussion illustrates how territorial expansion exhausted the labor force of local administrative units. Given the massive scale of mobilization, the burden of infrastructure construction and food supply likely did not fall on Qianling county alone. Rather, they had to be shared by administrative units within the purview of Dongting commandery as well as its adjacent regions. Inasmuch as convict laborers were the most reliable and intensive production units of the Qin government, it is plausible that the enormous demand for convict laborers easily offset the efforts made to increase their supply.

The unsustainability of the Qin's new policies may also account for their failure. Among the types of laborers deployed by the regime, convict laborers had the highest maintenance cost. The state was not only required to satisfy the livelihoods of convict laborers (food rations, accommodations, clothing) but also needed to provide for their oversight costs. Given the lifelong sentencing of convict laborers and the rarity of amnesty during the Qin era, the vast number of convict laborers must have placed immense pressure on state finances.[104] Peripheral regions such as Qianling county, which often relied on staples imported from more productive regions, were conceivably the hardest hit. The severe fiscal condition of these administrative units immediately calls into question the sustainability of the convict labor system. In fact, to reduce food supply expenses, Qianling officials often thinned the food rations of convict laborers. This way of cutting corners might have negatively affected the physical condition of convict laborers and accounted for their high turnover rate.[105]

Another piece of evidence concerning the unsustainability of the convict labor system is the frequent abscondence of convict laborers. The policies discussed above usually entailed long-distance transmission that took days or even months to accomplish. Along the way, there were plenty opportunities for convict laborers to flee. Transmitted literature reveals that Liu Ji escorted a group of convict laborers to Mount Li 驪山

from Pei county, but many of these convicts absconded along the way.[106] A fragmentary formal statement drafted by a Scribe Director of Qianling also reports the abscondence of a convict laborer during a mining mission.[107] The high policing cost incurred by deploying convict laborers inevitably undermined the effectiveness of the new allocation policy.

In addition, the unsustainability might come from the careless policy design of the central government. Consider Qianling county. Although the Qin authorities did increase the supply of convict laborers of the region by establishing Dongting commandery as one of the main destinations for such labor, the new laborers were not necessarily suited to the tasks they were assigned. The following report records one such case:

> (A) In the twenty-eighth year, in the first month, which began on a day *xinchou*, on the *dingwei* (seventh) day, Jing, the Overseer of Erchun commune, presumes to report: As for followers who are wall-builders, all of them do not know [the way of creating] swidden fields,[108] but they should be capable of engaging in handicraft work and repairing buildings for the county offices. Here I call upon you to order all these followers to engage in handicraft at such offices, as well as carrying earth and assisting in the production of ceramics; and to send all males who previously assisted in carrying earth to cultivate the field. In addition, since conscripts guarding the city walls and those black-headed ones who [have been punished] according to their crimes all know [the way of creating] swidden fields, I call up the superior to decide to dispatch those who can cultivate fields from the military camp and do not order my office (Erchun commune) to single-handedly dispatch those who can cultivate fields. I call upon your reply. This I presume to report.

> (C) Now Jing is receiving his laborers on the *renzi* (twelfth) day of the first month, [and we] will not reply [to this report].

> (B) In the evening of the *renzi* (twelfth) day [of the first month], Assistant Hei arrived [with this document]. Chu opened it. (A) X handles [this document].

> (A) 廿八年正月辛丑朔丁未，貳春鄉敬敢言之：從人城旦皆非智（知）篈田殹，當可作治縣官府，謁盡令從人作官府及負土佐

甄，而盡遣故佐負土男子田。及乘城卒、諸黔首抵辠（罪）者皆智（知）篆田，謁上財（裁）自敦（屯）遣田者，毋令官獨遣田者。謁報。敢言之。

(C) 今敬正月壬子受徒，弗報。

(B) 壬子夕，佐黑以來。 /除半。　　(A) □[109]手[110]

This letter indicates that Dongting indeed received some followers of former aristocrats as prescribed in the ordinance. The commandery then delivered them to Qianling, where they were assigned the task of creating swidden fields. Probably due to their prestigious former social status or different cultural background, these followers did not possess such a skill. As a result, Ji, then Overseer of Erchun commune, applied for a reassignment of their duties. Furthermore, he asked the county government to send him convict laborers who actually knew how to make swiddens. Although the Qianling government approved Ji's request and dispatched laborers accordingly, time was wasted on administrative communication. This report provides an excellent example of the discrepancy between the ideals and the realities of government policies.

Even if a policy is thoroughly designed, it may still fall apart in the face of poor execution. As I have discussed in chapter 2, the competence and motivation of the "officials in the new territories" were questionable. In a lawsuit against Yan 厭, then Overseer of Convict Labor of Qianling, regarding his negligence in field cultivation, the Dongting Governor stated that the county did not start field cultivation until 218 BCE, four years after its establishment as a Qin administrative unit. Another example comes from a report that an Overseer of the Office of Field Cultivation had repeatedly sent back the convict laborers assigned to him and was seemingly under investigation for "not working diligently in nourishing field cultivation and encouraging fieldwork" (不勉力調護，勸勉作之).[111] The official's incompetence and lack of motivation likely led to policy failure.[112]

Conscripts

The third area of human resource shortage was conscripts. As the Qin Empire was a highly militaristic state, its male subjects, most of whom were farmers, were subject to conscription. Levying conscripts was one of the paramount duties of government administration. Textual sources indicate that Qin developed an intricate conscription system. In addition to the regular conscripts such as "conscripts in-shift" (*gengshu* 更戍) and "long-term conscripts" (*rongshu* 冗戍),[113] convicts were often conscripted to perform military duties to repent of their crimes. With the exception of long-term conscripts, who were recruited soldiers with longer service terms, no other types of conscripts were entitled to government rations. If these conscripts could not provide their own food, they could borrow food from the government, and in exchange, their terms of service would be extended.[114]

The military force of a county was in the hands of the Commander. A fragmentary evaluation conducted by the County Commander of Qianling reveals that the county controlled 626 conscripts, 143 of whom were long-term conscripts.[115] One fragment even mentions that the number of long-term conscripts once reached or exceeded 200.[116] No information about other types of conscripts stationed in Qianling county has been found. Plausibly, these conscripts were supposed to conduct everyday military routines and fill martial positions such as Sergeant Major (Shi Li 士吏), Constable (Jiao Zhang 校長), and Thief Catcher.

Similar to the case of officials, most traceable conscripts of Qianling came from the old territories, although evidence suggests that local governments also levied locals to undertake military service. Case 18 of the *Book of Submitted Doubtful Cases* reveals that Cangwu commandery conscripted new subjects in a failed scrimmage against Chu insurgents from that region.[117] Moreover, the Liye corpus constitutes a dozen wooden slips that were inscribed with the personal information of their recipients, all of whom were residents of villages in Qianling. Since these wooden slips all end with the phrase "the order has been received" (*shuoling* 受令) that usually appeared in the context of mobilization or statuary labor service, they were presumably notices or confirmation letters pertinent to military or labor services.[118] In short, a mixture of local and external conscripts was common in the new territories.

SHORTAGE OF CONSCRIPTS AND JEOPARDIZED MILITARY LOGISTICS

The following letter from the Temporary Constable of Tang post 唐亭 reveals the shortage of conscripts in the formative stage of the Qin Empire:

(A) In the twenty-sixth year, in the second month, which began on a day *guichou*, on the *bingzi* (twenty-fourth) day,

Zhuang, the Temporary Constable of the Tang Post, presumes to report: Near the Tang Post, there are robbers numbering approximately thirty persons. Given that I[119] have too few conscripts [stationed at the post], I am not capable of tracing [the robbers] because the Post cannot be left empty. I call upon [the county] to send conscripts to pursue [these robbers]. This I presume to report.

(C) On the *xinsi* (twenty-ninth) day of the second month, Dunhu, the Acting Vice-Prefect of Qianling, presumes to inform the Commander, and inform the Overseers of communes: Act according to the statutes and ordinances. The Commander hands down [this letter] to posts and forts and has stationed the Sergeant Major to carefully prepare [for the robbers]. Erchun commune submits [this letter] to the Vice-Prefect of the Major [of Dongting commandery]. Ting [handled it]

(D) On the same day, order runner Tu to forward this letter.

(B) On the *xinsi* (twenty-ninth) day of the second month, Xu, who ranks *bugeng* and is from Yu Village, arrived with [this letter]. Cheng [opened it]. (A) Zhuang [handled it].

(A) 廿六年二月癸丑朔丙子，唐亭叚校長壯敢言之：唐亭旁有盜可卅人，壯卒少，不足以追，亭不可空。謁遣卒索。敢言之。

(C) 二月辛巳，遷陵守丞敦狐敢告尉，告鄉主：以律令從事。尉下亭鄣，署士吏謹備。貳【春】鄉上司馬丞。／亭手／ (D) 即令走涂行。

(B) 二月辛巳，不更輿里戌以來／丞半。 (A) 壯手。[120]

Tang post was likely located near or in Erchun commune and was at some distance from the county seat. In his report, Zhuang requested reinforcements from the County Commander since the small number of conscripts that he commanded were not capable of tracing the gang of robbers in his area of responsibility. Although we do not know if the Qianling government succeeded in eliminating the gang, an investigative report reminds us not to overestimate the state's effectiveness. The investigation focused on the failure of a military action against a group of insurgents. The official in question seemed to ascribe the Qin's defeat to the disparate defense forces and unorganized defensive strategy in "posts and forts of outlying communes" (離鄉亭障).[121] Conceivably, the Qianling government did not pay much attention to the defense of these regions.

This proposition also conforms to other examples. We are told that Erchun commune at that time only controlled eight conscripts,[122] despite being the second most populous commune in Qianling.[123] The garrison size of other communes and fortifications was likely even smaller. Given the modest number of soldiers in outlying communes, the main body of troops probably were mustered within the jurisdiction of Capital commune, where the county seat and the County Commander dwelled.[124]

While Zhuang's report was drafted one year after the establishment of the Qin administration in Qianling and does not necessarily indicate a normal situation, another fragmentary report states that "All . . . [new black-?]headed ones are barbarians who often come and steal the fields and salt owned by black-headed ones and convict laborers, and we do not have officials and conscripts . . ." (☒〔新黔〕首皆蠻夷，時來盜黔首、徒隸田、鹽，毋吏卒☒).[125] Despite being undated, the fragment suggests that this particular shortage of conscripts was not an isolated case. Due to the small number of troops in Qianling county, it is possible that they could not have effectively covered the whole region and thus had to seek help from the commandery office. This could also explain why Qianling decided to deploy its major military force in the Capital commune to protect the local administrative center.

The shortage of conscripts seemed to force the Qianling government to take several expedient measures. An incomplete multi-piece manuscript records a lawsuit case file concerning a minor *shangzao* 上造 (the second rank) from Yang 陽 village in Capital commune called Shuo (or Yue) 說, who was appointed by the County Commander as a Thief Catcher.[126] What is relevant here is that Shuo was appointed to this position despite his young age and nonconscript identity. Evidence from Liye indicates that the post of Thief Catcher was usually held by long-term conscripts.[127] That the County Commander assigned a nonconscript minor such as Shuo to this post suggests an abnormal or even unlawful situation. A "Statute on Government Service" (Yao lü 徭律) stipulates that counties should not employ people who have reached the age of exemption for statutory labor (*mianlao* 免老) or stalwart youths (*aotong* 敖童) in government service.[128] Similarly, a county should not levy people who reach the age of exemption for statutory labor or minors who are not yet enrolled for government service.[129] These regulations indicate that Shuo's appointment was extraordinary. I suspect that this was caused by the shortage of long-term conscripts, which forced the Commander to appoint a minor to fill the vacancy.

EFFORTS TO INCREASE THE NUMBER OF CONSCRIPTS IN THE NEW TERRITORIES

The measures that the Qin implemented to tackle the conscript shortage mirror those it employed for handling convict laborers. First, to increase the number of available conscripts, the Qin rulers extended the service terms for conscripts whose conscriptions were part of the punishment for their crimes. In the preimperial Qin legal texts, the longest term of service for this type of conscript was usually two years.[130] Nevertheless, a lawsuit case from the Yuelu manuscripts reveals a new regulation for their terms of service. In a lawsuit that occurred in 221 BCE, the minister suggested punishing some of the deserting soldiers by sending them to garrison duty on the frontier for four to eight years.[131] It is worth noting that the recommended terms of service for these soldiers were longer than those seen in the Shuihudi manuscripts. One can imagine that after the implementation of this new regulation, the number of soldiers serving on the frontier would have increased.[132]

Indeed, in the *Statutes and Ordinances of the Second Year*, there are a plethora of other conditions under which the punishment of serving garrison duty on the frontier was deployed. It was stipulated that if commanding officials were unable to arrest robbers who used short-range weapons to kill or injure them or their men,[133] if functionaries unintentionally let criminals carry gold out through a pass or the frontier or if they failed to search them,[134] if two persons played a *bo* 博 game but one stole the other's cash or one acted as the broker or host of the game,[135] or if someone who was neither an official nor personally serving the Emperor at court recommended and endorsed a corrupt or incompetent person as an official,[136] in every case, they were sentenced to two years of garrison duty on the frontier, in combination with other punishments.

Additionally, a "Statute on the Composition of Judgments" (Ju lü 具律) even says that there were punishments warranting four years of garrison duty on the frontier, although none of the statutes in *Statutes and Ordinances of the Second Year* records such a punishment.[137] Given that the early Western Han regime was largely modeled on the Qin legal system, it is conceivable that most of the aforementioned prescriptions were inherited from the Qin dynasty.[138] In view of the severe conscript shortages of the empire, these regulations were most likely enacted during or after the unification war to increase the number of servicemen on the frontier.

REFORMS TO IMPROVE THE LOGISTICAL EFFICIENCY OF THE CONSCRIPTION SYSTEM

The Qin regime invented a new mobilization system, with which conscripts from the old Qin regions could be more effectively deployed to the new territories. This crucial institutional change is documented in the Qin ordinance below:

> [Chancellor] Wan petitioned to approve [the above deliberation], but to order [those who come from] the counties within the central region to be stationed in Donghai commandery; from Taiyuan [commandery] to be stationed in Sichuan commandery; from Dong, Sanchuan, or Yingchuan commandery to be stationed in Jianghu commandery;[139] from Nanyang or Henei commandery to be stationed in Jiujiang commandery; from Nan or Shangdang commandery, as well as from dependent states and marches, [and originally] matched conscription to the former border in the east to be stationed in Hengshan commandery.

> 綰請: 許，而令中縣署東晦（海）郡，泰原署四川郡，東郡、叁川、穎川署江胡郡∟，南陽、河內署九江郡，南郡、上黨、屬邦、道當戍東故徼者，署衡山郡。[140]

The ordinance provides some vital information in relation to the new dispatchment policy for "penal conscripts" (*fashu* 罰戍), who had to serve in the frontier as part of the punishment.[141] The above measure was suggested by the Chancellor (Chengxiang 丞相). It covers the dispatchment of conscripts from the northern regions and Jianghan Plain to the Huai River Basin, especially to newly established commanderies such as Sichuan, Jianghu, Jiujiang 九江, and Hengshan 衡山.[142] These commanderies were situated in the former Chu territory, where insurgencies were strong. One of the major purposes of strengthening the supply of conscripts in these regions was probably repressing potential threats from the periphery.

The former Chu region was the most dangerous area of the empire. A "Statute on Collation of Lawsuit" (Yujiao lü 獄校律) states that government personnel can be "conscripted as a solider and serve in the commanderies of the Jiangdong or Jiangnan regions for four years" (以卒戍江東、江南四歲) if they erred during penal proceedings.[143] Due to the complex landscape and the empire's tenuous control in these regions, Jiangdong and Jiangnan were hotbeds or even the powder keg of anti-Qin revolts. One of the best examples of such danger was the clan of Xiang Liang, who fled to Kuaiji commandery from Xianyang, served as the leader of his community, and awaited a chance to overthrow the Qin regime.[144] Hence, it is understandable that the Qin rulers had paid extra attention to enhancing security within Jiangnan and Jiangdong by increasing the number of troops therein.

The cited ordinance indicates that the mobilization system was characterized by long-distance transportation over at least several hundred kilometers. The longest route was between Yingchuan and Jianghu commanderies, which is over 1,000 kilometers as the crow flies, whereas the straight-line distance between Taiyuan and Sichuan commanderies is approximately 624 kilometers. In addition to the transportation routes listed in the above ordinance, profiles of conscripts stationed in Qianling county reveal that both Shu and Yingchuan commanderies were prevalent sources of conscripts delivered to Dongting commandery. The biography of Chen Sheng in the standard histories also mentions that he was escorting exile conscripts (zheshu 謫戍) en route from Daze 大澤 commune in Qi 蘄 county to Yuyang 漁陽 commandery. Suffice to say that the mobilization system was updated concomitantly with the expansion of the Qin Empire.[145] One can imagine that after the acquisition of the Yue and Ordos regions, more routes would have been created to transfer conscripts to the periphery.

Overextended Empire and the Dissipation of Military Power

Although Qin promulgated multiple measures to alleviate the paucity of conscripts, this problem lingered at the end of the Qin Empire. The continued shortage of conscripts was partly because the Qin regime often used conscripts to fill the gaps left by other types of human resource shortages. Ostensibly, the Qin's policies increased the number of conscripts serving in the empire. However, the newly recruited conscripts did not necessarily perform their assigned duties. This paradox was caused by the characteristics of conscripts as a type of human resource. In Qin government organizations, conscripts were not mere soldiers who assumed only military tasks. Rather, they were substitutes for other human resources. Conscripts in-shift often took up the tasks of convict laborers, such as cooks or servants. One fragmentary official letter describes that many conscripts in Qianling served as officials' servants.[146] Specifically, a Scribe Director called Tang 唐 was assigned to accompany Judicial Scribe De 德 on an official trip, during which a convict laborer was supposed to serve as their cook or servant.[147] The commandery eventually sent Shun 順, a conscript in-shift who held the *shiwu* status, to Tang because they currently had "no laborers in the office" (守府毋徒).[148]

In addition, a Register of Convict Labor reveals that long-term conscripts stationed at the Office of Crossbow Shooting (Fanu 發弩) needed to forward documents or worked at the Office of Convict Labor like convict laborers.[149] One fragmentary report also states that long-term conscripts had cultivated at least 800 *mu* 畝 (ca. 36.88 ha) of fields in Qianling county as of 214 BCE.[150] These bits of information suggest that tasks to which conscripts were assigned overlapped significantly with those assigned to convict labor.

The placement of penal conscripts and "expelled conscripts" (*feishu* 廢戍)—who were often former officials who had engaged in serious misconduct and supposedly could never work for the government again[151]—contrasts quite significantly with long-term conscripts and conscripts in-shift. Often such conscripts were former officials. With such rare virtues as writing skills and administrative experience, they could be reappointed as officials in the new territories. Two transaction tallies record the identity of Han 悍 as a penal conscript and a Corporal (Tun Zhang 屯長), respectively.[152] Since the two tallies were produced within a month of each other, it is unclear whether Han was appointed to Corporal later or if he held the position as a penal conscript. Either way, this suggests that penal conscripts could have become officers.

A similar story also happened with Qu 詘, who worked as an Assistant in the Qianling government in 213 BCE:

(A) In the thirty-fifth year, in the third month, which began on a day *gengyin*, on the *dingyou* (ninth) day, Zi, the

Overseer of Erchun commune, presumes to report: Assistant Qu self-reported that "I held the *shiwu* status and lived in Yigu village of Niyang [county]. Formerly I was an expelled conscript stationed in Ruyin [county], and now . . . [it has been] four years." Here I call upon you to inform the Prefect of Niyang that Qu . . . I fear that the previous document did not [arrive] . . .

(B) On the evening of the *renxu* (fourth) day of the fourth month, conscript Ji arrived [with this document]. Tam opened this document. (A) Qu handled it.

(A) 卅五年三月庚寅朔丁酉，貳春鄉茲敢言之: 佐詘自言: 士五，居泥陽

益固里，故廢戍，署女陰。‧今□□☑

四歲。謁告泥陽令，【詘】□☑

前書畏其不☑

(B) 四月壬戌日入，戍卒寄以來。瞫發。 (A) 詘手。¹⁵³

Since this letter was handled by Qu himself, it could in some measure be classified as a personal statement. According to it, Qu was an "expelled conscript" and originally served in Ruyin county. Despite the fragmentary status of the tablet, it seems that after completing his four-year term, Qu was appointed as an Assistant and was probably sent to Qianling in 213 BCE, together with another Assistant named Ruyi 如意, who also came from Qu's village.¹⁵⁴ The reason that the Overseer of Erchun requested that his superior delivered a message to Niyang county is unclear. Given that Niyang was Qu's domicile, it might have something to do with his appointment. Qu's case proves that expelled conscripts could have held official positions, which radically contradicts the notion of "expelled."

More importantly, some of the aforementioned practices were even strictly prohibited by law. Employing someone who held the *shiwu* status as an officer-cook violated the prescription of a "Statute on Government Service" from the Yuelu corpus, which states indisputably that administrators should not "order holders of the *shiwu* status to be officer-cook or to feed horses" (毋令士五為吏養、養馬).[155] However, as shown above, such an arrangement was by no means exceptional at Qianling county. The insufficient number of convict laborers likely accounts for this violation of the law.

Evidently, conscripts were deemed the "master key" in fulfilling the demands of other government organizations during times of labor shortages. At one point in Qianling county, "there were twenty-three conscripts who were fulfilling the tasks of convict laborer" (戍卒給徒隸事者廿三人).[156] If we compare this figure with the total number of conscripts (about 626) in the region, the percentage of conscripts substituting for convict laborers may not seem consequential. That said, this number excluded conscripts who undertook positions such as administrators. Therefore, the overall percentage of conscripts providing nonmilitary services was likely higher. In other words, although the Qin's administrative reforms were intended to mitigate the labor shortage of local governments, they probably widened the gap in the state's military power.

Equally importantly, the long-term shortage of conscripts likely resulted from the empire's incessant military actions and demand for conscripts. The relationship between the Qin's territorial expansion and overstretched military power has been well discussed. The Yue campaign alone was said to input over 500,000 soldiers; over 100,000 men were conscripted in the northern campaign, stationed at the new frontier, and built the Great Wall. Although these numbers might be inflated, the empire likely mobilized large numbers of troops. During the second expansion, most of the forces should have been sent to the Lingnan 嶺 南 region. In view of the shifted strategic focus, administrative units such as Qianling were almost destined to be short of military power. As a comparison, the size of the regular force stationed at the county was even smaller than that of the group of exile conscripts whom Chen Sheng and Wu Guang escorted to Yuyang commandery on the northeastern frontier. This seems to suggest a lopsided distribution of military power between the frontier and other parts of the new territories.

A more profound detrimental effect of the discussed institutional reforms and the new deployment policy was the dissipation of the military power wielded by the state. While the military power of the Qin Empire was in theory under the total command of the state apparatus, the regime's reforms might nevertheless have provided chances for local strongmen to usurp the empire's military power. The deployment of both conscripts and convict laborers (who could be equipped as soldiers) entailed the long-distance movement of armed forces. The potential danger of this action is illustrated in the story of Chen Sheng and Wu Guang. While the transmitted account might be overdramatic, evidence from Liye indicates that the abscondence of conscripts was common. A letter from the Linju 臨沮 County Commander reveals that a long-term conscript of Qianling called Zhao went missing after returning to Linju during his leave. Although the letter does not mention this explicitly, it implies that Zhao had fled.[157] A formal statement submitted by a Constable reveals that a conscript called Liaoke 繚可 absconded and the Constable was "afraid that he would become a robber" (恐為盜賊). Since Liaoke was fully armed, the fear was well founded.[158]

The rise of anti-Qin insurgency also reflects the danger of the long-distance movement of convict laborers. The anecdote of Liu Ji is worth a second look. Standard histories state that after realizing that he would have lost all his convict laborers by the time they arrived on Mount Li, Liu, instead of restricting his men and completing the escort mission, decided to free all remaining convicts and absconded himself.[159] Moved by Liu Ji's generosity, a dozen convicts were willing to join him. Liu's gang hid in the mountains and marshes and later turned into one of the strongest insurgencies challenging Qin rule. Aside from Liu, the *Shiji* also records that Ying Bu 英布, a valiant warrior and general, was once sentenced to the punishment of being tattooed and dispatched to Mount Li as a convict laborer. On his way to Mount Li, he became acquainted with the leaders of convict laborers, persuaded them to abscond with him, and founded a gang of robbers with them.[160]

These lively accounts reveal the dissipation and decentralization of military power of the empire. Although the Qin authorities strictly prohibited unauthorized travel—especially that of new subjects—to prevent social instability,[161] the long-distance transportation of large gangs of desperados allowed a significant room for conspirators to maneuver. The unstable sociopolitical landscape of the new territories drained away the empire's military forces, who often ended up joining anti-Qin insurgencies. The military power that the state sought to monopolize now flowed to the hands of militia led by ambitious local strongmen. The emergence of local militia not only eroded the military prowess of the Qin's local governments in the new territories, which were often plagued by insufficient numbers of conscripts, but also proved to be a huge threat to state security during the anti-Qin movement. The dissipation of military power and the uneven distribution of troops may account for the military failures at the end of the Qin Empire. In this respect, a side effect of Qin's military reforms and new policies was to endanger the security of the empire.

The situation was further exacerbated because of Qin's disarmament policy. The defortification of mega-cities in Luoyang Basin, with their well-constructed city walls, hampered the progress of the Qin conquest. While the defortification hindered the potential resistance from the new territories, it also diminished the defensive capacity of the empire in times of war. The destruction of infrastructure evidently explains why important cities in the eastern regions such as Suiyang 睢陽, Waihuang 外黃, and Handan 邯鄲 were easily seized during the anti-Qin uprisings and the subsequent intermediate period. In view of the drawbacks of overdefortification, shortly after the founding of the Western Han dynasty, Emperor Gaozu decreed that counties and settlements within the empire should build their own walls.[162] Such an order seems to attest to the authenticity of the earlier Qin policy, which inadvertently gave rise to a gap in the military power of the state.

Policy Failure and Persisting Personnel Shortages

Extant Qin legal regulations and administrative records reveal that the rapid expansion of the empire engendered severe shortages of officials, convict laborers, and conscripts. Cautious about these threats, the Qin rulers orchestrated manifold institutional reforms and new measures to meet these challenges. Their efforts can be summarized as follows.

First, the Qin were eager to increase the number of functionaries in the new territories. Former officials were appointed the "officials in the new territories," followers of aristocrats from eliminated polities were delivered to peripheral regions, and the service periods of conscripts were extended. On top of these measures, local governments also attempted to incorporate indigenous people into the administrative system to enlarge the reservoir of eligible personnel such as writing specialists.

Second, the Qin regime attempted to enhance the logistical efficiency of deploying human resources. Administrative units situated in the new territories became the primary destinations of convict laborers and conscripts. Procedures revolving around the distribution of convict laborers were simplified, and new organizations were set up, thereby improving the logistics of convict laborers. Along the same line, a new system of mobilization pertinent to the allocation of conscripts was introduced. In theory, these reforms should have facilitated a more effective distribution of conscripts from the old territories to the peripheral regions.

Nevertheless, most of the abovementioned policies had little impact on improving labor shortages. The case of Qianling county shows that the paucity of human resources persisted until the end of the Qin Empire. The Qin's policy failure could be ascribed to the perpetual demand caused by infrastructure construction and territorial expansion, which far outpaced any attempts to increase the supply of personnel, and to the careless policy design of the regime and the poor execution by local officials.

Regardless of the reasons behind Qin's policy failure, the loopholes caused by the persisting personnel shortages evidently wrecked the normal processes of administrative procedures (political power), hindered the production activities and resource extraction (economic power), and undermined the security (military power) of the empire. While Qianling was only a small and remote county surrounded by mountains, it was an excellent indicator of the level of Qin political power in the peripheral regions. The example of Qianling suggests that the empire's power was far from steadfast in reaching its periphery, and the empire's administrative units in its new territories were misfunctioning long before the outbreak of the anti-Qin movement in 209 BCE. Again, this reminds us not to overestimate the effectiveness of Qin governance in the new territories.

Although administrative misfunction is believed to be among the elements that can trigger organizational collapses,[163] it is facile to assume that labor shortages alone led to the fall of the whole empire, because the collapse of complex societies and organizations can hardly be ascribed to a single factor. In the next chapter, I will further gauge the limits of the Qin state power by examining the efficiency of the empire's administration in conveying its power along regional networks.

Chapter 4

Inefficient Logistics of State Power
and Communication Gaps
in the New Territories

> When Xiao He entered the Qin [capital], he collected the adminis-
> trative documents, and it is by their power that the Han managed
> to subjugate the nine provinces (Sinitic proper). With administrative
> documents, [the founders of the Western Han Empire] harnessed all-
> under-heaven, and comparing the wealth of that with the property
> of family members, which one is richer?
>
> 蕭何入秦，收拾文書，漢所以能制九州者，文書之力也。以文書御天下，
> 天下之富，孰與家人之財？
>
> —Wang Chong 王充, *Lun Heng* 論衡, 13[1]

For the Eastern Han (25–220 CE) philosopher Wang Chong, administrative documents were *the* source of state power, through which the
Western Han founders managed to conquer and administer the realm.
Wang's words should not be taken at face value. He refers to "administrative documents" not as artifacts but as the carrier and transmitter of
information produced by administrative units. In this fashion, one may
say that the real source of state power that Wang Chong describes is
the written information transmitted through administrative documents.
Wang's proposition not only demonstrates the prominent role of written
communication in the Qin-Han government but, more profoundly, reveals
the awareness of a contemporary about this fact.

Nevertheless, Wang Chong's understanding is incomplete. While communication is indeed a fundamental part of the infrastructure of political, ideological, economic, and military power sources,[2] what Wang does not realize is that communication entails more than the production and transmission of information. A state will have no power if it fails to effectively convey commands, deliver personnel, and dispatch resources and troops. Rather than written communication per se, it is the system that facilitates the communication between regional networks that warrants a close look. In the ancient world, efficient transmission of communication was often achieved by virtue of well-organized infrastructure (both tangible and intangible) and the proper maintenance of such infrastructure, both of which were highly dependent upon the capacity of the state. From this perspective, the efficiency of communication is a useful measuring rod for examining state power.

Since it is impossible to address all these networks of state power at once, I have decided to focus on administrative communication because of the availability of more concrete and reliable evidence than other perspectives. Despite this limitation, administrative communication involves more than just political power. The compliance of personnel handling the production and transfer of administrative documents is enforced by the authoritative political power of the state, as well as the ideological power that encouraged the personnel to perform according to official standards. The logistics of delivering administrative documents rest upon the physical infrastructure of the state, which is dependent on political and economic power. Also, the military presence of the state in places along major postal routes is a key element in ensuring a smooth delivery process; this, needless to say, relates to the military power of the state. Hence, administrative communication serves as a lens through which one can observe the overall state power of the Qin Empire.

Like earlier chapters, Qianling county is again featured as a major case study. That said, my concern is by no means confined to the internal and external logistical efficiencies of Qianling's administrative communication,[3] but extends more broadly to other administrative units of Dongting commandery and beyond. In contrast to the perception that the Qin government ensured efficient communication between the emperor and his subjects,[4] this chapter reveals that the administrative communication between Qianling county and other administrative units of Dongting commandery was by no means logistically efficient. Such a phenomenon differs strikingly from the internal logistical efficiency within the organizations of Qianling. The low external administrative efficiency seemed to suggest that the Qin Empire was stricken by inefficient logistics because of the precarious social landscape and labor shortages. These factors probably ignited serious administrative communication gaps during the large-scale mobilization of troops or revolts.

Definition, Infrastructure, and Methodology of Efficiency Analysis

Several questions must be answered before starting our analysis. What is "efficiency"? In what ways can efficiency be observed and measured? How can we determine the efficiency of government organizations? What kinds of infrastructure were needed to facilitate administrative communication? This section clarifies these basic issues, so that a more grounded discussion can then be built.

Defining "Efficiency"

Modern public administration theories predominantly understand the term *efficiency* to mean "technical efficiency"; that is, "a comparison between observed and optimal values of its output and input."[5] If organization A can attain a better outcome (more products, shorter time, etc.) than organization B by employing identical resources, and provided that all other factors are equal, one may say that organization A has better efficiency than organization B.[6] This understanding of the term, however, was not popularized until the early twentieth century,[7] and the classical meaning of *efficiency* is not limited to technical efficiency but also includes any agents aiming to achieve the final objective.[8] Along this line, the labor shortages discussed in the last chapter can also be regarded as a manifestation of administrative inefficiency.

In this chapter, I further observe the efficiency of Qin government organizations from the perspective of logistical efficiency of administrative communication.[9] There are two practical reasons for this choice: (1) it is one of the rare "yardsticks" that carry measurable, comparable, and legible qualities, which are crucial in generating relatively objective outcomes; and (2) sources in relation to the logistical efficiency of communication are relatively sufficient. Adopting such a measuring rod also implies that the analysis of efficiency in this chapter is close to the analysis of technical efficiency. While it is hard to know the full potential of an organization or individual, one can observe the best practices and their changes across time. By comparing the "efficient" performances of the collected samples, one can see if their performances surpass or fall short of efficient performance, thereby demonstrating the relative efficiency of the samples.[10] Hence, although technical efficiency does not represent the entirety of the concept of efficiency, it nonetheless serves as a viable instrument for our study.

INFRASTRUCTURES OF COMMUNICATION LOGISTICS

The foundation of communication is the assurance of the smooth movement of people, goods, or information from one place to another. This goal can only be achieved through a set of supporting measures from the state. On the one hand, the state must guarantee the availability of physical infrastructure such as roads, riverways, and facilities along the transportation routes, thus establishing a communication network. On the other hand, "software" such as official standards must be formulated to regulate the operation and maintenance of the network.

Physical Infrastructure

The arteries for conveying state power are the roads and waterways connecting regional political and economic nodes with smaller administrative units. For example, the development of the Roman road system and the maintenance thereof are believed to be instrumental in connecting the Roman government with local communities across the empire, thereby spreading Roman culture and enhancing its infrastructural power.[11] For the Qin Empire, two of its major construction projects were the building of the Imperial Highways (Chidao 馳道) and of the Direct Road (Zhidao 直道). The former were to connect the existing thoroughfares of the states eliminated by the Qin and to form an empire-wide transportation network, whereas the latter was a special highway connecting the capital with the northern frontier.[12]

While horses and carts were the major modes of transportation in northern regions, in the southern areas of the empire, there was likely a very different story. Given its marshy, watery, and mountainous landscape, riverine transport, such as boats and ships, likely held a prominent status there because of its lower average cost and larger shipping capacity.[13] A Qin text entitled the *Document of Roads and Distances* (*Daoli shu* 道里

書) in the possession of Peking University documents the distances of thoroughfares within Nan commandery in present-day Hubei.[14] The text begins with a meticulous enumeration of the transit speeds of ships, which varied due to seasonal changes, the load of the ship, the use of large or small rivers, and whether the ship was sailing upstream or downstream.[15] These detailed regulations prove the prevalence of riverine transport in the empire's south.

Another important part of the hardware of the transportation network was transportation facilities. To ensure a safe voyage, facilities such as piers would be created, obstacles in the water (e.g., dangerous reefs) would be removed, and, ideally, river courses would be widened. For overland transport, strings of official postal and courier stations and checkpoints were set up to both facilitate and restrict the transmission of information and mobility of the people along major roads. Despite their heterogeneous functions, these facilities mostly targeted functionaries who undertook missions such as transferring urgent administrative documents.

Among them, the most important facility was the postal station (*you* 郵). To maximize the delivery speed of express mail, postal stations were set up according to the distances stipulated in official standards. Personnel serving in these stations were all trained Postmen who supposedly performed their relay jobs on foot and had to deliver their burdens under strict time limits. In return for their service, they were exempt from annual statutory labor.[16] In regions that were too remote and had no established postal stations, conscripts and Thief Catchers at the "police stations of the gates" (*menting* 門亭), as well as special "fleet-footed runners" (*lizu* 利足), were alternatives for postal stations and Postmen.[17]

While express mail could be sent through official postal stations, ordinary mail was delivered by administrative units along postal routes.[18] Evidence from Liye indicates that documents of the central government, prior to their arrival at the seat of Dongting commandery, were first delivered to Nanyang commandery in Nanyang Basin and then to Nan commandery to the south. Upon receiving the information from the central government, the headquarters of the Commandery Governor would disseminate it to subordinate counties according to the intraregional postal network.

Administrative documents from Qianling record that when the seat of Dongting commandery was at Linyuan, in the downward communication between Dongting and its subordinate counties, the Governor sometimes disseminated messages through Suo 索, Menqian 門淺, Linyang 零陽, and Shangyan 上衍 counties. Scholars observe that each of these four counties was the starting point of a postal route traveling in different directions.

After the arrival of the Dongting document, these four counties had to forward it to the next stop on their respective route.[19] Qianling county was at the end of the Linyang route, which successively passed through Linyang, Chong 充, and Youyang 酉陽 counties before finally reaching Qianling.[20] Understanding the sequence of transmission is helpful in determining the modes of transportation that were being used, as well as how an intraregional postal network was created to facilitate information exchange.

Official Standards Prescribing the Logistical Efficiency of Administrative Documents

In addition to physical infrastructure, the Qin authorities also designed various performance standards to regulate the logistical efficiency of administrative documents. Extant Qin and Han legal texts reveal that to ensure the timely delivery of documents and to keep the dispatched documents on track, the Qin and early Western Han regimes promulgated thorough regulations with respect to (1) the retention of transferring and (2) the delivery speed for administrative documents. These stipulations represented

Map 4.1. "Linyang route," which passed through Linyang, Chong, Youyang, and Qianling counties. Map based on "Map 1" of Guo, "Wenshu xingzheng yu Qindai Dongting jun de xian jiwangluo," 166. Author's own material.

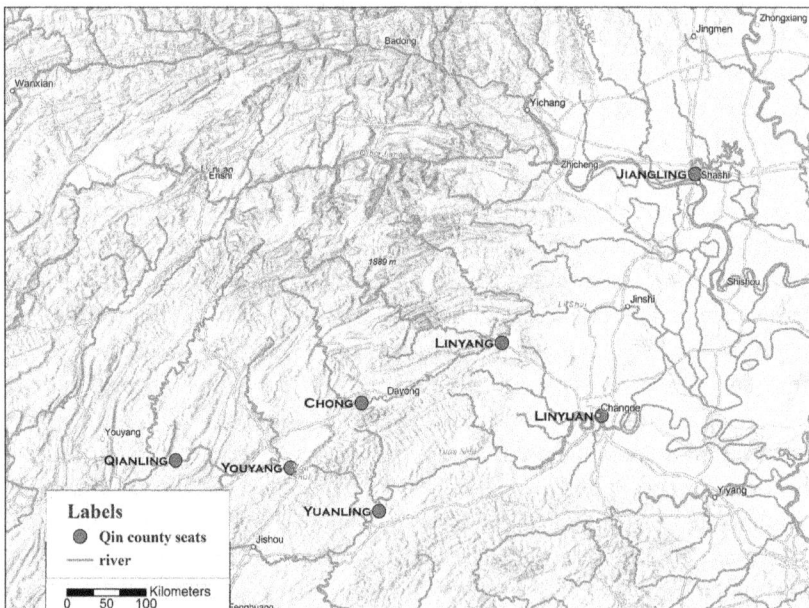

the grand design of the Qin rulers to their empire. In this regard, the numbers prescribed in these regulations could be deemed as the optimal, efficient performance standards that the Qin rulers envisioned for administrative communication and are thus valuable for our efficiency comparison.

To begin with, Qin ordinances reveal that the punishments for delaying an in-transit official document depend on three factors: the identity of the dispatcher, the duration of delay, and the level of urgency of the delayed mail.

Table 4.1 reveals that punishments inflicted on Postmen for delaying the delivery of administrative documents were much more severe than

Table 4.1. Punishment for retaining the delivery of official documents

Retention period (days)	Mails forwarded by Postmen[1]	Ordinary mail[2]
0.5	Fine one shield	Fine two sets of armor (urgent mail); No punishments (nonurgent mail)
1–1.5	Fine one set of armor	Fine two sets of armor (urgent mail); No punishments (nonurgent mail)
2–2.5	Fine two sets of armor	Fine two sets of armor (urgent mail); No punishments (nonurgent mail)
3	Redemption fee for shaving beard (shu nai 贖耐)	Fine two sets of armor (urgent mail); Fine one shield (nonurgent mail)
3.5	Shave the beard (nai 耐)	Fine two sets of armor (urgent mail); Fine one shield (nonurgent mail)
4 or above	Shave the beard (nai 耐)	Fine two sets of armor (urgent mail); Fine one set of armor (nonurgent mail)

Author's own material.

1. The punishments and figures in this column derive from the regulations listed in the *Yuelu*, vol. 5, 112, slip 133.

2. The punishments and figures of this column derive from the regulations listed in the *Yuelu*, vol. 4, 131–32, slips 192–93.

those on ordinary personnel. Even if a Postman delayed a document for only an extra half a day, he was still fined one shield. On the one hand, this arrangement is probably because Postmen were special express couriers who enjoyed exemption from statutory labor service, and as a result, their services had to be evaluated according to a much higher standards than those of ordinary personnel. On the other hand, given that only essential and urgent mail was qualified to be delivered by Postmen, the severe punishments may also be attributed to the nature of the mail. The requirement was so uncompromising that Postmen would fake arrival records to evade punishment.[21]

For ordinary mail, further demarcations could be made between urgent and nonurgent mail. Urgent mail had to be delivered immediately; otherwise, the dispatcher would be published. While nonurgent mail was supposed to be transferred within one day, couriers would not be punished until the third day of retention.[22] In other words, they were granted a 2.5-day grace period if we count the extra time to the nearest half day.

The regulations related to the retention of official documents were much more nuanced than the standards discussed above, which focus on official mail whose transmission process had already begun. The newest material reveals that special regulations were formulated regarding delayed forwarding of official documents that were ready but were stuck at their respective offices. An unspecified Qin statute from the Yuelu collection reveals that the punishments for such misbehavior diverge from those listed in table 4.1. An official would be fined one set of armor for retaining a drafted official mail for at least five full days.[23] Again, if we count the retention time to the nearest half day, the grace period under this circumstance was 4.5 days. Such a threshold is clearly higher than that determining the punishment for not forwarding nonurgent ordinary mail on time.

Nevertheless, this does not imply that the punishments for keeping drafted documents from dispatch were necessarily lighter. Under these regulations, the amount of an offender's fine increased concomitantly with the retention period. Thus, an offender's liability was in theory unlimited. Such divergences in sentencing principles bespeak different foci between the two statutes. The regulations in table 4.1 compelled a speedy transmission of official mail, whereas the above statute aimed to prevent the stacking of drafted but unsent documents.

The abovementioned Qin statute was followed by a supplementary ordinance dated to 220 BCE, which indicates that the Qin regime's relatively low expectations changed during the imperial period.[24] In the Qin legal system, if a functionary accidentally committed multiple offenses of a similar nature, his or her sentences could be combined, thereby equating to a much lighter punishment.[25] However, under the new regulation, each delay was to be considered a separate offense, and the punishment would be exacted aggregately. Without the principle of combined punishments, if an official did not send out three documents eleven days after drafting them, he would be fined six sets of armor. This amount (which equates to 8,064 cash[26]) could have easily caused the family of a low-level official or soldier to go broke.[27] This implies that personnel were not allowed to accumulate multiple official documents and send them all at once, thus reducing the possibility of retention.

The second category of standards focuses on the delivery speed of administrative documents. A "Statute on the Forwarding of Documents" (Xingshu lü 行書律) indicates that Postmen were expected to travel 200 li (83.16 km) in one full day. Since the Qin and Han dynasties adopted a sixteen-hour clock, Postmen had to walk 12.5 li (5.2 km) per hour (3.47 km/modern hour). Given that documents were transmitted in relay and that in theory there would be a postal station every ten li (4.16 km), in modern time conventions and measurements, if every Postman could finish his route (4.16 km) in about 72 minutes, the required speed would be met. If a Postman was behind this standard, he would be caned or fined according to the retention period.[28]

The practicality of the required speed listed above is confirmed by administrative records unearthed from the northwestern frontier of the Western Han Empire. One "Evaluation of Documents Delivered by Postal Stations" (youshu ke 郵書課) found in the northwestern frontier of the Western Han Empire record that a soldier managed to finish 39.5 km under an average speed of 3.17 km per hour.[29] Although this figure is slightly lower than the standard speed listed in the cited "Statute on the Forwarding of Documents," it suggests that the delivery speeds enumerated in the official standards were not impossible. Instead, they were the manifestation of optimal performance, allowing us to determine the level of logistical efficiency of communication achieved by an organization.

It is worth noting that the standards for travel speeds were somewhat flexible. One of the decisive factors was the topography of the region. In areas endowed with a more suitable natural environment and better economic conditions, postal stations were to be set up every ten li (4.16 km) on average. By contrast, from the south of Yangzi River in Nan commandery to the southern boundary of Suo county, postal stations could be twice as far apart as in other areas.[30] For Beidi 北地, Shang 上, and Longxi 隴西 commanderies along the northern frontier, the designated distance between the two postal stations was as far as 30 *li* (12.47 km).[31] Although these prescriptions do not state so explicitly, the required speed assigned to Postmen serving in peripheral regions might have decreased in proportion to the distance between postal stations.[32] That is, for the region between the south of Yangzi River in Nan commandery and the southern boundary of Suo county, the required transfer speed of documents was 100 *li* (41.58 km) per day, while in remote areas such as Beidi, Shang, and Longxi, it was 66.67 *li* (27.72 km) per day.

METHODOLOGY

This section discusses the methodology behind this chapter's efficiency analysis. In the Liye manuscripts, administrative documents are often inscribed with their drafting, dispatchment, or arrival dates. Although these three elements seldom simultaneously appear in one single document, their existence yields valuable information about the communication between senior officials and their subordinate offices, from which ample data regarding the duration of drafting, processing, and delivering an official document can be drawn.

Based on the nature of the organizations involved in communication, we can further dichotomize the logistical efficiency of communication as internal and external. "Internal logistical efficiency" refers to the performance of communication among internal organizations under the umbrella of the same administrative unit, including senior officials, offices (communes included), and bureaus, whereas "external logistical efficiency" is characterized by intraregional communication between the commandery headquarter and its subordinate counties or among subordinate counties, as well as interregional communication either between the central and local governments, or among commanderies or, from time to time, among counties of different commanderies.

The calculation of statistics is done according to the following principles:

1. All data in this chapter are rounded to the nearest two decimal places.

2. To avoid statistical fluctuations, if a dataset constitutes more than three samples, the calculation of figures such as the mean or standard deviation will exclude the highest and lowest values.[33]

3. For documents that were delivered to their recipients on the same day, their dispatchment duration is treated as zero day.

As noted earlier, the efficiency of an organization is evaluated through a comparison with optimal performance, or at least a couple of "efficient" cases. There are two feasible sources from which ideal or "efficient" administrative communication can be determined: (1) a comparison of official norms and actual performance of communication and (2) a comparison among different local administrative units.

Comparison between Official Norms and Actual Communication Performances

The speed of transmission differs between urgent mail carried by a relay of Postmen and ordinary mail. Evidence from Liye indicates that through the postal relay system, letters from Youyang county could arrive at Qiling commune in three days.[34] Since documents from Qiling required an average of 4.12 days to be processed and sent to the seat of Qianling county (figure 4.3), one can infer that Youyang documents sent via postal service took approximately seven days to arrive at the seat of Qianling. On the other hand, multiple sources reveal that the ordinary administrative communication between Qianling and Youyang ranged from fourteen to twenty-two days (table 6 in appendix 2), which is considerably longer than for those dispatched through the postal station.[35] Because of this difference, it is necessary to demarcate between mail sent through the postal station and by ordinary personnel.

On the other hand, the distinction between overland and riverine transportation was less important. While Qin and early Western Han official norms highlight the possible influence of topography on the delivery speeds of mail, the records never stipulate *how* mail should be transferred. This indicates that the Qin regime was wise enough to grant some liberty to local functionaries and let them accomplish their tasks in their own novel solutions. Insofar as one could send mail to its destination at the targeted speed and within the legally permissible range, it did not matter if it was done by riding a horse and/or sailing a boat or other possible means. From this perspective, the issue of overland or riverine transport is not particularly important in studying the logistical efficiency of communication.

Naturally, the crux of the comparison lies in the average speed of communication. Since direct evidence is extremely rare, these data are often reconstructed based on two important factors: (1) the distance between Qianling county and other administrative units documented in postal records, and (2) the length of the delivery time for administrative documents.

With regard to the first factor, extant Qin sources comprise route distance records compiled by government personnel. Accordingly, the distance between Linyuan 臨沅 county, presumably the seat of Dongting commandery from 221 to 214 BCE, and Qianling county is 910 *li* (378.38 km).[36] These records provide crucial information for the reconstruction of the average delivery speed of administrative communication between the Dongting and Qianling seats. Apart from the route distance records, archaeological evidence is another important reference. Benefiting from recent archaeological discoveries, archaeologists have already identified the locations of some of the ancient settlements listed in postal records. These new pieces of information are also instrumental in estimating the distance between Qianling and other administrative units.

For the delivery times for administrative documents, the calculation is the same as that for the internal organizations; that is, the period between the latest drafting date and the document's arrival date. If there is a delay in communication, only the date on the last letter is considered. By dividing the estimated distance between two parties at both ends of the communication by the duration of transmission, we can reconstruct the average delivery speed.

Comparison among Local Administrative Units

While official norms are useful references for comparison, it is unidimensional if we treat them as the only criterion for determining the logistical efficiency of communication in the Qin Empire. Consider the aforementioned norms regarding delivery speed. Since the pace of delivery was often affected by the topography of different regions, it is arbitrary to assume that the Metropolitan Area experienced more efficient communication than a commandery in the periphery *simply* because the former could deliver mail at a faster speed because in the mentality of the Qin rulers, the slower speed of the latter was an expected and accepted fact. To compensate for this drawback, in addition to comparing data on Qianling's administrative communication with that on official norms, it seems necessary to analyze such data across local administrative units.

As far as communication among internal organizations of county-level administrative units goes, although other counties did not produce as many administrative records as Qianling, the Liye manuscripts comprise manifold documents sent from administrative units outside Qianling, from which one can derive information pertinent to retention period and delivery speed. For example, the ration certificate below records the following:

> In the first year [of the Second Emperor of Qin] (209 BCE), in a seventh month that began with a day *gengzi*, on the *dingwei* (eighth) day, Tang, the Overseer of Granary, presumes to report: Judicial Assistants Bian and Ping, Sergeant Major He are [bringing] a completed lawsuit dossier to a county office. Their food will last until the fifteenth day (*jiayin*). Here I call upon the counties and communes subsequently on their way to continue their food rations. When there is either a delay because of rain, or [the conveyance station is full and they] cannot lodge an accommodation, supply their food. [This document is a] round-trip pass. The fields of Linyang can provide their food [within the jurisdiction of Linyang]. Should this document be copied, (copy it). The expected period of this trip is 30 days. Here I presume to report.
>
> On the *wushen* (ninth) day of the seventh month, Gong, the Prefect of Linyang, transfers [this document] to the counties and communes on the way [of Bian, Ping, and He]. Yi [handles it].

元年七月庚子朔丁未，倉守陽敢言之：獄佐辨、平，士吏賀具獄縣官，食盡甲寅。謁告過所縣、鄉，以次續食。雨留、不能投宿，齎。來復傳。零陽田能食。當騰。期卅日。敢言之。 ／ 七月戊申，零陽𬀩移過所縣、鄉。 ／ 齮手。[37]

This document includes both a request from the Overseer of Granary on the eighth day and a cover letter from the Linyang Prefect on the following day. The report of the Overseer was handled by the Prefect in one day. As a result, the interval, that is, the aggregated number of both the retention and transmission periods, can be calculated. By comparing the interval of other county-level organizations with the same statistics from the Qianling side, one can see the comparative efficiency of Qianling county.

A similar method can be applied to the communication between Qianling and external organizations, such as commanderies and other counties. In the third section of this chapter, the adjacent Nan commandery north of Dongting, which was annexed by the Qin regime more than sixty years before 221 BCE, serves as the main comparative administrative unit. This choice is primarily under the consideration that Nan commandery had similar topography to Qianling, so that we can avoid the comparison being biased by geographical differences. Additionally, comparing an administrative unit in the empire's old territories like Nan commandery can also emphasize Qianling's position as a newly conquered region.

Internal Logistical Efficiency of Administrative Communication

Most embodied administrative communications in the Liye manuscripts comprise correspondence between Qianling county's senior officials and their subordinates. The communications can be divided into two categories based on the senders' identities. The first one belongs to senior officials, predominantly the Vice-Prefect, and provides information on the retention of communications. The second category features offices and bureaus and is more concerned about the delivery speed of official documents. Given the relative proximity between these government organizations, internal communication was generally conveyed as ordinary mail.

Documents sent by the Prefect and the Vice-Prefect were not always handled instantly after their arrival and might have been stuck at their respective offices after completion. Hence, we should differentiate between (1) the retention period of administrative documents from the Prefect or the Vice-Prefect to offices outside the county seat, and (2) the processing period for administrative documents forwarded by the Prefect or the Vice-Prefect. A typical model is as follows:

(B) On the *jiaxu* (seventh) day of the eighth month, Acting Vice-Prefect Shanzhi presumes to inform the person in-charge of the Office of [the County] Commander: Act according to the statutes and ordinances; deliver [the original] and make a copy of this document.[38] Erchun [commune] is to hand down [this document] to the Chief of Conscripts and the Office of?. Ji(?)[39] handled it.

(C) On the *bingzi* (ninth) day of the eighth month, at the time of breakfast, runner Yin forwards this document.

(A) [In the twenty-eighth year,] on the *gengwu* (third) day of the eighth month, at the time when the water level [of the water clock] was down to the fifth marker, Ci from the Ping village of Dangqu march holding the *shiwu* status arrived [with this document]. Chao opened it. Dong . . .

(B) 八月甲戌，遷陵守丞膻之敢告尉官主：以律令從事，傳、別書。貳春下卒長、□[40]官 ╱□手 ╱ (C) 丙子旦食，走印行☑

(A) ☑【八】月庚午水下五刻，士五宕渠道平邑疵以來。 ╱ 朝半 洞☑[41]

The cited text demonstrates the two aforementioned differences. Arriving on the third day of the eighth month, the Acting Vice-Prefect did not handle the document until four days later; its delivery was further retained for two days. If we ignore the four-day processing period and concentrate only on the retention time, it is likely that the eventual analysis will overestimate the efficiency of Qianling in administrative communication. To present a more complete picture, I will examine these two figures as two separate datasets respectively in figures 4.1 and 4.2 below.

STATISTICAL ANALYSIS OF INTERNAL COMMUNICATION

The published Liye manuscripts comprise forty-eight samples concerning the retention of administrative documents, of which the mean was 0.6 days and the standard deviation was 1.14. Among these samples, over 60 percent (31) of them were delivered on the day they were drafted. As shown in table 1 in appendix 2, the longest delay was eighteen days, which was for a report to Dongting commandery dated to 213 BCE.[42]

Since the report concerns possible changes to the length of roads within the purview of the Qianling government, its delay may be due to the complexity of verifying the relevant data. Regardless, retaining a document for eighteen days undoubtedly broke with protocol, and the responsible officials were likely fined. Interestingly, the second longest delay was also observed in a letter to Dongting commandery.[43] Replying to the inquiry about the whereabout of an administrator called Zhou 周, the Acting Vice-Prefect waited six days before finally delivering the report.

Nevertheless, this does not imply that Qianling officials tended to delay documents bound for Dongting commandery. If we arrange the forty-eight samples according to their respective recipients and treat each of these organizations as a disparate dataset, a pattern like that shown in figure 4.1 appears.

The longest average retention period (two days) occurred for documents sent to Capital commune and Langzhong 閬中 county. In contrast, after eliminating extreme cases, mail to Dongting commandery was kept for only 0.67 days on average, which is far lower than mail bound for Capital commune and Langzhong. Notably, all these figures are within the range of the four-and-a-half-day grace period after the drafting of official documents.

Figure 4.1. Average retention of the administrative documents handled by Qianling Prefect or Vice-Prefect. Author's own material.

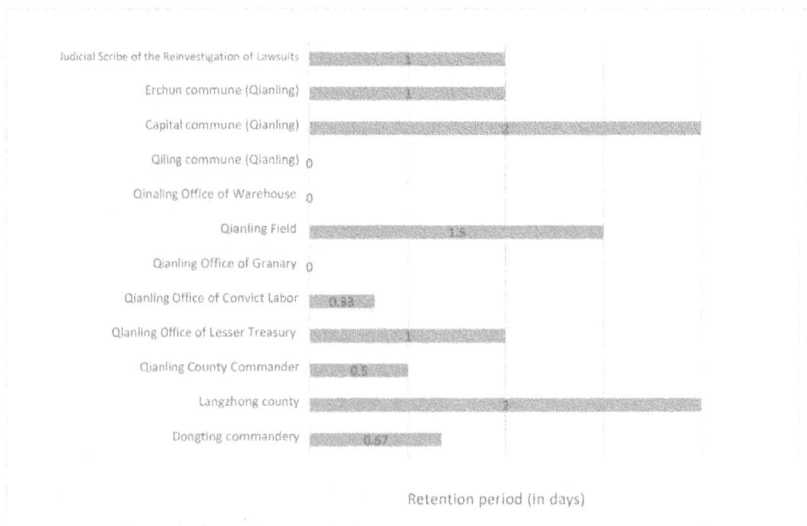

	Retention period (in days)
Judicial Scribe of the Reinvestigation of Lawsuits	1
Erchun commune (Qianling)	1
Capital commune (Qianling)	2
Qiling commune (Qianling)	0
Qinaling Office of Warehouse	0
Qianling Field	1.5
Qianling Office of Granary	0
Qianling Office of Convict Labor	0.33
Qianling Office of Lesser Treasury	1
Qianling County Commander	0.5
Langzhong county	2
Dongting commandery	0.67

The enforcement of the above standards is confirmed by administrative records from Qianling county. At the end of several documents, the senders reported whether the documents were not immediately delivered, and, if so, the number of day(s) and reason for their retention. Even if retentions occurred because of investigations or inquiries on certain issues, the documents were always delivered within two days; that is, the legally permissible grace period.[44] Overall, the listed statistics seem to imply that the Prefect and Vice-Prefect of Qianling generally followed the protocol when handling administrative documents.

However, other statistics suggest that the county seat did not handle administrative documents as efficiently as it appears here. Table 2 in appendix 2 presents the "processing periods" for the administrative documents, within which time the Prefect or Vice-Prefect of Qianling had to either reply or forward the documents to a third party. The figures are calculated according to the time difference between the arrival of a document and the point at which it proceeded to the next procedure. If we separate the thirty-nine specimens listed in Table 2 in appendix 2 based on their recipients, their respective processing periods can be seen in figure 4.2.

Figure 4.2. Average processing period of the administrative documents handled by Qianling Prefect or Vice-Prefect. Author's own material.

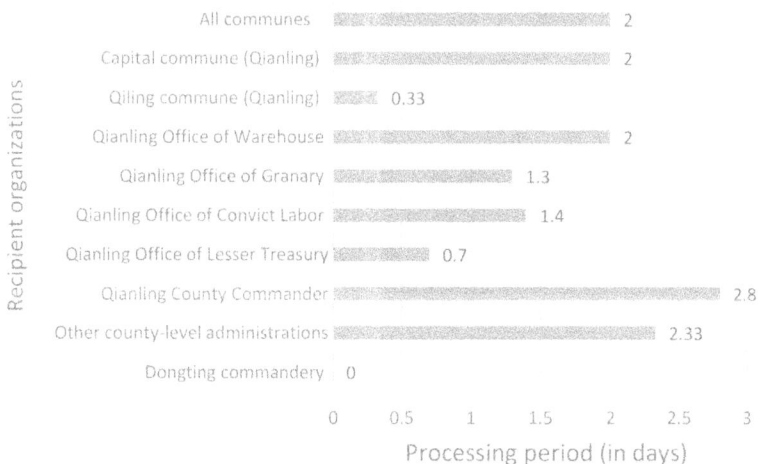

Recipient organizations	Processing period (in days)
All communes	2
Capital commune (Qianling)	2
Qiling commune (Qianling)	0.33
Qianling Office of Warehouse	2
Qianling Office of Granary	1.3
Qianling Office of Convict Labor	1.4
Qianling Office of Lesser Treasury	0.7
Qianling County Commander	2.8
Other county-level administrations	2.33
Dongting commandery	0

The average processing period for these organizations was 1.5 days. Unfortunately, due to the small number of usable examples, the datasets pertaining to Capital commune, the Office of Warehouse, and Dongting commandery consist of only one sample each (table 2 in appendix 2). As a result, they do not yield a complete picture.

That said, existing sources indicate that Qianling's Prefect and Vice-Prefect seemed to require more time to process their documents than to deliver them. While the documents to the Office of Granary were generally dispatched within a day, they took approximately 1.3 days to be processed. Likewise, the average processing period (2.8 days) of the documents sent to the County Commander was almost six times as long as the average retention period. Moreover, the processing period for those documents sent to other county-level administrative units was 2.33 days, which is second only to that of the County Commander.

Figure 4.2 reveals that documents sent to organizations that were not directly subordinate to Qianling tended to have a longer processing period. Although it is far from certain that the Prefect and Vice-Prefect gave priority to the administrative affairs of their direct subordinates over those of the County Commander and other county-level organizations, these figures nonetheless suggest that the administrative communication of Qianling was not as efficient as figure 4.1 indicates.

The last important element underlying the logistical efficiency of the Qianling government is the transmission period of mail. To date, the Liye manuscripts comprise sixty-nine examples of mail delivered to the Qianling county seat from its subordinates. Since most of these documents only contain the drafting and arrival dates, it is impossible to know how long they were kept after being drafted. Thus, the data in figure 4.3 illustrate the maximum days of transmission (from drafting to arrival), and the actual time spent in transit might have been shorter.

Regarding the calculation of statistics, specific treatments are given to documents that were resent. The calculation of their transmission periods is based only on the later sending dates, which are closer to the actual drafting dates of such letters. Of the seventy samples, the average transmission period for documents from outlying communes such as Qiling 啓陵 and Erchun 貳春 was 4.68 days, whereas that of other organizations was merely 1.7 days. If we further categorize the statistics according to the sending organizations, figure 4.3 will emerge.

Unsurprisingly, outlying communes required a much longer time to transfer documents to the Qianling county seat than organizations

Figure 4.3. Maximum duration of transmission of documents delivered to Qianling county seat from its subordinate organizations. Author's own material.

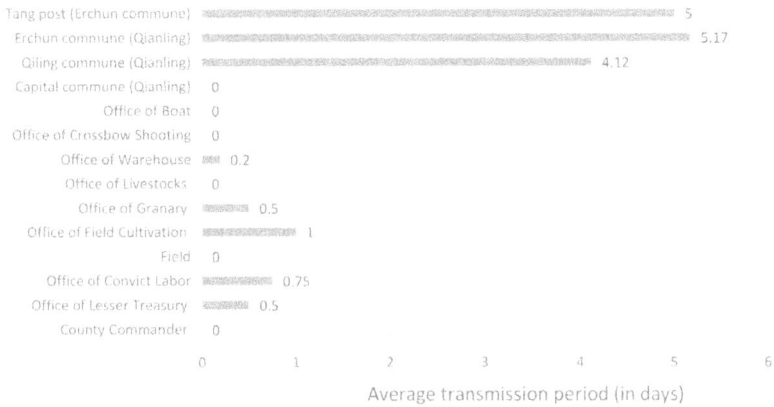

near the seat. Since we do not know the distance between each outlying commune and the seat, it is impossible to examine the average speed of transmission. The transmission periods listed in figure 4.3 nonetheless suggest that in addition to the organizations in the outlying communes, documents from other organizations could reach the county seat within a day. Specifically, among the forty-two examples that fall into this category, only three spent more than one day in transit. In this light, two observations can be made. First, while these organizations might not have been situated within the walled town, they were likely scattered across the jurisdiction of Capital commune, where the county seat was located. Second, these organizations, like their superiors, seldom delayed internal administrative communication.

Assessment of the Internal Communication Logistics of Qianling County

According to the figure in the preceding section, mail drafted by the Prefect and Vice-Prefect of Qianling was mostly delivered within two days, which conforms to the official standards on the transmission time for nonurgent administrative documents. For the delivery speed of administrative documents, it is difficult to estimate whether the internal organizations within Qianling met the prescribed standards. But considering that those organizations situated within the jurisdiction of Capital commune were able to transfer their documents to the county seat in one day, it seems difficult to imagine more efficient performances. Simply put, officials in Qianling seemed to follow the standards established by the Qin regime quite faithfully.

That said, the above analysis may be delusional. Taking the retention period of documents into consideration, while the Prefect and Vice-Prefect of Qianling seemed to follow the official standards, they actually spent a much longer time handling the administrative documents, especially those from organizations that were not under their direct control. The reason behind this phenomenon may be ascribed to the institutional design of the Qin Empire. While the regime established thorough standards and protocols to prevent delays in delivering administrative documents, extant Qin legal enactments include no regulations on the processing period for official documents. Such a loophole in the legislation gave officials leeway to maneuver and allowed them to avoid fulfilling their duties without breaking the law. Therefore, to examine the logistical efficiency of administrative communication in Qianling, we must opt for another measures, that is, a comparison of the interval (processing period + transmission period) of document delivery between Qianling and other county-level administrative units.

Table 6 in appendix 2 lists nineteen examples that show the interval of administrative document delivery from offices of other county-level governments to their respective county seats. After adjustments, the mean of these samples was 3.13 days with a standard deviation of 1.81. This figure is almost identical to that for Qianling, which was equal to [1.5 + 1.7] = 3.2 days. Since these numbers do not consider the difference in sampling size of each organization, they can only serve as a rough reference.

To enhance this comparison, a more accurate picture can be reached by comparing the interval periods of different offices. Figure 4.4 compares the internal communication speed between Qianling and other county-level governments. The outlying communes are excluded to minimize the statistical fluctuation caused by the spatial factor. In this way, the comparison concentrates solely on the interval between the Qianling county seat and subordinate offices inside Capital commune, whose documents could arrive at the seat within a day. In the end, four internal organizations are taken as examples, namely, the Office of

Convict Labor, the Office of Warehouse, the Office of Granary, and the County Commander.

Statistics for three of the four organizations suggest that Qianling had a longer interval than other county-level administrations. However, given that Linyang, Chong, and Linju 臨沮 counties, Bo 僰 march, and another unknown county are each mentioned in only one example, these figures may not represent the internal communication of these administrative units.

In contrast, the dataset of Yangling 陽陵 county is a more reliable source. The Yangling examples are collected from a set of twelve debt-reckoning documents forwarded by the county to Qianling through the Commandant of Dongting commandery. Given that these documents were produced in the same year (214 BCE) and the figures are stable, they likely reflect the situation of Yangling more accurately than other datasets. The interval period in Qianling was only two-thirds that in Yangling county. As such, one may conclude that Qianling's internal administrative communication was at least as efficient as that of Yangling.

By means of a comparative study with the official standards and with the data from other county-level administrative units, two remarks on the internal logistical efficiency of Qianling county can be made.

First, the statistics on Qianling county indicate that its Prefect and Vice-Prefect handled their documents within the legally permissible

Figure 4.4. Interval between Qianling and other county-level administrative units. Author's own material.

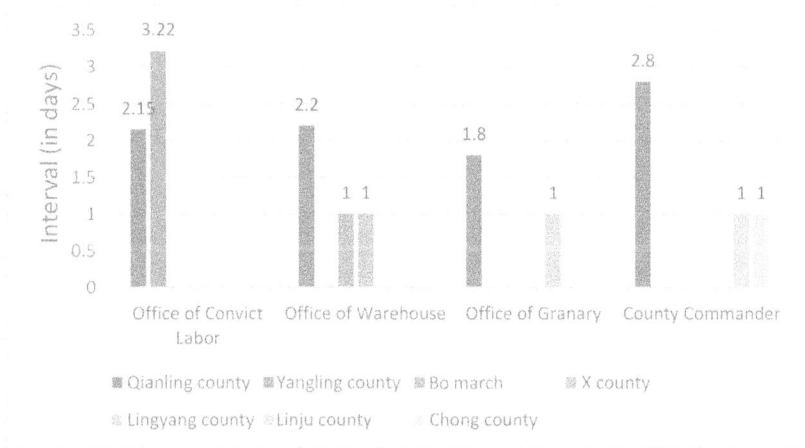

range of retention. Although no information can be found regarding the distance between outlying communes and the Qianling county seat, the swift delivery of mail sent to the seat from those organizations in its environs suggests that Qianling government personnel mostly accorded with official protocols. Second, a comparative study also demonstrates that Qianling's internal administrative communication was as efficient as that of other counties. Taken together, the internal administrative communication of Qianling county was in line with the definition of *efficiency* given at the beginning of this chapter.

External Logistical Efficiency of Administrative Communication

Now let us turn to the external side of this issue. The analysis in this section is mostly devoted to the delivery speed of administrative documents between Qianling and Linyuan (which was once the seat of Dongting commandery), whose direct mail could be transferred via the Yuan and You Rivers. In addition, it also delves into the communication between Qianling and other counties within the Dongting region, especially that between administrative units along the "Linyang route." Since all county seats were near riverbanks (map 4.1), it is conceivable that riverine transport was the main mode of transportation everywhere but between Chong and Youyang counties, where overland transport seems to have been a more sensible option.

STATISTICAL ANALYSIS OF EXTERNAL COMMUNICATION

The reconstruction of the average speed of communication is contingent on a combination of two elements: (1) the estimated duration of information transmission, and (2) the distance between parties on either end of the communication. Additionally, the estimation should differentiate between urgent mail delivered via postal stations and ordinary mail.

Table 6 in appendix 2 lists the estimated transmission periods of documents that were sent to the seat of Qianling from external organizations. Among them, examples from Dongting commandery and Youyang county are particularly noteworthy. First, the sampling size of these two groups is relatively large and thus can form more reliable datasets. Second, records related to Dongting and Youyang are more complete, so we can explore the differences between ordinary mail and that sent via postal stations.

In addition to these two datasets, two individual cases from Linyang and Linju counties should also be considered. Liye tablet 5-1 is a travel certificate issued by Linyang for the official trip of three functionaries. Since Linyang was the starting point on the postal route between Linyang and Qianling, mail from Linyang naturally had a longer transmission period than that from Youyang, all other factors being equal. Given that this letter took fifteen days to arrive in Qianling and the duration equates to the average mailing time between Youyang and Qianling, it is conceivable that tablet 5-1 was delivered via postal stations.

Figure 4.5 displays the significant difference in the transmission periods between mail sent via Postmen and ordinary mail, revealing that the former was indeed a much quicker mode than the latter. The dataset regarding the ordinary mail from Dongting commandery totally encompasses four specimens dated between 221 and 214 BCE, two of which amount to the lengthy duration of 85 and 87 days. If we exclude

Figure 4.5. Estimated transmission period of documents sent from external organizations to the Qianling county seat. Author's own material.

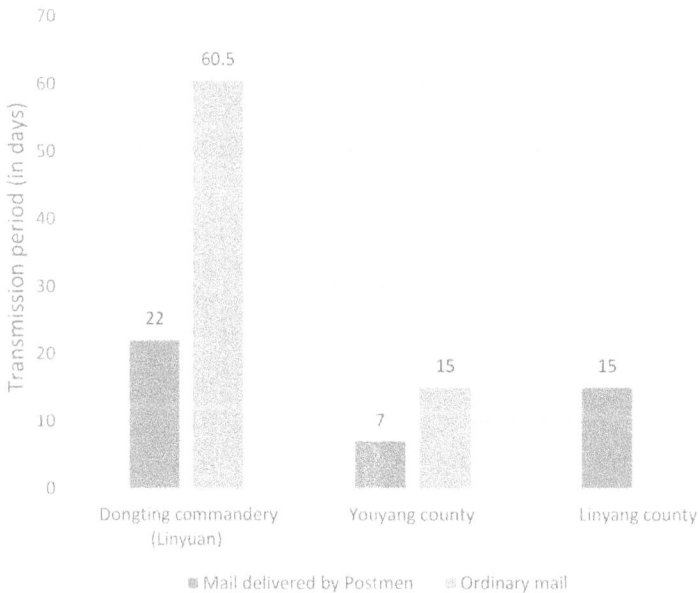

these two samples from the analysis, the average duration drops to 34.5 days. The next step in the reconstruction of average delivery speed is determining the distances between Qianling and the administrative units listed in figure 4.5. Inasmuch as the official distance between Linyuan and Qianling calculated by the Qin regime was 910 *li* (378.38 km), the projected average speeds of communication by post between Dongting and Qianling were as shown in table 4.2.

The variance is significant, to the extent that the pace of communication by post has a fluctuation of 37.87 percent, whereas the gap among ordinary mail is almost three times as large. These data indicate that the speed of information transmission between administrative units—especially for ordinary mail—was rarely stable even when the same route and transportation mode were used. Moreover, sometimes the difference in speed between mail sent via post and ordinary mail was not as large as what figure 4.5 illustrates.

This conclusion can be further contested by the information transmission between different segments along the "Linyang route." Since we do not have the same luck regarding information on the distances between Qianling and other administrative units along this route, we must seek another method to estimate these. First, I acquire the distances between the Liye site and those of other county seats using the "ChinaXmap 8.0"

Table 4.2. Performances of administrative communication between Dongting (Linyuan) and Qianling

	Mail delivered by Postmen	Ordinary mail
Best performance observed	50.51 *li* (21 km)/day	27.58 *li* (11.47 km)/day
25th percentile (estimated figure)	43.33 *li* (18.02 km)/day	26.43 *li* (10.99 km)/day
Median (estimated figure)	41.37 *li* (17.2 km)/day	18 *li* (7.48 km)/day
75th percentile (estimated figure)	39.57 *li* (16.43 km)/day	10.59 *li* (4.4 km)/day
Worst performance observed	31.38 *li* (13.05 km)/day	10.46 *li* (4.35 km)/day

Author's own material.

database (hereafter the Map), which suggests that the total distance of between Linyuan and Qianling counties on a modern map is about 276 km (663.78 *li*) as the crow flies, which is considerably shorter than the documented Qin route of 910 *li* (378.38 km). This may be caused by the meandering waterways of the region, the possibility of route changes from ancient to modern times, and potential errors of the reconstructed route. Regardless, this divergence indicates that it is both anachronistic and difficult to directly convert such figures to the Qin measurement.

To obtain more accurate estimations, I apply the ratio between the modern and Qin routes (1:1.37) to the modern distances and then calculate the traveling speed based on these adjusted figures (table 4.3). For example, the Map shows that the distance between Wangcun Town and the Liye site is about 64 km as the crow flies. Applying the 1:1.37 ratio to this distance, the adjusted ancient route distance was about 211.01 *li* (87.74 km).

Table 4.3 records the statistics derived from communication between two different segments of the "Linyang route." One reconstructed administrative communication between Youyang and Qianling (30.14 *li*/day)

Table 4.3. Estimated communication speed between Qianling and other counties along the "Linyang route"

Qin administrative unit	Present-day location	Estimated ancient route distance from Qianling	Travelling speed per day (in *li*)
Youyang county	Wangcun 王村 Town, Yongshun County[1]	211.01 *li* (87.74 km)	By Postmen: 30.14 *li* (12.53 km) By ordinary mail: 14.07 *li* (5.85 km)
Linyang county	Baigongcheng 白公城, Cili County[2]	678.74 *li* (282.22 km)	45.25 *li* (18.81 km)

Author's own material.

1. Zhong Wei 鐘煒, "Liye Qinjian suojian xian yi kao" 里耶秦簡所見縣邑考, *Henan kejidaxue xuebao* 河南科技大學學報 2 (2007): 18.

2. Zhong, "Liye Qinjian suojian xian yi kao," 19.

delivered by post is slower than even the worst speed between Dongting and Qianling (31.38 *li* per day) when using the same mode of delivery. Another reconstruction featuring Linyang and Qianling, however, observes an above-average performance of 45.25 *li* per day. Both figures are not far removed from the range of average speed shown in table 4.2. Whereas such estimations are indicative at best, the proximity of their results somewhat verifies the validity of the estimations of delivery speed between Dongting and Qianling listed in table 4.2.

ASSESSMENT OF THE EXTERNAL COMMUNICATION LOGISTICS OF QIANLING COUNTY

Now I examine the logistical efficiency of external communication between Qianling county and other administrative units. The reconstructed average communication speed by post between Dongting commandery (Linyuan) and Qianling was much slower than the prescribed speed of 200 *li* (83.16 km) per day in the "Statutes on the Forwarding of Documents." Even if we apply the standard of those commanderies along the northern frontier, whose minimum delivery speed might only have been one-third that of well-equipped regions, the best observed speed of the administrative communication between Dongting and Qianling—50.51 *li* (21 km) per day—is still subpar. Judging by the numbers prescribed in official standards and by the performances of other administrative units in the Dongting region, the external communication between Qianling and Dongting was quite inefficient.

Logistical Efficiency of the Communication between Dongting and Nan Commanderies

Now I compare the performance of units in the Dongting region with those in Nan commandery, supplemented by a couple of examples from Nanyang commandery. The most direct evidence of Nan commandery's communicative efficiency is a figure recorded in a judicial dossier datable to 220 BCE from the *Book of Submitted Doubtful Cases*. In it the scribe(s) listed that the traveling speed of responsible judicial officials was ca. 85.77 *li* (35.66 km) per day. We are also informed that such a speed was achieved by adopting overland and riverine transport concurrently. This figure is almost twice as fast as the best recorded performance of the Dongting region.

This finding can be confirmed through other indirect evidence. In the "Event Calendar of the Thirty-Fourth Year of the First Emperor (213 BCE)" unearthed in tomb no. 30 of Zhoujiatai 周家臺, it is recorded that the user stayed in Jingling 競陵 county on the first day (*bingshen*) of the second month; the next day (*dingyou*), he arrived at Jinghan 井韓 commune, and the third day (*wuxu*), he came to Jiangling 江陵 county (map 4.2).[45]

These three places also appear in the *Document of Roads and Distances* mentioned earlier. Jinghan commune was 106 *li* (44. 07 km) east of the eastern city of Jiangling, and the distance between Jinghan and Jingling amounted to 98 *li* (40.75 km).[46] As Xin Deyong 辛德勇 points out, Jiangling, Jinghan, and Jingling were stops on a major overland thoroughfare east of Jiangling.[47] Nevertheless, considering that this route basically overlapped with the waterway of the Yang 楊 River (map 4.2), travelers could also go by boat and/or ship. Either way, since the traveler managed to finish his 204 *li* (84.82 km) itinerary in two days, his average speed was 102 *li* (42.41 km) per day.

Map 4.2. Reconstructed transportation routes of Nan and Nanyang commanderies. Map based on Xin, Shishi sheng yan, 93. The location of Jingling is adjusted according to Wang Zuoxi 王琢璽, "Zhoudai Jianghan diqu chengyi dili yanjiu" 周代江漢地區城邑地理研究 (PhD. diss., Wuhan University, 2019), 61. Author's own material.

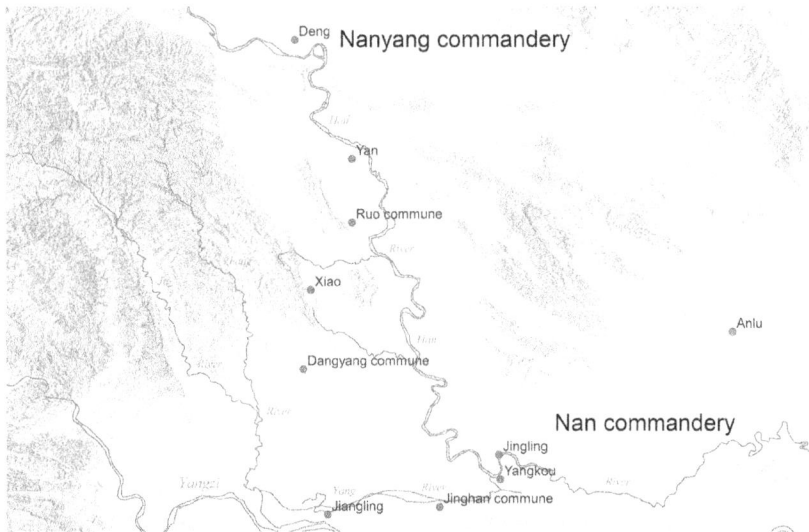

Comparatively, the "Event Calendar of the Twenty-Seventh Year of the First Emperor (220 BCE)" from the Yuelu collection reveals a similar itinerary but one that almost certainly involved riverine transportation. The calendar documents that on the *dingwei* (thirteenth) day of the fifth month the user stayed "inside the county," which likely refers to Jiangling county. He was delayed by flooding the following day and arrived at the mouth of the Yang River two days later (*gengshen*).[48] Correspondingly, an entry from the *Document of Roads and Distances* reads, "Altogether traveling from Jiangling to the mouth of Yang River is 194 *li*" (凡江陵到楊口百九十四里) (80.67 km).[49] This was almost certainly the distance of the riverway between Jiangling and the mouth of Yang River.[50] Excluding delays, it took the traveler two days to complete his trip; hence, the average speed of riverine transportation in this journey was 97 *li* (40.33 km) per day.

Another Qin event calendar records an itinerary pertaining to overland transportation. The "Event Calendar of the Thirty-Fifth Year of the First Emperor (212 BCE)" of the Yuelu manuscripts reveals that the traveler lodged at an accommodation at Dangyang 當陽 on the *jiwei* (first) of the fourth month and arrived in Xiao 鄁 the next day (*gengshen*), after which (*xinyou*) he stayed in Ruo 箬 commune.[51] The *Document of Roads and Distances* states that the distance of the route between Dangyang and Ruo communes was 189 *li* (78.17 km),[52] which implies that the traveler went an average of 94.5 *li* (ca. 39.29 km) per day. As shown in map 4.2, this itinerary should have been completed mostly if not entirely via overland transportation. Unlike Postmen, who transported mail via relay, traveling officers had to complete the whole journey themselves. Regardless of how the traveler achieved such an impressive speed (probably with the help of vehicles such as carriages or, though quite unlikely, horses), one can imagine that Postmen might have even managed a quicker average speed because of their professionalism and stamina advantages. This example provides us an important reference for the speed of overland transportation in Nan commandery.

In sum, the mean of the recovered communication speeds of the four cases discussed above was 94.82 *li* (39.42 km) per day.[53] Notably, the average traveling speed of riverine transportation had no salient advantage over its overland counterpart. The two cases of riverine transport averaged 99.5 *li* (41.37 km) per day, whereas one overland example had a pace of 94.5 *li* (39.29 km) per day. The difference is less than 5.5 percent.

Although the speeds observed in these cases relate to the official trips of functionaries rather than the delivery of mail, they were a vital part of the overall administrative communication. To give a later example, a slip unearthed from the Xuanquan postal station (Xuanquanzhi 懸泉置) records that an official garrisoning on the northwestern frontier of the Western Han Empire once traveled 100 *li* (41.58 km) per day,[54] which was slower than the required speed for mail delivered by post. Therefore, the delivery of administrative documents by post was conceivably as quick as (if not quicker than) that of official travel.

Evidently, the external communication of the Dongting region was inefficient in comparison with that of the Nan commandery. The recovered communication speeds between counties of Dongting commandery for mail delivered by post were merely 41.37 *li* (17.2 km) per day on average; even the best performance was just 50.51 *li* (21 km) per day. Both figures are far below the numbers stipulated in the official standards.

The gap between the logistical efficiency of the administrative communication of Nan and Dongting regions is equally significant even when the transportation mode is taken into consideration. The topography of Qianling county suggests that much of its external communication was transmitted via riverine transportation. The 41.37 *li* per day figure aligns with this supposition. This number is twice as slow as the average mobility speed (94.82 *li* per day) of personnel serving in the administrative units of Nan commandery who traveled by boat. Such a notable gap signals that the Nan region maintained better infrastructure at both the physical and institutional levels. By contrast, the Qin seemed to be unable to effectively convey its power in new territories such as Dongting.

Logistical Efficiency of the Communication between Nan and Nanyang Commanderies

In addition to information from Dongting and Nan commanderies, the Liye manuscripts also include an example pertinent to the communication logistics between Nan and Nanyang commanderies, both of which were situated in the semiperiphery of the empire. Initially sent from Handan 邯鄲 to Nanyang commandery, an official letter was delivered by post and subsequently forwarded to Dongting commandery, whose seat then disseminated it to subordinate counties such as Qianling.[55]

As with other documents bearing similar formulaic language, the sender of this letter specified the division of labor among counties in Nanyang with regard to its dissemination. Deng 鄧 county was responsible for forwarding it southward to Nan commandery. Presumably, Postmen delivering this document would have traveled along the famous "Nanyang-

Nan commanderies avenue" (map 4.2), which was a pivotal overland thoroughfare connecting Nanyang Basin and Jianghan Plain and is well documented in the transmitted texts.[56]

According to the *Document of Roads and Distances*, the total distance between Deng and Jiangling was 532 *li* (221.21 km). Also, the abovementioned Nanyang letter records that the interval after the letter was copied by Deng was eight days. Taken together, these figures indicate that the average communication speed was approximately 66.5 *li* (27.65 km) per day. Since the total processing period constituted the duration of both the delivery and the retention periods, this figure possibly underestimates the communication speed between the two locations. At the very least, one can argue that the logistical efficiency of the communication of Nanyang commandery was between that to the Dongting region and to the Nan region.

This case offers an opportunity to compare the logistical efficiency of the communication of administrative units in the old territories. Given that both Nanyang and Nan commanderies were established by the Qin decades before the unification in 221 BCE, and that both commanderies were north of the southern boundary of Suo county, they should have abided by the regulation of 200 *li* per day prescribed in the "Statutes on the Forwarding of Documents." The average communication speeds reconstructed above, though much better than that of the Dongting region, clearly indicate that administrative units within the two regions failed to uphold this standard. While it would be difficult to argue that such a failure was pervasive among the Qin Empire, these examples suggest that the regulations designed by the Qin regime might have deviated from actual practice. In this respect, the findings in this section call into question the logistical efficiency not only in the Qin Empire's new territories but also in its old ones.

COMMUNICATION GAPS BETWEEN THE ADMINISTRATIVE UNITS IN THE DONGTING REGION

In line with the theme of scrutinizing the external logistical efficiency of communication, this section is devoted to a series of communication gaps—both internal and external—involving the administrative units of Dongting commandery between 214 and 212 BCE, during which time the Qin Empire mobilized an enormous number of troops for its military campaign in the far south. I contend that the communication gaps were directly linked to the concurrent military campaign. Considering that Dongting commandery was one of the logistical bases of the southern campaign, counties within that region likely had to supply extra labor for tasks such as road construction and food transfer. These duties not only exacerbated the already severe paucity of human resources, but also hampered information transmission among administrative units because of the movement of troops. From this perspective, the unfavorable conditions in the new territories engendered communication gaps during times of urgency and widened the capacity gap of the empire.

Types of Communication Gap

In the Qin administrative system, there were multiple occasions where official documents were resent, sometimes more than once, after their initial dispatchments. One of the distinct features of this type of document lies in its formulaic language. An additional cover letter containing paratexts such as "to pursue" (*zhui* 追) or "to duplicate" (*zhong* 重) or the sentence "I fear that the previous document did not arrive" (前書畏其不到) would be attached after the main text. While the act of resending does not necessarily imply that documents were actually missing, extra labor had to be spent to produce and deliver the follow-up document(s).

In general, there are two circumstances under which communication gaps between the sender and recipient organizations can be observed: (1) when a document was previously sent but the recipient had not replied; and (2) when the sender wanted to guarantee that a crucial document would be delivered to its recipient appropriately. Either way, these two actions indicate procrastination in sharing information between parties involved in the communicative process, on the one hand, and on the other hand, the sender's effort to remedy the failure of communication that had occurred.

A typical example of the first category of communication gaps is shown in the protocols of transmission of the following multi-piece document dated to 213 BCE.[57] These three protocols were attached after the lawsuit against the Overseer of Convict Labor named Yan discussed in the previous chapter. The original sender of the document was Li, who was the Governor of Dongting commandery and drafted this letter on the twenty-second day of the sixth month. Since Qianling did not reply to Li's quest, Acting Governor Yi 繹 followed up eighteen days later and made a second attempt after a seventeen-day interval. Finally, the third follow-up letter attached to a multi-piece scroll was delivered thirteen days after the second attempt. It is notable that the tone of each of the pursuing letters became increasingly aggressive, thereby manifesting the commandery's loss of patience in the course of the communication breakdown.

The other type of communication gap is more subtle. Unlike the first category, which always required the recipient to reply, resending documents was intended to guarantee the transmission of a message. To this end, it was characterized by multiple dispatchments within a period that was too short for the recipient to provide a response. Such a communication gap can be observed in three official letters dated to 220 BCE.[58] On tablet 16-5, the Vice-Prefect of Qianling wrote that "the previous document has been handed down. Now I duplicate; listen to this document to carry out the affair" (前書已下。重,聽書從事). This indicates that the Qianling official received an earlier letter, which was probably tablet 16-6. Given that both letters were produced by the headquarter of Dongting commandery on the same day and that Qianling received the documents on the third and eighth days of the third month, the commandery likely dispatched the two letters to its subordinate counties concurrently.

To ensure the delivery of the message, the Governor resent another copy (tablet 9-2283) just two days after the earlier letters in the mode of the "constantly notated document" (*hengshu shu* 恒署書), which were to be delivered by the supposedly more reliable Postmen. Although this type of communication was produced when a failure of communication had not yet taken place, it reflects the sender's anxiety that the communication would have failed. For this reason, I still classify it as a type of communication gap.

Distribution of Communication Gaps

Altogether, there are twenty-seven cases of communication gaps in the published Liye material, all of which are dated between 221 and 209 BCE (see table 7 in appendix 2). As shown in figure 4.6, an overwhelming number of them were concentrated between 214 and 212 BCE, and only four examples come from the first three years. This distribution is extremely uneven.

The so-called "Yangling dossier" partly accounts for the predominant number of cases of communication gaps between 214 and 212 BCE.

Figure 4.6. Distribution of communication gap cases from 221 to 212 BCE. Author's own material.

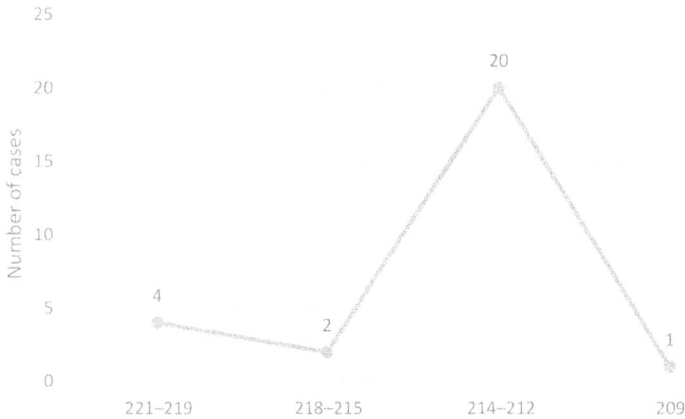

This dossier comprises twelve documents concerning the debt-reckoning process of conscripts from Yangling county, which pursued the debt of some of the conscripts who were allocated to Dongting commandery. The original letters of these documents were drafted across a mere eight-day span. Since Yangling, the creditor, did not know the county in which the debtors were stationed, the debt-reckoning requests were first sent to the Commandant of Dongting commandery, who was responsible for the distribution of conscripts, and he was asked to forward these messages to the appropriate locations. Apparently, the Yangling official received no response from Qianling, the corresponding county; hence, he decided to launch a second attempt after fourteen months. Although local governments in the Qin Empire seemed to give debt-reckoning documents an extremely low priority for processing, it rarely took the receiving county one and a half years to reply.[59] In view of this peculiarity, these letters should be classified as the first type of communication gap.

The cases of communication gaps embodied in the Yangling dossier are extraordinary. Given the strict regulations on the retention of administrative documents, the twelve original letters in the Yangling dossier were probably delivered to the Dongting Commandant soon after their completion. Since these documents were drafted under a tight schedule (eight days), that all of them eventually failed to convey their messages to Qianling officials implies that the cases of communication gaps between Yangling and the Dongting region from 214 to 212 BCE were not random or isolated events. Rather, there was a serial delay in information exchange.

This supposition also conforms to the processing of the Yangling dossier. All letters in this dossier were forwarded to Qianling on the same date, and the intervals between the cover letters of the Yangling official and the Dongting Commandant were extremely lengthy, ranging from 272 to 307 days. While these figures indicate the transmission period of these letters, which was naturally longer because of the distance between the Yangling and Dongting regions, the time for processing was still too long to be considered normal.[60]

There are several possibilities for explaining this phenomenon. First, it may have been a decided action taken by the Dongting Commandant, in the sense that he might have intentionally left these documents unprocessed until he accumulated a sizable number of the same kind of documents.[61] Second, it could also have resulted from an inevitable force that greatly disturbed the normal communication between the Yangling and Dongting regions. This implies that either (1) the Commandant received the twelve documents—all of which were redelivered within a one-and-a-half-month time span—almost simultaneously and handled them at once, or (2) the documents from Yangling arrived at different times, but the turbulence of information transmission in the region nonetheless prohibited the Commandant from immediately forwarding them to Qianling. Instead, he was compelled to process them concurrently until communication channels were restored. Either way, this case bespeaks the abnormal communication between the two regions.

With respect to the first possibility, the analysis under "Statistical Analysis of Internal Communication" above reveals that the Prefect and Vice-Prefect of Qianling on average spent just 2.33 days processing documents sent from other county-level organizations. This time span is much shorter than one and half months. In this light, the slow processing the Yangling dossier seems more likely a consequence of accidental communication lapse due to external factors than a calculated decision.

Liye tablet 9-2314 is a duplicate that comprises two pieces of correspondence involving the Office of Convict Labor of Qianling, the Qianling county seat, and Langzhong county.[62] The first correspondence dates to mid-214 BCE. A letter of the Office of Convict Labor took thirty-seven days to arrive at the county seat. Note that this letter was following up on an earlier report, meaning that there was another letter sent to Qianling. The second correspondence was sent seven months later in early 213 BCE, when the Office of Convict labor resubmitted another follow-up letter to the county seat, which did not handle it until forty-seven days later.

The duration of the first letter's transmission and the processing period of the second indicate abnormal communication. As noted earlier, the average transmission period for communication between the Office of Convict Labor and the Qianling county seat was 0.75 days. That the first letter from the Office of Convict Labor required over one month to be transferred is by itself an extraordinary phenomenon. Likewise, although documents delivered to other county-level administrative units often required a longer processing time, forty-seven days was completely outside reasonable expectations when compared to the 2.33-day average. This suggests that the communication documented on tablet 9-2314 had been derailed.

Cases of communication gaps were not confined to Qianling county. An official letter records that an Overseer of the Office of Warehouse in an unknown county delivered five successive letters in twenty-six days.[63] That the Overseer had to submit his report four additional times indicates an extraordinary scenario. Since the date of this letter (214 BCE) coincides with those of the Yangling dossier and tablet 9-2314, it serves as further evidence that the cases of communication gaps between 214 and 212 BCE were not isolated incidents.

This section unveils the distributional pattern of communication gaps in the Dongting region. The communication gaps occurred predominantly between 214 and 212 BCE. Specifically, the Yangling dossier reveals that there were serial communication gaps between Yangling and Dongting commandery and Qianling county. Other sources datable to 214 and 213 BCE even hint that the communication gaps were a regional phenomenon that also occurred in other administrative units in Dongting commandery. In what follows I unveil the possible reasons behind this serial lapse of communication and how it affected the decision-making process of the Qin Empire.

Assessment of Communication Gaps in the New Territories

One possible reason behind the communication gaps between administrative units in the Dongting region may relate to human resources shortages. One fragment records that "many have absconded along the way, and, as such, [government] affairs have been delayed by three to four (times?)" (☑□多道亡，事以故留，或至三四).[64] While the exact context of this fragment is unclear, the content seems to suggest that government affairs were repeatedly delayed because of the abscondence of personnel, presumably convict laborers or conscripts, who constituted the major workforce behind mail delivery in the empire.

Another possible factor for the serial communication gaps between 214 and 212 BCE was the Yue campaign occurring during that time. The campaign and its preparation probably deteriorated the already inefficient external communication. As is well documented in the transmitted sources, the initial encounter in this campaign resulted in one of worst military failures in Qin history and Tuwei was killed in the counterattack organized by the Yue people after three years of arduous fighting.[65] Subsequently, large numbers of exile conscripts across the realm were deployed to Lingnan as reinforcements in 214 BCE. This time, the empire finally managed to conquer the Yue tribes.

As a bridgehead of the Qin Empire's Yue campaign, Dongting commandery likely accepted considerable extra conscripts within its purview. Conceivably, the large-scale mobilization could have significantly disrupted the usual administrative communication in the Dongting region. This is not only because the troops occupied thoroughfares that Postmen and other relevant personnel used to transmit administrative documents, but also because most personnel were assigned to meet the more imminent demand for road construction and food transportation. These reasons could explain the chaotic and serial failures of communication between 214 and 212 BCE, during which time the southern campaign was at white heat. The cases of communication gaps thus demonstrate the negative effect of the Qin's expansionist policy.

The challenges in administrative communication undoubtedly hindered the efficiency of decision-making in the Qin Empire. While the external logistical efficiency of communication in the new territories was already quite low, what has been discussed in this section suggests, if not proves, that the logistics of imperial power in the new territories were vulnerable to sudden changes in situational factors. An abrupt increase of troops passing through a region already affected the efficiency of communication and, to some degree, partly paralyzed the communication network.

State Power and Administrative Inefficiency
in the New Territories

This chapter examines the logistical efficiency of the communication of administrative units in the new territories. Through a quantitative analysis of over two hundred examples in the Liye manuscripts, I have discovered that although the Qianling government maintained a relatively high internal logistical communicative efficiency, its external efficiency was low. In hindsight, these phenomena were hardly surprising, as in premodern societies, communication between different administrative units was mainly mediated through manual labor. While internal efficiency may be achieved due to the relative spatial proximity of organizations, the external communication of ancient states tended to vary because of the limitations of communication technology and longer traveling distances. Therefore, the efficiency of communication in a vast empire such as the Qin was inevitably uneven because of the uneven distribution of state power across its territories.

Although both historical records and archaeological evidence suggest that the Qin Empire invested an untold amount of resources in developing a whole system of infrastructure—with both physical and intellectual components—to facilitate the logistics of communication, given the cost of creating and maintaining these basic infrastructures, the level of efficiency was determined by the capacity of the state to establish roads, highways, and conveyance facilities, as well as to enforce its performance standards. The stronger the state power in a region was, the better the area's infrastructure and logistical efficiency likely were. The ephemeral rule of the Qin, the complicated topography, and the serious labor shortages in the new territories made Qin's project a per-petual work-in-progress, especially in regions such as Dongting, where the state presence was weak. In view of these constraints, it was rather natural that the short-handed local governments failed to construct an adequate communication network and achieve efficient logistics in external administrative communication in most of the empire's new territories.

Such communication deficiencies radically contradict the perception that the Qin Empire attained an effective government after the reforms of Shang Yang. The correlation between communication gaps among the administrative units of Dongting commandery in 214–213 BCE and the empire's concurrent southern campaign is especially striking.

Such a pattern suggests that the external communication between administrative units in the periphery could not have withstood sudden external changes. When black-swan events emerged, the connection between local governments—which were linked only by various fragile inter- and intra-regional networks—would be severed. Eventually, these administrative units became isolated islands surrounded by the sea of Qin haters. This may account for the slow response of the Qin central authorities to the revolts in the east and south (as they probably did not receive timely notification from the local governments) as well as the disorganization and vulnerability of Qin local governments in the face of the anti-Qin movement.

Conclusion

Gaps in State Power:
The Structural Problem and the Fall of the Qin Empire

This book has discussed three dynamics of state power in the imperial Qin period:

1. There were tensions between the "moral-legalist suprem-acism" ideology and the Qin's sociopolitical reforms and identity formation. Not only was the oppressive and supremacist nature of this ideology detrimental to the autonomy of communities and suffocating the incentives for government officials, but it also deterred the develop-ment of a universal ruling class.

2. The labor shortages of administrative units in the face of rapid territorial expansion partly account for the regime's incapacity to extract resources in the new territories and incorporate indigenous populations into the power networks controlled by government organizations. The measures to fill these loopholes did little to mitigate these problems, which hampered the completion of administrative tasks, the conduct of production activities, and the stabilization of security in the Qin Empire.

3. The regime had inefficient logistics for exercising state power in the new territories. The case of Qianling county indicates that external administrative communication was inefficient and that the communication system connecting

administrative units in the periphery could not have met sudden challenges. As a result, some of the Qin local governments might have had inoperable external administrative communication.

The theoretical framework developed in chapter 1 interprets these dynamics as the catalyst for a gap between the actual state power the Qin regime commanded and the level of state power necessary to govern the size of territory that it had claimed. Such an emergent gap in state power, if not overcome, can cause a state to collapse. Since state power is the capacity of a state to exercise its despotic and infrastructural power over and through ideological, economic, military, and political organizational networks, these dynamics—as well as the gap in state power that they precipitated—also stemmed from the interaction of these intersected and interrelated power networks.

To contextualize the eclectic nature of these dynamics, I analyze and simultaneously summarize their collective impact on the Qin collapse under the framework of legitimacy, capacity, and security gaps. Then, I conclude this book by remarking on the relationship between the structural problems of the Qin Empire and its collapse.

Legitimacy Gap

The legitimacy gap is mostly associated with gaps in ideological and political power. The revolts in the east and south of the Qin Empire were a prelude to its demise. Widespread rebellion was the best indication that the Qin regime was facing a serious legitimacy gap, which did not form in a vacuum. Many anti-Qin insurgencies were led by former elites of eliminated polities, who often acted as leaders of local communities. These people often teamed up with local militia or other influential figures to form various strong anti-Qin coalitions. The activities of these former elites (e.g., Xiang Liang and Zhang Liang) preceded the rebellion of Chen Sheng and Wu Guang. These results indicate that the legitimacy gap of the Qin Empire emerged as early as its founding. The Qin's failure to either engage with or eradicate these former aristocrats evinces the insufficient infrastructural and political power of the empire.

Despite this shortcoming, the Qin rulers were by no means unaware of this legitimacy crisis. The institutional reforms and policies elaborated in chapters 2 and 3 were among the many measures that they orchestrated in an attempt to soften social tensions and create a universal Qin cultural identity, thereby strengthening the infrastructural power of the state. Had their program succeeded, the legitimacy crisis could have been mitigated. What they failed to foresee, however, was that this social engineering project in turn widened their legitimacy gap.

The "moral-legalist supremacism" ideology adopted by the Qin regime was partly responsible for this failure. Scholars often consider austere punishment and the exhaustion of labor to be major sources of social tensions during the imperial Qin period. Both issues could be attributed to the abovementioned state ideology. First, since "Legalist" doctrines often emphasize the importance of stern punishments in statecraft, this mentality affected the decisions of bureaucrats, who were required to assign harsh punishment even though there were less radical options available. Ultimately, the strong "Legalist" mentality might have curtailed the effect of lenient policies and backfired on the Qin regime. Second, the territorial expansion of the empire, which exhausted much of the empire's labor, was prompted by the supremacist civilizing mission of the Qin regime.

In addition to these more explicit factors, the social tensions might also have been rooted in the radical social engineering project of the empire, whose design and enforcement were influenced by the "moral-legalist" mentality. Under this ideology, the social reforms of the Qin regime likely led to active and direct state interference in individuals' social lives and to the declining autonomy of local communities. In this respect, the state ideology and the social reforms might have escalated social tensions among the populace and made the new territories in the east and south a hotbed of social unrest. Rather than building a utopian society, the First Emperor's schemes presumably resulted in a horrific dystopia that was governed through terror rather than the devotion, reverence, kindness, and love that he envisioned. This probably gave rise to an even more serious legitimacy gap.

The oppressive state ideology affected not only ordinary masses but also elites. To protect themselves from the suffocating ideology and secure their own welfare, Qin administrators, especially officials in the new territories, simply concealed the reality of their respective jurisdictions from their superiors. An official report from Qianling county hints at such intrigues. While this kind of behavior likely lowered the capacity of government administration, the reluctant attitude of these political elites implied the rejection of the regulations and despotic power of the state. From this perspective, the situation reflects the legitimacy gap between the Qin regime and some of its ruling elites.

This leads to another important facet of the issue of legitimacy: the inability of the Qin regime to construct a universal ruling class. It is evident that the "old" Qin people, as conquerors, held a condescending attitude toward the new subjects. The discrimination by the "old" Qin people, coupled with an ideology and policies encouraging Qin cultural superiority, might have ignited or strengthened the new subjects' awareness of their former cultural identities. This likely hindered the development of an immanent morale and the commitment of the new subjects to the Qin regime. This can partly explain why the Qin Empire failed to form a universal ruling class like that of the Western Han and Roman Empires, despite its various attempts to publicize a universal Qin identity.

Capacity Gap

Over the course of nine years, the Qin state expanded to twice the size of its former territory. The rapid expansion gravely challenged the capacity of the Qin Empire to fulfill its basic state functions for its subjects. As I have stressed repeatedly in this book, the Qin regime displayed serious capacity gaps in the political, military, and economic spheres.

The capacity of the newly founded empire in its new territories was tenuous. The central authorities reacted terribly slowly toward rebellions in the east and south, whereas administrators in local governments were either incompetent or deceitful in handling the crises. In the end, the whole of the Qin administration was in disarray.

Indeed, both transmitted and excavated sources reveal that the Qin local governments were incapable of fulfilling some of their core functions. Evidence from Liye suggests that prior to the outbreak of the uprisings in 209 BCE, the government of Qianling county suffered immensely from a lack of personnel such as officials, convict laborers, and conscripts. The personnel shortages not only hampered the completion of mundane administrative tasks and production activities, the extraction of economic resources, and the assurance of state security, but also led to inefficient external communication among administrative units. In all likelihood, Qianling endured an inexorable capacity gap. Considering the manifold reforms and new policies designed to tackle these issues,

Qianling's struggle was likely shared by many similar administrative units in the new territories rather than being an isolated case.

As with the legitimacy gap, the Qin rulers were cautious about the capacity gap stemming from the state's lack of political, economic, and military power. Measures were contemplated to increase the number of feasible personnel and to facilitate the logistics of state power. Nevertheless, most of these efforts proved futile. The reason for such policy failure lies partly in the brevity of the Qin Empire, which prevented some of the policies from achieving their desired ends. For example, although the Qianling government began to train former Chu scribes to write in the Qin script and employed locals to serve in the government, the short-lived empire simply could not have survived to observe the impact of this policy.

The most significant factor behind such policy failure, nevertheless, was the incessant expansion of the Qin Empire. Most of the known institutional reforms and measures entailed reshuffling former government personnel from the old territories to politically peripheral regions. These people included convicts who committed minor crimes or debtors who were unable to repay their debts. Their terms of service in the new territories were substituted for the punishments they would otherwise have received. Since these potential personnel were also conscripted to engage in military campaigns, Qin's territorial expansion inevitably directed these human resources away from filling vacancies in the government to serving as imperial soldiers. From this perspective, the expansion of the empire made labor shortages a structural problem.

The military expansion of the Qin Empire also brought about administrative breakdown. Military actions rely on logistics, which hinge on infrastructure construction that guarantees the mobility of troops and the transfer of resources. Building infrastructure in one region rests upon the presence of state power there. In the new territories where the natural environment was challenging, infrastructure was insufficient, and personnel were lacking, inefficient logistics were almost inevitable. Moreover, when the available laborers were deployed for infrastructure building, the labor shortages in the government were likely exacerbated. In addition, given that troops and Postmen used the same roads, large troop movements potentially disrupted the transmission of information. The serial communication lapse during the Qin's Yue campaign from 214 to 212 BCE presumably resulted from the collective effects of the aforementioned factors.

Inefficient administrative communication likely made it difficult for policy-makers to utter timely responses to urgent matters, on the one hand, and deterred local administrators from reporting the reality of their situation to the central authorities in the face of unforeseeable crisis, on the other. Such conditions may account for the sloppy and chaotic decision-making between the central and local governments during the anti-Qin movement.

All these facts demonstrate that the Qin regime was incapable of ensuring the fulfillment of its core functions. Given its large capacity gap, the state power did not suffice to withstand sudden changes in external factors.

Security Gap

The security gap relates mainly to military power. It is hard to imagine that the Qin Empire, which was known for its superlative military prowess, was afflicted with a security gap. However, multiple sources indicate that one of the struggles of the Qin Empire was its incapacity to ensure state security in the periphery. Here, I am talking about the empire's inability to curb the earth-shattering rebellions that ended the Qin rule, the catastrophic first Yue campaign in 217 BCE, and the more chronic and detrimental gap in the Qin Empire's security that arose from multiple small military failures, such as the failed counterattack against the Chu insurgency documented in the *Book of Submitted Doubtful Cases*, and from the incapability of local administrative units to recruit enough laborers to maintain local security. This bespeaks the existence of a chronic security gap from the founding of the Qin Empire.

Like their solutions to the capacity gap, the Qin implemented reforms to increase the size of the military and facilitate the efficient logistics of military servicemen. The effects of these reforms were nonetheless questionable. On the one hand, this was because in Qin government organizations, conscripts were often used as substitutes for other forms of human resources. On the other hand, the territorial expansion guided by or disguised as a civilizing mission generated everlasting demand for military personnel and soldiers. These factors undermined the effectiveness of the empire's measures.

A security gap also arose due to the uneven distribution of troops. Since most military forces controlled by the state were garrisoned on the new frontier in the far south and north, the size of regular forces stationed in administrative units in the new territories annexed between 230 and 221 BCE was conceivably small. This shifted strategic focus, coupled with the defortification of large cities in the new territories, led to the emergence of a military imbalance in different parts of the empire. Such a lopsided distribution of military power created a security gap in the new territories of the Qin Empire. Thus, it was not a coincidence that these regions were where the anti-Qin rebellion started.

An equally concerning impact of the regime's new policies to reduce the shortages and improve the logistics of conscripts was the dissipation of state-controlled military power, which aggravated Qin's security gap. The new deployment scheme entailed the long-distance movement of armed conscripts and convict laborers; the transmission process was usually time-consuming. It is evident that quite a few soldiers simply fled to escape from their military burden. Multiple transmitted accounts reveal that vigilantes often absconded with their followers during the journey. These people formed multiple militias that later became some of the major participants in the anti-Qin insurgency. From this perspective, the policies of the Qin regime aimed at improving military efficiency ironically resulted in the decentralization of military power and widened the security gap of the empire.

Taken together, the evidence suggests that the Qin Empire was plagued by a security gap emanating from its rapid expansion and from anti-Qin insurgency. While the issue of state security often encompasses different power relations, the situation of the Qin Empire specifically related to the new measures meant to mitigate the state's lack of military power. These policies not only failed to fulfill their objectives but also surged the maintenance cost of social stability and imposed negative effects on the defense capacity of the state. The insufficient military personnel, the imbalance in the army's distribution, and the emergence of local militias led to a serious security gap, which can partially explain the failure of the Qin Empire to tackle the rebellion in the east.

Final Remarks

The collapse of the Qin Empire was like a dam failure. When a dam collapses, people often say that the dam failed because there was too much water. The underlying rationale of this statement, of course, does not simply ascribe the dam's failure to the volume of water. The phrase "too much water" implies that the water exceeded the maximum capacity of that dam, thereby exerting excessive pressure on the dam structure and eventually tearing it apart. In other words, in investigating dam failure, what matters the most is not the water level. Did the designer of the dam miscalculate the necessary capacity? Did the design of the dam fail to account for sudden increases in the amount of water? Was the quality of the dam structure good enough to withstand the pressure exceeding the water level? Did the ecosystem surrounding the dam aggravate the velocity of the water? Did the managers of the dam make the right decision in attempting to mitigate the crisis?

While state collapse is far more complicated than a dam failure, these questions in some sense mirror the concerns of this book. Like the dam failure analogy, the Qin collapse was not caused by the personal desire of the Qin emperors, the state's oppressive ideology, weak territorial control, expansion, or inefficient logistics. This is not to say that these dynamics did not contribute to the final result. Rather, my point is that it is more appropriate to evaluate their collective impact on a larger ground: state power.

Simply put, the Qin Empire fell because its state power failed to sustain its expansion and maintain efficient territorial control. While the reader may find this conclusion a truism, it is not to be taken for granted, at least not in the study of the Qin collapse or, to a large extent, the Qin Empire, whose mighty image has not been challenged until recently. This seemingly simple conclusion serves as another reminder of the fundamental limit of the Qin's power.

Indeed, the statement "the Qin Empire fell because of its state power failed to sustain its expansion" is much more nuanced than it sounds, as *state power* is an umbrella term constituting a broad variety of networks of social relations. Specifically, the Qin regime exhibited severe legitimacy, capacity, and security gaps, which stemmed from the intersection of four sources—ideological, economic, military, and political—of social power. By examining the interrelation of these power networks, I have discerned the collective impact of both idealist and materialist factors in the rapid collapse of the Qin Empire.

More importantly, this book is concerned about the *changes* made by the Qin regime to narrow the state's legitimacy, capacity, and security gaps. While earlier scholarly works either reduce the Qin rulers to inhumane, brainless, and greedy individuals who intended to use only violence to govern their people and had no idea what was happening in their territories, or regard them as adherents of the Zhou cultural tradition and values, I offer a more balanced account. I contend that although the Qin rulers instigated a plethora of social and institutional reforms to soften social tensions and spread social values on the ground, to improve the efficiency of its administrative system, and to forge an ideal social order and a uniform empire, most of these well-intended, potentially beneficial measures probably engendered bad outcomes. Their ramifications in turn aggravated the legitimacy, capacity, and security gaps of the empire.

Now let us return to the question I raised at the beginning of chapter 3: Why did the Qin Empire fail to contain a small-scale revolt before it grew and became a disaster? Taking the discussions in this book into consideration, I argue that the military disaster of the Qin Empire possibly emanated from the interplay of these three gaps. The legitimacy gap generated chronic social tensions in the eastern and southern territories of the empire and turned them into a hotbed of rebellion. The capacity gap manifesting in the misfunction of local governments hindered information transmission across the empire and inhibited timely responses and the suppression of small-scale social unrest. The security gap worsened by the sociopolitical and military reforms undermined the empire's proficiency in organizing defense against the rebels. The military failure of the Qin Empire between 209 and 207 BCE epitomized its inability to govern and its low level of state power.

On account of these facts, it seems that the problems the Qin Empire faced were long-term and structural. The positive impact of efforts designed to narrow the gaps between the actual and necessary state power was often negated by the ramifications of, notably, oppressive state ideology, weak territorial control, misfunction of administrative units, and inefficient logistics. To take this one step further, the Qin regime might have faced the following paradox: Even though its policies and reforms could have in theory improved the governance of the empire, they simultaneously triggered larger legitimacy, capacity, and security gaps. In the end, the combined effect of these factors created a perfect storm that tore the Qin Empire apart.

The Qin Empire collapsed, and this was not without consequences. I have already enumerated the immediate aftermath of this historic event in the introduction, but its far-reaching impact was not limited to the Huaxia ecumene. The collapse of ancient empires such as that of the

Qin often profoundly affected contemporaneous interstate politics. One of its short-term implications would be that it gave room for neighboring political units to expand their territories and form more powerful states. The fall of Qin and the concomitant retreat of its troops from the newly occupied lands at the north bend of the Yellow River not only allowed the formerly defeated Xiongnu to reclaim their lost grasslands, but more importantly, propelled the formation of the first nomadic empire in the eastern Eurasian Steppe. In a similar vein, the power vacuum in the Yue region after the disintegration of the Qin central authorities gave rise to the establishment of the Nanyue 南越 kingdom, which was founded by a Qin official called Zhao Tuo 趙佗 from the north.

In the long run, the collapse of complex organizations like empires often formed the collective memory not only of those who personally experienced such events but also of later people. Often such events would have stimulated vibrant discussions, reflections, and critiques in the generations to come. Gradually, historical details would be forgotten and what people remembered was but a few reduced tropes. As a trope, the "Qin collapse" has been perceived as the dramatic breakdown of a polity flawed by the poor governance of its tyrannical, incompetent rulers. Such an image was mostly constructed by the early Western Han thinkers and their followers, who often adopted the "Qin collapse" as a negative example when debating contemporaneous political and social issues. Despite the nuanced differences among the discourses of these thinkers, the seeming repetition of the "Qin collapse" trope strengthened the stereotypical image of the Qin Empire. In the end, the symbolized trope of "Qin collapse" was transformed into the long-term cultural memory, the absolute past shared by the whole East Asia, which was under strong Sinitic influences. This whole dialectic will be the subject of future research.

Notes

Introduction

1. Patricia A. McAnany and Norman Yoffee, "Why We Question Collapse and Study Human Resilience, Ecological Vulnerability, and the Aftermath of Empire," in *Questioning Collapse: Human Resilience, Ecological Vulnerability, and the Aftermath of Empire*, ed. Patricia A. McAnany and Norman Yoffee (Cambridge: Cambridge University Press, 2010), 4.

2. For recent reviews of essential theories, models, and frameworks in relation to the collapse of ancient states and complex societies, see Guy D. Middleton, *Understanding Collapse: Ancient History and Modern Myths* (Cambridge: Cambridge University Press, 2017), 1–50, especially 22–29.

3. For a summary of recently discovered Qin archaeological evidence, see Zhongguo shehui kexue yuan kaogu yanjiusuo 中國社會科學院考古研究所, ed., *Zhongguo kaoguxue: Qin Han juan* 中國考古學: 秦漢卷 (Beijing: Zhongguo shehui kexue, 2010), 32–173.

4. Such concerns are also expressed in Norman Yoffee, *Myths of the Archaic State: Evolution of the Earliest Cities, States and Civilizations* (Cambridge: Cambridge University Press, 2005), 131–32.

5. There are a few excellent summaries exploring the rise and fall of the Qin from different perspectives. Using transmitted sources and then recently excavated manuscripts from the Shuihudi tomb no. 11, Derk Bodde strives to portray a holistic picture of Qin history, discussing issues such as the founding of the Qin polity, the regime's various social and political reforms from the fourth century BCE onward, and the reasons underlying the triumph and demise of the Qin Empire. Instead of providing a comprehensive account like that of Bodde, Mark Edward Lewis focuses on the roles played by a few Warring States Qin ministers such as Shang Yang and Fan Ju 范睢. Special attention has been given to Shang Yang, whose policies of turning the Qin state into a giant, perpetual military machine account for both the regime's success and its dramatic fall

in 207 BCE. In contrast, Li Feng is concerned more with the material culture and archaeological findings of the Qin, such as its infrastructure projects and artifacts. Interested readers can refer to them to obtain more comprehensive background information. See Derk Bodde, "The State and Empire of Ch'in," in *The Cambridge History of China*, vol. 1, *Ch'in and Han Empires*, ed. Denis Twitchett and Michael Loewe (Cambridge: Cambridge University Press, 1986), 34–45, 81–85; Mark Edward Lewis, *The Early Chinese Empires: Qin and Han* (Cambridge, MA: Belknap Press of Harvard University Press, 2007), 30–74; Li Feng, *Early China: A Social and Cultural History* (Cambridge: Cambridge University Press, 2013), 234–58.

6. For a summary of Shang Yang's reforms and how they transformed the environment in Guanzhong Basin, see Brian Lander, *The King's Harvest: A Political Ecology of China from the First Farmers to the First Empire* (New Haven, CT: Yale University Press, 2021), 133–53.

7. For a detailed account of the Qin's annexation and incorporation of the Sichuan Basin, as well as how this contributed to the Qin unification, see Steven F. Sage, *Ancient Sichuan and the Unification of China* (Albany: State University of New York Press, 1992), 112–152.

8. Robin D.S. Yates, "Reflections on the Foundation of the Chinese Empire in the Light of Newly Discovered Legal and Related Manuscripts," in *Dongya kaoguxue de zaisi: Zhang Guangzhi xiansheng shishi shi zhounian jinian lunwenji* 東亞考古學的再思: 張光直先生逝世十週年紀念論文集, ed. Chen Kwang-tsuu 陳光祖 (Taipei: Academia Sinica, 2013), 483–84.

9. Miyake Kiyoshi, "The Military History of Qin and the Composition of Its Expeditionary Forces," trans. Yao Zhuming, *Bamboo and Silk* 1 (2018): 143–46.

10. To avoid confusion, although the Qin polity became a de facto empire roughly a century prior to 221 BCE, this book still applies the year 221 BCE as the turning point, thus referring the Qin polity prior to 221 BCE as the "Qin state" or "preimperial period" and that after 221 BCE as the "Qin Empire" or "imperial era."

11. For the changes that the Qin rulers made in their appellations during the Warring States period and the political implications of the title "Huangdi," see Sun Wenbo 孫聞博, *Chubing tianxia: Qin junzhu jiquan yanjiu* 初併天下: 秦君主集權研究 (Xi'an: Xibei daxue, 2021), chapter 3, especially 138–47.

12. *Shiji* 史記 (Beijing: Zhonghua, 2014), 6.303–8, 326–27. For the instrumental role of the standardization of measurements, infrastructure projects, and ritual ceremonies in facilitating the communication between the Qin Empire and the general populace, see Charles Sanft, *Communication and Cooperation in Early Imperial China: Publicizing the Qin Dynasty* (Albany: State University of New York Press, 2014), 57–121. One nonetheless should not overestimate the Qin's capability in empire-wide implementation of the new system of standardization. As Summy Li notes, "diverse systems are only to be expected" regarding

the measurement system after the Qin conquest. See Kin Sum (Sammy) Li, "To Rule by Manufacture: Measurement Regulation and Metal Weight Production in the Qin Empire," *T'oung Pao* 103 (2017): 31.

13. Zhou Zhenhe 周振鶴, Li Xiaojie 李曉傑, and Zhang Li 張莉, *Zhongguo xingzhengquhua tongshi: Qin Han juan* 中國行政區劃通史: 秦漢卷 (Shanghai: Fudan daxue, 2017), vol. 1, 12. For the distribution of major spatial units established by the Qin Empire see map I.1.

14. For summaries of government organizations in the Qin local administrative units, see You Yifei 游逸飛, *Zhizao "difang zhengfu": Zhanguo zhi Hanchu junzhi xin kao* 製造「地方政府」: 戰國至漢初郡制新考 (Taipei: Guoli taiwan daxue, 2021), chapter 5; Wu Fangji 吳方基, *Xinchu Qinjian yu Qindai xianji zhengwu yunxing jizhi yanjiu* 新出秦簡與秦代縣級政務運行機制研究 (Beijing: Zhonghua, 2021), chapter 1.

15. Nakayama Shigeru 仲山茂, "Shin Kan jidai no 'kan' to 'so': Ken no bukyoku soshiki" 秦漢時代の「官」と「曹」: 県の部局組織, *Tōyō gakuhō* 82, no. 4: 35–65; Guo Hongbo 郭洪伯, "Baiguan yu zhucao: Qin Han jiceng jigou de bumen shezhi" 稗官與諸曹—秦漢基層機構的部門設置, *Jianbo yanjiu* 簡帛研究 2013 (Guilin: Guangxi shifan daxue, 2014), 101–27.

16. Lai Ming Chiu 黎明釗 and Tong Chun Fung 唐俊峰, "Liye Qinjian suojian Qindai xian guan, cao zuzhi de zhineng fenye yu xingzheng hudong—yi ji, ke wei zhongxin" 里耶秦簡所見秦代縣官、曹組織的職能分野與行政互動——以計、課為中心 (revised version), in *Liye Qinjian yanjiu lunwen xuanji* 里耶秦簡研究論文選集, ed. Liye Qinjian bowuguan 里耶秦簡博物館 (Shanghai: Zhongxi, 2021), 455–56.

17. Aoki Shunsuke 青木俊介, "Riya Shinkan ni mieru ken no bukyoku soshiki ni tsuite" 里耶秦簡に見える県の部局組織について, *Chūgoku shutsudo shiryō kenkyū* 中國出土資料研究 9 (2005): 107–9.

18. Chun Fung Tong, "The Construction of Territories in the Qin Empire," *T'oung Pao* 107 (2021): 509–54.

19. This fact is keenly observed by the celebrated Qing 清 (1644–1912 CE) historian Zhao Yi 趙翼 by means of the composition of core members of the faction of Liu Bang, the founder of the Western Han dynasty; see *Nianershi zhaji jiaozheng* 廿二史札記校證, punctuated and edited by Wang Shumin 王樹民 (Beijing: Zhonghua, 2013), 36–37. For more on this issue, see also Jack L. Dull, "Anti-Qin Rebels: No Peasant Leaders Here," *Modern China* 9, no. 3 (1983): 285–318.

20. *Shiji*, 48.2371.

21. Norman Yoffee, "Orienting Collapse," in *The Collapse of Ancient States and Civilizations*, ed. Norman Yoffee and George L. Cowgill (Tucson: University of Arizona Press, 1988), 14.

22. George L. Cowgill, "Onward and Upward with Collapse," in *The Collapse of Ancient States and Civilizations*, 255–56; Joseph Tainter, *The Collapse of Complex Societies* (Cambridge: Cambridge University Press, 1988), 39–42.

23. McAnany and Yoffee, "Why We Question Collapse and Study Human Resilience, Ecological Vulnerability, and the Aftermath of Empire," 10–11.

24. Tang Xiaofeng 唐曉峰, "The Evolution of Imperial Urban Form in Western Han Chang'an," in *Chang'an 26 BCE: An Augustan Age in China*, ed. Michael Nylan and Griet Vankeerberghen (Seattle: University of Washington Press, 2015), 55–59.

25. Tang, "The Evolution of Imperial Urban Form in Western Han Chang'an," 60–64.

26. Shaanxi sheng kaogu yanjiusuo 陝西省考古研究所, *Qin du Xianyang kaogu baogao* 秦都咸陽考古報告 (Beijing: Kexue, 2004), 721.

27. Colin Renfrew lists "abandonment of palaces and central storage facilities" and "settlement shift and population decline" among the general features of system collapse; see Renfrew, *Approaches to Social Archaeology* (Cambridge, MA: Harvard University Press, 1984), 368.

28. Gideon Shelach and Yuri Pines, "Secondary State Formation and the Development of Local Identity: Change and Continuity in the State of Qin (770–221 B.C.)," in *Archaeology of Asia*, ed. Miriam T. Stark (Malden, MA: Blackwell, 2006), 217–19.

29. Martin Kern, *The Stele Inscriptions of Ch'in Shih-huang: Text and Ritual in Early Chinese Imperial Representation* (New Haven, CT: American Oriental Society, 2000), 155–56.

30. Edwin G. Pulleyblank, "The Roman Empire as Known to Han China," *Journal of the American Oriental Society* 119, no. 1 (1999): 71.

31. For example, the People's Republic of China still uses cultural designations such as "Han ethnicity" (Han zu 漢族) and "Han people" (Han ren 漢人) as official ethnicities to differentiate such groups from other "non-Han" ethnics residing within its claimed territories.

32. A similar phenomenon also emerged after the Persian conquest of Babylonia in the six century BCE; see Yoffee, *Myths of the Archaic State*, 154–60.

33. The conventional English translation of *Fajia*—"Legalism"—is problematic. In full awareness of the controversies surrounding the terms *Legalism*, *Legalist*, and the like, I do not completely abandon these terms for the sake of convenience; however, their application is restrained. The reader is reminded that under the current context, they primarily designate the philosophical discourses of Shang Yang and Han Fei, and less to Shen Dao, Shen Buhai, or others.

34. This traditional view is sometimes partly endorsed by modern scholars. See, for example, Randall Peerenboom, *Law and Morality in Ancient China: The Silk Manuscripts of Huang-Lao* (Albany: State University of New York Press, 1993), 242–48.

35. Kanaya Osamu 金谷治 notes that prominent early Western Han ministers and thinkers were heavily influenced by the so-call "Legalist" ideas. He therefore suggests that the *Huang-Lao* ideology was a variant of the "Legalist"

school; see Kanaya, *Shin Kan shisōshi kenkyū* 秦漢思想史研究 (Tōkyō: Heirakuji, 1992), 64–102.

36. For details of this transition, see Maxim Korolkov, "Fiscal Transformation during the Formative Period of Ancient Chinese Empire (Late Fourth to First Century BCE)," in *Ancient Taxation: The Mechanics of Extraction in Comparative Perspective*, ed. Jonathan Valk and Irene Soto Marín (New York: New York University Press, 2021), 232–43.

37. Miyake Kiyoshi 宮宅潔, *Chūgoku kodai keiseishi no kenkyū* 中国古代刑制史の研究 (Kyoto: Kyōto daigaku, 2011), 153–55.

38. For the jurisdiction of regional kingdoms in the early Western Han period, see Li Kaiyuan 李開元, *Han diguo de jianli yu Liu Bang jituan: Jungong shouyi jieceng yanjiu (zengding ban)* 漢帝國的建立與劉邦集團: 軍功受益階層研究 (增訂版) (Beijing: Sanlian, 2023), 87–94; Chen Suzhen 陳蘇鎮, *Liang Han Weijinnanbeichao shi tanyou* 兩漢魏晉南北朝史探幽 (Beijing: Peking daxue, 2013), 139–56.

39. The term *Nei Shi* can represent both the administrative region itself and the title of the chief administrator of this region. To avoid confusion, I call the region "Metropolitan Area" and its chief administrator the "Metropolitan Scribe."

40. On the administrative geography during the early years of Emperor Gaozu's reign, see Zhou, Li, and Zhang, *Zhongguo xingzhengquhua tongshi*, vol. 1, 121–26.

41. For the development of political system during the early Western Han period, see Li Feng, *Early China*, 260–64; Li Kaiyuan, *Han diguo de jianli yu Liu Bang jituan (zengding ban)*, 280–83.

42. For the commonalities between the political system of the Han central government and that of regional kingdoms, see Hans Bielenstein, *The Bureaucracy of Han Times* (Cambridge: Cambridge University Press, 1980), 105–6; Kamada Shigeo 鎌田重雄, *Shin Kan seiji seido no kenkyū* 秦漢政治制度の研究 (Tokyo: Nihon gakujutsu shinkōkai, 1962), 152–59; Kamiya Masakazu 紙屋正和, "Zenkan shokō ōkoku no kansei" 前漢諸侯王国の官制, *Kyushu Daigaku Toyoshi ronshu* 九州大学東洋史論集 3 (1975): 17–26.

43. *Hanshu* 漢書 (Beijing: Zhonghua, 1962), 28a.1543; *Hou Hanshu* 後漢書 (Beijing: Zhonghua, 1965), 40a.1323.

44. Traits of such cultural exchanges could be observed in the material culture of the Qin region as early as the late Warring State period; see Teng Mingyu, "From Vassal State to Empire: An Archaeological Examination of Qin Culture," trans. Susanna Lam, in *Birth of an Empire: The State of Qin Revisited*, ed. Yuri Pines, Gideon Shelach, Lothar von Falkenhausen, and Robin D.S. Yates (Berkeley: University of California Press, 2014), 89–92.

45. In reference to examples of cultural integration and regional variation within Han material culture, see Gideon Shelach, *The Archeology of Early China: From Prehistory to the Han Dynasty* (Cambridge: Cambridge University Press, 2015), 325–36; Teng, "From Vassal State to Empire," 75, 80.

46. Huang Yijun, "Chang'an's Funerary Culture and the Core Han Culture," in *Chang'an 26 BCE*, 156–57.

47. Textual records date the foundation of the Qin state to around 771–770 BCE, after the retreat of the Zhou court to the east. For the early history of and Western Zhou influence on the Qin polity, see Li Feng, *Landscape and Power in Early China: The Crisis and Fall of the Western Zhou, 1045–771 BC* (Cambridge: Cambridge University Press, 2005), 262–78; Lothar von Falkenhausen, *Chinese Society in the Age of Confucius (1000–250 BC): The Archeological Evidence* (Los Angeles: The Cotsen Institute of Archaeology Press, 2006), 233–43, 328–36.

Chapter 1

1. For an outline of some of their propositions, see Anthony J. Barbieri-Low, *The Many Lives of the First Emperor of China* (Seattle: University of Washington Press, 2022), 29–40; Chun Fung Tong, "Framing the Qin Collapse: Redaction and Authorship of the *Shiji* 史記," *Asiatische Studien/Études Asiatiques* 75, no. 4 (2021): 910, 918–22.

2. Yan Zhenyi 閻振益 and Zhong Xia 鐘夏, *Xinshu Jiaozhu* 新書校注 (Beijing: Zhonghua, 2000), 5.183–84.

3. Consider Zhen Dexiu 真德秀, an influential Southern Song (1127–1279 CE) *daoxue* scholar-official who cites verbatim the "Bao Fu" chapter in his celebrated *Daxue yanyi* (大學衍義; *Extended Meaning of the Great Learning*); see *Daxue yanyi*, ed. Zhu Renqiu 朱人求 (Shanghai: Huadong shifan daxue, 2010), 41.671–74.

4. For a summary of the virtue politics see James Hankins, *Virtue Politics: Soulcraft and Statecraft in Renaissance Italy* (Cambridge, MA: Belknap Press of Harvard University Press, 2019), 37–38.

5. Chun Fung Tong, "The Reformation of Social Order in the Qin Empire," *Asia Major*, 3rd ser., 36 no. 1 (2023): 98–134.

6. The translation is modified from *The Grand Scribe's Records*, revised vol. 1, ed. William H. Nienhauser Jr. (Bloomington: Indiana University Press, 2018), 296. Note that similar viewpoints are widely shared by modern scholars. Mark Edward Lewis remarks that "the most insightful discussion of this catastrophe is also the earliest" prior to his summary of Jia Yi's views. He then ascribes the collapse of the Qin to its failure to transform from a military state into a more civilian government, and to wasting the empire's strength on useless military campaigns and external expansions. In a similar vein, Li Kaiyuan even proclaims that no historical evaluation concerning the fall of Qin he has read is better than Jia Yi's "On the Fault of Qin." See Lewis, *The Early Chinese Empires*, 71; Li Kaiyuan, *Qin beng: cong Qin Shihuang dao Liu Bang* 秦崩: 從秦始皇到劉邦 (Taipei: Lianjing, 2010), 395–98.

7. Bodde, "The State and Empire of Ch'in," 85–90; Robin D.S. Yates (Ye Shan 葉山), "Jiedu Liye Qinjian: Qindai difang xingzheng zhidu" 解讀里耶秦簡: 秦代地方行政制度, *Jianbo* 8 (2013): 119.

8. Gideon Shelach, "Collapse or Transformation? Anthropological and Archaeological Perspectives on the Fall of Qin," in *Birth of an Empire*, 113–38.

9. System theorists often assume that complex societies are formed by compartmental yet interdependent systems. These systems are hierarchical and the vulnerability of a system is often considered to be related to the internal connectedness between its subsystems; see Ronald K. Faulseit, "Collapse, Resilience, and Transformation in Complex Societies: Modeling Trends and Understanding Diversity," in *Beyond Collapse: Archaeological Perspectives on Resilience, Revitalization, and Transformation in Complex Societies,* ed. Ronald K. Faulseit (Carbondale: Southern Illinois University Press, 2016), 10.

10. Cowgill, "Onward and Upward with Collapse," 253. Skepticism about system theory is expressed more bluntly by Michael Mann, who entirely refutes the existence of any closed or open social system. Mann affirms that there is no "single bounded society in geographical or social space," and "because there is no system, no totality, there cannot be 'subsystems,' 'dimensions,' or 'levels of such a totality." See Mann, *The Sources of Social Power*, vol. 1: *A History of Power from the Beginning to AD 1760* (Cambridge: Cambridge University Press, 2012), 1.

11. A similar view can also be found in textbooks of Chinese history. See, for example, Harold M. Tanner, *China: A History* (Indianapolis: Hackett, 2009), 87.

12. Yates, "Jiedu Liye Qinjian," 119; Kim Jonghi 金鍾希, "Qin Han difang sifa yunzuo yu guanzhi yanbian: yi guanfu de jiquanhua xianxiang wei zhongxin" 秦漢地方司法運作與官制演變: 以官府的集權化現象為中心 (PhD dissertation, Peking University, 2021), 201–3; Maxim Korolkov, "Empire-Building and Market-Making at the Qin Frontier: Imperial Expansion and Economic Change, 221–207 BCE" (PhD dissertation, Columbia University, 2020), 304.

13. Cowgill, "Onward and Upward with Collapse," 251.

14. The cornerstones of resilience theory are the adaptive cycle and panarchy. An adaptive cycle constitutes four phases: exploitation, conservation, release, and reorganization. Collapse occurs when a system becomes overconnected, rigid, and internally focused and loses its resilience capacity to unexpected external disturbances. This leads to the reorganization of a system in the wake of a drastic, transient release phase. A panarchical structure comprises various nested adaptive cycles of heterogeneous time scales, and there is no hierarchy between large-and-slow and small-and-fast adaptive cycles, each of which can influence the other; see Faulseit, "Collapse, Resilience, and Transformation in Complex Societies," 12–16.

15. Theda Skocpol, *States and Social Revolutions: A Comparative Analysis of France, Russia, and China* (Cambridge: Cambridge University Press, 1979), 26–28.

174 | Notes on Chapter 1

16. Michael Mann, "The Autonomous Power of the State: Its Origins, Mechanisms and Results," *European Journal of Sociology* 25, no. 2 (1984): 187–88.

17. Skocpol, *States and Social Revolutions*, 29–31.

18. Skocpol, *States and Social Revolutions*, 1.

19. Mann, *The Sources of Social Power*, vol. 1, 22–27.

20. Mann, *The Sources of Social Power*, vol. 1, 188. The different rhythms of different sources of power are exemplified in what he calls the first "empire of domination" of Sargon of Akkad, whose empire "depended overwhelmingly on a militaristic organization of both state and economy embodying 'compulsory cooperation,' as defined by Spencer. This led to a further burst of economic development, to a further immanent diffusion of ideological power within the dominant groups, and to the long-term consolidation of the empire and a ruling class." Ibid., 174. This, however, does not mean that every ancient state had to undergo the same process.

21. Mann, *The Sources of Social Power*, vol. 1, 5–6.

22. Mann, *The Sources of Social Power*, vol. 1, 26.

23. Mann, "The Autonomous Power of the State," 188–89.

24. Mann, *The Sources of Social Power*, vol. 1, 26.

25. Mann, *The Sources of Social Power*, vol. 1, 6–8.

26. Dingxin Zhao, *The Confucian-Legalist State: A New Theory of Chinese History* (Oxford: Oxford University Press, 2015), 33–36.

27. Zhao, *The Confucian-Legalist State*, 14–15.

28. Kern, *The Stele Inscriptions of Ch'in Shih-huang*, 188; Yuri Pines, "The Messianic Emperor: A New Look at Qin's Place in China's History," in *Birth of an Empire*, 268–273.

29. Seth Richardson, "Before Things Worked: A 'Low-Power' Model of Early Mesopotamia," in *Ancient States and Infrastructural Power: Europe, Asia, and America*, ed. Clifford Ando and Seth Richardson (Philadelphia: University of Pennsylvania Press, 2017), 18; Seth Richardson, "Early Mesopotamia: The Presumptive State," *Past & Present* 215 (2012): 3–49.

30. Richardson, "Before Things Worked," 19.

31. Joyce Marcus, "The Peaks and Valleys of Ancient States: An Extension of the Dynamic Model," in *Archaic States*, ed. Gary M. Feinman and Joyce Marcus (Santa Fe: School for Advanced Research Press, 1998), 59.

32. Marcus, "The Peaks and Valleys of Ancient States," 94.

33. Tainter, *The Collapse of Complex Societies*, 120–21.

34. Tainter, *The Collapse of Complex Societies*, 124–26.

35. Tainter, *The Collapse of Complex Societies*, 110–18.

36. Mark Elvin, *The Pattern of the Chinese Past: A Social and Economic Interpretation* (Stanford: Stanford University Press, 1973), 18.

37. Elvin, *The Pattern of the Chinese Past*, 19.

38. This point is also raised in Elvin, *The Pattern of the Chinese Past*, 19.

39. Yang Kuan 楊寬, *Zhanguo shi* 戰國史 (Shanghai: Shanghai renmin, 2003), 416–19.

40. Bodde, "The State and Empire of Ch'in," 49–52; Lewis, *The Early Chinese Empires*, 46.

41. Yang, *Zhanguo shi*, 441-49; Yuri Pines, *Envisioning Eternal Empire: Chinese Political Thought of the Warring States Era* (Honolulu: University of Hawaii Press, 2009), 50–53, 220; Pines, "The Messianic Emperor," 259–63.

42. Tong, "The Reformation of Social Order in the Qin Empire," 129–34.

43. Charles T. Call, "Beyond the 'Failed State': Toward Conceptual Alternatives," *European Journal of International Relations* 17, no. 2 (2010): 308.

44. The provision of security connotes the ability of a state to provide infrastructure that is instrumental in enforcing security—for example, the construction of roads to ensure the logistical movement of troops, production of arms, and ability to conscript and mobilize troops. On the other hand, a "security gap" is more about the performance of a military force on the battlefield; that is, its ability to defend or attack enemies of the state, which is not necessarily equal to the ability of provisioning.

45. Call, "Beyond the 'Failed State,'" 306.

46. Call, "Beyond the 'Failed State,'" 307.

47. Call, "Beyond the 'Failed State,'" 306.

48. Call, "Beyond the 'Failed State,'" 306.

49. For an example of such an approach, see Ian Morris, *The Measure of Civilisation: How Social Development Decides the Fate of Nations* (Princeton: Princeton University Press, 2013), 25–52.

50. For an introduction to the archaeological context and contents of the hoard, see Robin D.S. Yates, "The Qin Slips and Boards from Well No. 1, Liye, Hunan: A Brief Introduction to the Qin Qianling County Archives," *Early China* 35 (2013): 291–329. For photos of published Liye manuscripts (strata 5, 6, 8, and 9) see *Liye Qinjian* 里耶秦簡, vol. 1–2, ed. Hunan sheng wenwu kaogu yanjiusuo 湖南省文物考古研究所 (Beijing: Wenwu, 2012, 2018).

51. Wicky W.K. Tse, *The Collapse of China's Later Han Dynasty, 25–220 CE* (Abingdon, UK: Routledge, 2018), 12–13; Andrew Chittick, "Thinking Regionally in Early Medieval Studies: A Manifesto," *Early Medieval China* 26 (2020): 3–18.

Chapter 2

1. The translation is modified from Paul R. Goldin and Elisa Levi Sabattini, *Lu Jia's New Discourses: A Political Manifesto from the Early Han Dynasty* (Leiden: Brill, 2020), 50–51.

2. In the transmitted *Xinyu*, the only personal attack was against the First Emperor of Qin's covetous grab for extravagance and luxury items, which, Lu believed, eventually wrecked norms and principles; see Wang Liqi 王利器, *Xinyu jiaozhu* 新語校注 (Beijing: Zhonghua, 1986), 4.67.

3. Tong, "The Reformation of Social Order in the Qin Empire," 98–134.

4. Mann, *The Sources of Social Power*, vol. 1, 267–70.

5. Mann also points out that the Han dynasty also "developed ruling-class cultural homogeneity," which "centered on the transmission of a predominantly secular culture (Confucianism) through literacy"; see Mann, *The Sources of Social Power*, vol. 1, 270. I suggest that a similar process might have taken place in the imperial Qin period, but was discontinued after the empire's collapse.

6. Regarding how the territorial and institutional consolidation brought about cultural cohesiveness among the population of Warring States polities and "a growing sense of alienation from the people of the neighboring states," as well as how the Qin elites tried to distinguish themselves from the Zhou (Huaxia) world and create a unique Qin cultural identity from fourth century BCE onward, see Yuri Pines, "The Question of Interpretation: Qin History in Light of New Epigraphic Sources," *Early China* 29 (2004): 32–41. For an alternative interpretation of the program by which the Qin distinguished different layers of cultural identities, see Watanabe Hideyuki 渡邉英幸, "Shin no jiko ishiki to tasha ninshiki" 秦の自己意識と他者認識, in *Shin teikoku no tanjō: kodai-shi kenkyū no kurosurōdo* 秦帝国の誕生: 古代史研究のクロスロード, ed. Momiyama Akira 籾山明 and Rōtāru fon Farukenhauzen ロータール・フォン・ファルケンハウゼン (Lothar von Falkenhausen) (Tokyo: Rokuichi, 2020), 33–47.

7. For a more detailed summary of this case, see Ulrich Lau and Thies Staack, *Legal Practice in the Formative Stages of the Chinese Empire: An Annotated Translation of the Exemplary Qin Criminal Cases from the Yuelu Academy Collection* (Leiden: Brill, 2016), 118.

8. Armin Selbitschka, " 'I Write Therefore I Am': Scribes, Literacy, and Identity in Early China," *Harvard Journal of Asiatic Studies* 78, no. 2 (2018): 463–65.

9. For the diminishing status of *shǐ* in policy-making since the Spring and Autumn period (770–481 BCE), see Kai Vogelsang, *Geschichte als Problem: Entstehung, Formen und Funktionen von Geschichtsschreibung im Alten China* (Wiesbaden: Harrassowitz, 2007), 49; Tsang Wing Ma, "Scribes in Early Imperial China" (PhD dissertation, University of California, Santa Barbara, 2017), 42–61.

10. The English translation of *Taishi Ling* is always controversial. Manifold proposals ranging from "Prefect of Grand Astrologer" to "Director of Archives" have been offered and each has its own advantages; for a review of some of the existing translations, see Stephen Durrant, Wai-yee Li, Michael Nylan, and Hans van Ess, *The Letter to Ren An and Sima Qian's Legacy* (Seattle: University of Washington Press, 2018), 18–21. In the Qin and Han legal texts, the major

tasks of Taishi Ling include supervising the training of hereditary scribal trainees and assigning suitable Scribes to different offices. Neither Prefect of Grand Astrologer nor Director of Archives can fully convey this aspect of the Taishi Ling's duties. Here I render the title "Prefect of Grand Scribe," which, despite not being an ideal term, seems generic enough to encompass the heterogenous duties of Taishi Ling.

11. The only high-grading Scribe in the Qin and early Han governments was Nei Shi (Metropolitan Scribe), who was a 2,000-bushel—then the highest salary grade—official. While the title Yu Shi Dafu (Chief Prosecutor) also carried the word "*shǐ*," a subfix "Dafu" was appended.

12. Vogelsang, *Geschichte als Problem*, 84.

13. Transmitted sources claim that Huwu Jing 胡毋敬, a Grand Scribe of the Qin dynasty, compiled a scribal primer called *Boxue* 博學, which was part of the official scribal curriculum. On the other hand, Christopher Foster suggests that the Qin regime might have tested scribal candidates by means of such texts as the *Wei li zhi dao* 為吏之道; see Ma, "Scribes in Early Imperial China," 66; Christopher J. Foster, "Study of the *Cang Jie pian*: Past and Present" (PhD dissertation, Harvard University, 2017), 239–48. To date, no contemporaneous Qin evidence can attest to the use of scribal primers or other types of texts in the scribal training during the Qin era.

14. For the types of documents that military officers and soldiers were required to prepare, see Michael Loewe, *Records of Han Administration*, vol. 1 (London: RoutledgeCurzon, 2002), 28–39. Regarding the level of literacy attained by soldiers and military officers, see Robin D.S. Yates, "Soldiers, Scribes, and Women: Literacy among the Lower Orders in Early China," in *Writing and Literacy in Early China*, ed. Li Feng and David Prager Branner (Seattle: University of Washington Press, 2012), 360–64; Enno Giele (Ji Annuo 紀安諾), "Handai biansai beiyong shuxie cailiao ji qi shehui shi yiyi" 漢代邊塞備用書寫材料及其社會史意義, *Jianbo* 2 (2007): 475–500.

15. Chen Yingjie 陳英傑, "Shi, li, shi, shi fenhua shidai cengci kao" 史、吏、事、使分化時代層次考, *Zhongguo wenzi* 中國文字 40 (2014): 174–77.

16. Li Feng, *Bureaucracy and the State in Early China* (Cambridge: Cambridge University Press, 2008), 55–58.

17. In reference to this process, see Yan Buke 閻步克, *Cong jue benwei dao guan benwei: Qin Han guanliao pinwei jiegou yanjiu (zengding ben)* 從爵本位到官本位: 秦漢官僚品位結構研究 (增訂本) (Beijing: Shenghuo, dushu, xinzhi sanlian, 2017), 48–55.

18. Vogelsang, *Geschichte als Problem*, 80–83.

19. For the latter point see Robin D.S. Yates, "The Empire of the Scribes," in *Birth of an Empire*, 145.

20. Anthony J. Barbieri-Low and Robin D.S. Yates, *Law, State, and Society in Early Imperial China: A Study with Critical Edition and Translation of the Legal*

Texts from Zhangjiashan Tomb no. 247 (hereafter cited as *LSS*) (Leiden: Brill, 2015), 1087–89.

21. For the former usage, see the term "臣史," in which "史" should connote the notion of "literate" and the binomen "臣史" likely refers to a type of literate slaves; see *Yuelushuyuan cang Qinjian (yi–san) shiwen xiudingben* 嶽麓書院藏秦簡 (壹–叁) 釋文修訂本, ed. Chen Songchang 陳松長 (Shanghai: Shanghai cishu, 2018), 146, slip 65; *Yuelushuyuan cang Qinjian* 嶽麓書院藏秦簡 (hereafter cited as *Yuelu*), vol. 5, ed. Chen Songchang (Shanghai: Shanghai cishu, 2017), 200–1, slips 308, 310, 311.

22. *Yuelu*, vol. 4, ed. Chen Songchang (Shanghai: Shanghai cishu, 2015), 154, slip 261.

23. The editors originally put slips 250–51 after this slip (249). This arrangement, however, hardly makes sense, as slips 250–51 stipulate excuses that existing officials make to be dismissed from their offices and are not tallied with the contents of slip 249. I suspect that slip 251 was part of the Grand Scribe's memorial and should therefore be preceded by slip 249.

24. *Yuelu*, vol. 6, ed. Chen Songchang (Shanghai: Shanghai cishu, 2020), 178–80, slips 248–55. For an alternative English translation of the latter part of this ordinance, see Robin D.S. Yates, "Dated Legislation in the Late-Qin State and Early Empire," *Asia Major*, 3rd ser., 35, no. 1 (2022): 159–60.

25. Lu Jialiang 魯家亮, "Liye Qinjian suojian 'xiaoshi' chuyi" 里耶秦簡所見「小史」芻議, in *Chutu wenxian de shijie: di liu jie chutu wenxian qingnian xuezhe luntan lunwenji* 出土文獻的世界: 第六屆出土文獻青年學者論壇論文集, ed. Chutu wenxian yu Zhongguo gudai wenming yanjiu xietong chuangxin zhongxin Zhongguo renmin daxue fenzhongxin 出土文獻與中國古代文明研究協同創新中心中國人民大學分中心 (Shanghai: Zhongxi, 2018), 99–101.

26. Kai Vogelsang also makes a similar observation using Western Han sources; see Vogelsang, *Geschichte als Problem*, 87. Note that a statute from the "Miscellaneous Regulations of Metropolitan Scribe" (Nei Shi Za 內史雜) in the Shuihudi Qin legal manuscripts stipulates that "a *xia li* who manages to write cannot venture into undertaking a scribe's duties" (下吏能書者，毋敢從史之事). Whereas this seems to suggest that low-level officials could not have served as scribes, other appearances of *xia li* in the Shuihudi corpus always list the term alongside hard laborers such as bondservants, wall-builders, and robber-guards. This indicates that *xia li* were not officials (at least not normal ones) but a type of convict. Hulsewé renders the term as "persons in detention," which is more appropriate; see A.F.P. Hulsewé, *Remnants of Ch'in Law: An Annotated Translation of the Ch'in Legal and Administrative Rules of the 3rd century B.C., Discovered in Yun-meng Prefecture, Hu-pei Province, in 1975* (Leiden: E.J. Brill, 1985), 61, A58, n. 1; 88, A102.

27. For a comparison between the three extant textual witnesses, see *Peking daxue cang Qin jiandu* 北京大學藏秦簡牘, ed. Peking daxue chutu wenx-

ian yu gudai wenming yanjiusuo 北京大學出土文獻與古代文明研究所 (Shanghai: Shanghai guji, 2023), 52–58.

28. Lau and Staack, *Legal Practice in the Formative Stages of the Chinese Empire*, 13–14; *Peking daxue cang Qin jiandu*, 1086–87.

29. For more detailed summaries of its content, see Daniel S. Sou, "Shaping Qin Local Officials: Exploring the System of Values and Responsibilities Presented in the Excavated Qin Tomb Bamboo Slips," *Monumenta Serica* 61, no. 1 (2013): 11–30.

30. For an analysis of the nonlinear feature of the *Way of Making a Good Official*'s textual form, see Matthias L. Richter, *The Embodied Text: Establishing Textual Identity in Early Chinese Manuscripts* (Leiden: Brill, 2013), 175–82.

31. The term "black-headed one" was used by the imperial Qin regime to replace "commoner" (*min* 民). See *Shiji*, 6.307.

32. The above reading is indebted to Chen Wei, "'Wei li zhi guan ji qianshou' 1531, 0072 hao jian shi du" 《為吏治官及黔首》1531、0072號簡試讀, Jianbowang, January 20, 2010.

33. Chen Kanli 陳侃理, "Shuihudi Qinjian 'Wei li zhi dao' ying gengming 'Yu shu': jian tan 'Yu shu' mingyi ji Qinjian zhong leisi wenxian di xingzhi" 睡虎地秦簡「為吏之道」應更名「語書」：兼談「語書」名義及秦簡中類似文獻的性質, *Chutu wenxian* 出土文獻 6 (2015): 256.

34. Chen, "Shuihudi Qinjian 'Wei li zhi dao' ying gengming 'Yu shu,'" 256.

35. Daniel S. Sou also posits a similar idea in his "Shaping Qin Local Officials," 5.

36. For the connection between officials' administrative tasks and arithmetic proficiency as well as hemerological and anatomical knowledge, see Robin D.S. Yates, "State Control of Bureaucrats under the Qin: Techniques and Procedures," *Early China* 20 (1995): 339–42; "The Empire of the Scribes," 147.

37. In fact, Western Han sources do use the term *daobi li* to describe Qin officials; see *Shiji*, 53.2452; 102.2330.

38. Tsang Wing Ma, "Between the State and Their Superiors: The Anxiety of Low-Ranked Scribes in the Qin and Han Bureaucracies," *Asia Major*, 3rd ser., 33 no. 2 (2020): 25–26.

39. Tsang Wing Ma, "Scribe, Assistant, and the Materiality of Administrative Documents in Qin–Early Han China: Excavated Evidence from Liye, Shuihudi, and Zhangjiashan," *T'oung Pao* 103, no. 4–5 (2017): 305.

40. Ma, "Scribe, Assistant, and the Materiality of Administrative Documents in Qin–Early Han China," 301–13.

41. In the present context, the term *junzi* should be understood as a denomination for low-level officials or holders of certain low meritorious rank; see Li Yuening 李玥凝, "Qinjian 'junzi' shenfen zaitan" 秦簡「君子」身份再探, *Guwenzi yanjiu* 古文字研究 33 (2020): 410; Saitō Ken 齋藤賢, "Mibun koshō to shite no 'kunshi'" 身分呼稱としての「君子」, in *Gakuroku Shoin shozō kan Shin*

ritsuryō (ichi) *yakuchū* 嶽麓書院所藏簡《秦律令（壹）》譯注, ed. Miyake Kiyoshi 宮宅潔 (Tokyo: Kyūko, 2023), 400–3.

42. *Yuelu*, vol. 4, 137–38, slips 210–11.

43. Ma, "Scribe, Assistant, and the Materiality of Administrative Documents in Qin–Early Han China," 304–5. Note that by legal definition, *xin fu* should have referred to persons over eighteen years old; see Ling Wenchao 凌文超, "Qindai fuji biaozhun xin kao: jian lun zizhan nian yu nianling jisuan" 秦代傅籍標準新考: 兼論自占年與年齡計算, *Wenshi* 128 (2019): 14.

44. *Liye Qin jiandu jiaoshi* 里耶秦簡牘校釋 (hereafter cited as *LQJJ*), vol. 2, ed. Chen Wei 陳偉 (Wuhan: Wuhan daxue, 2018), 167–68, tablet 9-633.

45. In addition, there are Commander Assistant (Wei Zuo 尉佐) to Commander Scribe (Wei Shi 尉史), Reassigned Assistant (Jun Zuo 均佐) to Reassigned Scribe (Jun Shi 均史); see Ma, "Scribe, Assistant, and the Materiality of Administrative Documents in Qin-Early Han China," 320–22.

46. *Shiji*, 53.2445; 54.2455.

47. There is no direct evidence regarding the ages of Xiao He and Cao Can. Nevertheless, since Xiao and Cao were of the same generation as Liu Ji, who was around thirty years old when the Qin Empire was founded, their ages should be similar. For a discussion of Liu Ji's age, see the first section of chapter 3.

48. *LQJJ*, vol. 1, 342, tablet 8-1514.

49. For the career path of Hun, see Lu Jialiang, "Liye Qinjian suojian Qin qianling xian liyuan de goucheng yu laiyuan" 里耶秦簡所見秦遷陵縣吏員的構成與來源, *Chutu wenxian* 13 (2018): 216–18.

50. Zhao Yan 趙岩 also uncovers four other possible examples of promotion from Assistant Director to Scribe Director. These officials are Shang 尚, Chao 朝, Han 悍, and Hua 華; see Zhao, "Qin lingzuo kao" 秦令佐考, *Ludong daxue xuebao (zhexue shehuikexue ban)* 魯東大學學報 (哲學社會科學版) 31, no. 1 (2014): 68–69.

51. Hunan sheng wenwu kaogu yanjiusuo 湖南省文物考古研究所 and Yiyang shi wenwuchu 益陽市文物處, "Hunan Yiyang Tuzishan yizhi jiuhao jing fajue baogao" 湖南益陽兔子山遺址九號井發掘報告, *Hunan kaogu jikan* 湖南考古輯刊, vol. 12 (Beijing: Kexue, 2016), 133.

52. In addition to manuscripts, the well also yielded 201 blank slips from strata 5, 7, and 8; see Hunan sheng wenwu kaogu yanjiusuo and Yiyang shi wenwuchu, "Hunan Yiyang Tuzishan yizhi jiuhao jing fajue baogao," 148.

53. For the Chu characteristics of the formulaic language of these slips, see Hirose Kunio 廣瀬薫雄, "Yiyang Tuzishan J9⑦chutu jiandu chutan" 益陽兔子山J9⑦出土簡牘初探, in Hirose, *Jianbo yanjiu lunji* 簡帛研究論集 (Shanghai: Shanghai guji, 2019), 141–53.

54. Hunan sheng wenwu kaogu yanjiusuo and Yiyang shi wenwuchu, "Hunan Yiyang Tuzishan yizhi jiuhao jing fajue baogao," 148–49.

55. Tian Wei 田煒, "Cong Qin 'shutong wenzi' de jiaodu kan Qinyin shidai de huafen he Qin Chu zhi ji guwen guanyin de panding" 從秦「書同文字」的角

度看秦印時代的劃分和秦楚之際古文官印的判定, in Tian, *Tian Wei yingao* 田煒印稿 (Shanghai: Zhongxi, 2018), 105–7. Tian's proposal is endorsed and elaborated by Hirose, "Yiyang Tuzishan J9⑦chutu jiandu chutan," 137–55.

56. Li Songru 李松儒, "Yiyang Tuzishan jiuhao jing jiandu zhong Chu Qin guodu ziti tanxi" 益陽兔子山九號井簡牘中楚秦過渡字體探析, *Zhongguo shufa* 中國書法 6 (2019): 54–56.

57. Most extant hollow bricks were found at sites and in tombs in north China, especially in present-day Shaanxi and Henan provinces; see Yang Chengliang 陽承良, "Yiyang Tuzishan yizhi chutu daxing kongxinzhuan xiangguan wenti chuyi" 益陽兔子山遺址出土大型空心磚相關問題芻議, *Hunan sheng bowuguan guankan* 湖南省博物館館刊, vol. 14 (Changsha: Yuelu, 2018), 350–51.

58. Hunan sheng wenwu kaogu yanjiusuo and Yiyang shi wenwuchu, "Hunan Yiyang Tuzishan yizhi jiuhao jing fajue baogao," 151.

59. Hunan sheng wenwu kaogu yanjiusuo and Yiyang shi wenwuchu, "Hunan Yiyang Tuzishan yizhi jiuhao jing fajue baogao," 131–32. I thank Jeanette Werning for pointing this detail out to me.

60. Although one cannot deny the possibility that strata seven and eight date to the Qin and Chu periods, respectively, it seems difficult to substantiate this claim based on the published material.

61. For the common anxieties and struggles of Qin and Han officials, see Ma, "Between the State and Their Superiors," 25–59.

62. In reference to the impact of low-level local officials on their communities, see Lai Ming Chiu 黎明釗, *Fucou yu zhixu: Han diguo difang shehui yanjiu* 輻輳與秩序: 漢帝國地方社會研究 (Hong Kong: The Chinese University Press, 2013), 383–400.

63. Donald Harper has entertained a similar definition of the term "elite," which he characterizes as a social status "associated with literacy and access to positions of authority in government. . . . Highly literate elite readers knew the technical literature of specialists on astrology, divination, or medicine, and they knew the popular hemerological literature." See Harper, "Daybooks in the Context of Manuscript Culture and Popular Culture Studies," in *Books of Fate and Popular Culture in Early China: The Daybook Manuscripts of the Warring States, Qin, and Han*, ed. Donald Harper and Marc Kalinowski (Leiden: Brill, 2017), 103.

64. The transmitted texts record the name of this commandery as "Sishui" 泗水. As various researchers have pointed out, this could be a transmission error of "Sichuan"; see Zhou, Li, and Zhang, *Zhongguo xingzhengquhua tongshi*, vol. 1, 35.

65. *Shiji*, 53.2446.

66. Robin D.S. Yates, "Cosmos, Central Authority, and Communities in the Early Chinese Empire," in *Empires: Perspectives from Archaeology and History*, ed. Susan E. Alcock, Terence N. D'Altroy, Kathleen D. Morrison, and Carla M. Sinopoli (Cambridge: Cambridge University Press, 2002), 351–53.

67. See *LQJJ*, vol. 1, 8, 10–11, slips 5-5, 5-7, 5-8, 5-9.

68. Zheng Wei 鄭威, "Liye bufen she Chu jiandu jiexi" 里耶部分涉楚簡牘解析, in *Chu wenhua yanjiu lunji* 楚文化研究論集, vol. 11, ed. Chu wenhua yanjiuhui 楚文化研究會, 345–46 (Shanghai: Shanghai guji, 2015).

69. *LQJJ*, vol. 2, 474, slip 9-2330.

70. For a list of the corresponding Chu and Qin month names, see Marc Kalinowski, "Hemerology and Prediction in the Daybooks: Ideas and Practices," in *Books of Fate and Popular Culture in Early China*, 156, Table 4.7.

71. *Yuelu*, vol. 7, ed. Chen Songchang (Shanghai: Shanghai cishu, 2022), 98, slips 111–13.

72. The term *Qinzhong* 秦中 literally means "within the Qin." During the Qin and Han dynasties, it was one of the synonyms for the Metropolitan Area, which was the heartland of the Qin polity.

73. *Shiji*, 7.396–97; the translation is modified from *The Grand Scribe's Records*, vol. 1, 327.

74. *Shiji*, 7.396–97.

75. As Wicky Tse notes, although the "Qiang" 羌 identity was initially an exonym adopted by the Han people, the protracted conflicts between the "Qiang" and Han might have caused the emergence of a common "Qiang" awareness and encouraged the "Qiang" people to define their differences from the Han to cement solidarity against their common enemy: the Eastern Han government; see Tse, *The Collapse of China's Later Han Dynasty, 25–220 CE*, 102.

76. Hunan sheng wenwu kaogu yanjiusuo, *Liye fajue baogao* 里耶發掘報告 (Changsha: Yuelu, 2007), 203–5, K1/25/50, K2/23, K4, K13/48, K17, K27.

77. With regard to the phrase "bugeng of Ji region," Hsing I-tien argues that it was the rank that Qin rulers awarded the Chu inhabitants in reference to their original Chu rank so as to gain the support of these new subjects. On the other hand, Zhang Rongqiang believes that these ranks were given to the Chu inhabitants because of their military achievements, or as part of an appeasement policy; see Hsing, "Longshan Liye Qin Qianling xiancheng yizhi chutu mou xiang Nanyang li hujijian shitan" 龍山里耶秦遷陵縣城遺址出土某鄉南陽里戶籍簡試探, Jianbowang, November 6, 2007; Zhang Rongqian 張榮強, *Han Tang zhangji zhidu yanjiu* 漢唐籍帳制度研究 (Beijing: Shangwu, 2010), 28–29.

78. *LQJJ*, vol. 2, 276, slip 9-1205.

79. Zhou, Li, and Zhang, *Zhongguo xingzhengquhua tongshi*, vol. 1, 61.

80. *Shiji*, 95.3234.

81. For a discussion of the regional confrontation in the Qin Empire, see also Zhang Jinguang 張金光, *Qin zhi yanjiu* 秦制研究 (Shanghai: Shanghai guji, 2004), 829–30.

82. Ōkushi Atsuhiro 大櫛敦弘, "En, Sei, Jin wa jitōshi: Shin Kan tōitsu kokka to tōhō chiiki" 燕・齊・荊は地遠し: 秦漢統一国家と東方地域, *Hainan Shigaku* 海南史學 55 (2017): 11–12.

83. *Shiji*, 55.2471–72.

84. *Shiji*, 7.385. For the anti-Qin sentiments among the Chu people, see Tian Yuqing 田餘慶, *Qin Han Wei Jin shi tanwei* 秦漢魏晉史探微 (Beijing: Zhonghua, 2011), 1–29.

85. Yuri Pines contends that both the Chu elites and commoners might have stronger attachement to a Chu cultural identity, whereas the intermediate social group *shi* might subscribe less to one because they often sought employment outside their native states and thus "prioritized the whole over its parts"; see Pines, "Chu Identity as Seen from Its Manuscripts: A Reevaluation," *Journal of Chinese History* 2 (2018): 26.

86. In reference to "immanent morale," Mann suggests that its major function is to intensify "the cohesion, the confidence, and, therefore, the power of an already established social group. Immanent ideology is less dramatically autonomous in its impact, for it largely strengthens whatever is there"; see Mann, *The Sources of Social Power*, vol. 1, 24.

87. Yuri Pines, *The Book of Lord Shang: Apologetics of State Power in Early China* (New York: Columbia University Press, 2017), 67–69.

88. Bodde, "The State and Empire of Ch'in," 50, 74–78; Kern, *The Stele Inscriptions of Ch'in Shih-huang*, 188l.

89. Tong, "The Reformation of Social Order in the Qin Empire," 109–27.

90. Here I follow Chen Wei's gloss of 苟若 (*gouruo*; "careless and rude"); see "*Yuelushuyuan cang Qinjian (wu)* jiaodu (xu si)" 《嶽麓書院藏秦簡〔伍〕》校讀 (續四), Jianbowang, March 31, 2018.

91. *Yuelu*, vol. 5, 133–34, slips 196–98.

92. Here the distinction between the original statute and the amending ordinance is vague. A parallel version in volume six of the Yuelu manuscripts nonetheless indicates that the section after the line "for those who have violated the statute" belongs to the supplementary ordinance; see *Yuelu*, vol. 6, 149–50, slips 194–97. For a comparison and analysis of this ordinance, see Ou Yang 歐揚, "Yuelu Qinjian hushi fushen ling chutan" 嶽麓秦簡戶時復申令初探, unpublished conference paper presented at "Dijiujie chutu wenxian yu falü shi yanjiu guoji xueshu yantao hui" 第九屆出土文獻與法律史研究國際學術研討會, Shanghai: East China University of Political Science and Law, October 11–13, 2019.

93. Case 21 of the *Book of the Submitted Doubtful Cases* enumerates two conditions under which a child would be classified as committing "filial impiety": (1) someone starves his father for three days; (2) someone disobeys his father; see Barbieri-Low and Yates, *LSS*, 1382–85, slips 189–91. Barbieri-Low and Yates suggest that the text might be "a literary story partially based on a real case," which is convincing (ibid., 1378). In this fashion, the legal regulations cited therein should be extracted from actual legal enactments, and "disobeying parents," coupled with mistreatment, cursing or negligence, were all classified as

filial impiety that warranted the death penalty (ibid., 443, n. 160). Although the punishment for "speaking to parents carelessly and rudely" is unclear, given its similarities to "disobeying parents," it may also be classified as unfilial.

94. Hulsewé, *Remnants of Ch'in Law*, 147, D85; 196, E18; Barbieri-Low and Yates, *LSS*, 402–5, slips 35–37; 1228–29, slips 49–50; Yun Jae Seug 尹在碩, "Qin Han lü zhong de buxiao zui susong yu hanyi" 秦漢律中的不孝罪訴訟與含義, in *Qin Han shi luncong* 秦漢史論叢, vol. 11, ed. Zhongguo Qin Han shi yanjiuhui 中國秦漢史研究會 (Changchun: Jilin wenshi, 2008), 318.

95. Xu Shihong 徐世虹, "Qin Han jiandu zhong de buxiao zui susong" 秦漢簡牘中的不孝罪訴訟, *Huadong zhengfa xueyuan xuebao* 華東政法學院學報 46 (2006): 128.

96. For a detailed comparison and discussion of this passage, see Oliver Weingarten, "Delinquent Fathers and Philology: *Lun Yu* 13.18 and Related Texts," *Early China* 37 (2014): 230–37.

97. For the activities and roles of grassroots leaders such as elders and "wandering gallants" (*youxia* 游俠) in the anti-Qin movement, see Moriya Mitsuo 守屋美都雄, *Zhongguo gudai de jiazu yu guojia* 中國古代的家族與國家, trans. Qian Hang 錢杭 and Yang Xiaofen 楊曉芬 (Shanghai: Shanghai guji, 2010), 142–59; Masubuchi Tatsuo 增淵龍夫, *Shinpan Chūgoku kodai no shakai to kokka* 新版 中國古代の社會と國家 (Tokyo: Iwanami, 1996), 77–118.

98. Shimokura Wataru 下倉涉, "Aru josei no kokuhatsu wo megutte: Gakuroku shoin zō Shin Kan 'Shiki kō En an' ni arawaretaru dorei oyobi 'Shagin' 'Ritan'" ある女性の告発をめぐって: 嶽麓書院藏秦簡「識劫婉案」に現れたる奴隸および「舍人」「里單」, *Shirin* 史林 99, no. 1 (2016): 39–80.

99. For the autonomy of grassroots societies and the role of communal leaders in ancient China, see Tu Cheng-sheng 杜正勝, *Bianhu qimin: Chuantong zhengzhi shehui jiegou zhi xingshi* 編戶齊民: 傳統政治社會結構之形式 (Taipei: Lianjing, 1990), 218–28.

100. *Yuelu*, vol. 4, 115–16, slips 142–46.

101. For example, an entry in the "Answers to Questions Concerning Laws" revolves around the meaning of "leaders and stalwarts" (*shuaiao* 率敖), to which the glossary refers as "leaders and stalwarts match the description of the village chief" (率敖當里典謂殹); see *Qin jiandu heji (Shiwen zhushi xiuding ben)* 秦簡牘合集 (釋文注釋修訂本), vol. 1, ed. Chen Wei 陳偉 (Wuhan: Wuhan daxue, 2016), 258, slip 198; Hulsewé, *Remnants of Ch'in Law*, 178, D177.

102. Chen Kanli 陳侃理, "Qin Han lili yu jiceng tongzhi" 秦漢里吏與基層統治, *Lishi yanjiu* 歷史研究 1 (2022): 57–62.

103. Chen, "Qin Han lili yu jiceng tongzhi," 63–65.

104. *Shiji*, 6.341; 8.445 and 459; 48.2366 and 2370. Chen Suzhen, *Chunqiu yu "Han dao": Liang Han zhengzhi yu zhengzhi wenhua yanjiu* 《春秋》與「漢道」: 兩漢政治與政治文化研究 (Beijing: Zhonghua, 2011), 37.

105. *Yuelu*, vol. 5, 150, slips 246–47.

106. *LSS*, 462–63, slips 55–56.

107. Tomiya Itaru 冨谷至, *Qin Han xingfa zhidu yanjiu* 秦漢刑罰制度研究, trans. Chai Shengfang 柴生芳 and Zhu Hengye 朱恒嘩 (Guilin: Guangxi shifan daxue, 2006), 34–37.

108. *LSS*, 500–3, slip 93.

109. In addition, a "Statute on Robbery" from *Statutes and Ordinances of the Second Year* also prescribes that if the judicial officer acted not uprightly by taking a bribe, his punishment should be increased by two degrees. This regulation was even harsher than the Qin prescription for a comparable offense. Given the inheritance of the early Western Han legal system from the preceding dynasty, this discrepancy might have resulted from a later amendment by the Qin rulers.

110. The abovementioned unnamed Qin ordinance comprises another section, which stipulates that if the relatives or acquaintances of a judicial officer took a bribe and successfully convinced the judicial officer to distort the fact in a lawsuit, this officer should be sentenced to the shaving punishment. If the punishment that the judicial officer warranted because of sparing the offender was heavier than shaving, he should instead be sentenced to the more serious punishment; see *Yuelu*, vol. 5, 149–50, slips 244–45.

111. The translation is modified from Ernest Caldwell, *Writing Chinese Laws: The Form and Function of Legal Statutes Found in the Qin Shuihudi Corpus* (Abingdon, UK: Routledge, 2018), 65.

112. *Qin jiandu heji (Shiwen zhushi xiuding ben)*, vol. 1, 29, slips 5–8.

113. Caldwell, *Writing Chinese Laws*, 65-66.

114. Zhang Menghan 張夢晗, "'Xindi li' yu 'Wei li zhi dao': yi chutu Qinjian wei zhongxin de kaocha" 「新地吏」與「為吏之道」：以出土秦簡為中心的考察, *Zhongguo shi yanjiu* 中國史研究 3 (2017): 69.

115. Chen Hong 陳洪, *Qin wenhua zhi kaoguxue yanjiu* 秦文化之考古學研究 (Beijing: Kexue, 2016), 231–32, 241–42.

116. Keum Jaewon 琴載元, "Fan Qin zhanzheng shiqi Nanjun diqu de zhengzhi dongtai yu wenhua tezheng: zailun 'wang Qin bi Chu' xingshi de juti cengmian" 反秦戰爭時期南郡地區的政治動態與文化特徵：再論「亡秦必楚」形勢的具體層面, *Jiandu xue yanjiu* 簡牘學研究 5 (2014): 131–39.

117. *Qin jiandu heji (Shiwen zhushi xiuding ben)*, vol. 1, 599, tablet 6. For a discussion of this private letter, see Keum Jaewon, "Qindai Nanjun bianhu min de Qin, Chu shenfen rentong wenti" 秦代南郡編戶民的秦、楚身份認同問題, *Jianbo yanjiu 2015 Qiudong juan* 簡帛研究 2015 秋冬卷 (Guilin: Guangxi shifan daxue, 2015), 78–92. Note that Chen Hong suggests that the occupant of tomb no. 4 as well as those of the adjacent tombs 5 and 6 were Qin migrants; see Chen, *Qin wenhua zhi kaoguxue yanjiu*, 238.

118. Keum Jaewon, "Fan Qin zhanzheng shiqi Nanjun diqu de zhengzhi dongtai yu wenhua tezheng," 132.

119. Hubei sheng wenwu kaogu yanjiuyuan 湖北省文物考古研究院 and Yunmeng xian bowuguan 雲夢縣博物館, "Hubei Yunmeng xian Zhengjiahu mudi 2021 nian fajue jianbao" 湖北雲夢縣鄭家湖墓地2021年發掘簡報, *Kaogu* 2 (2022): 20.

120. For the text see Li Tianhong 李天虹, Xiong Jiahui 熊佳暉, Cai Dan 蔡丹, and Luo Yunbing 羅運兵. "Hubei Yunmeng Zhengjiahu mudi M274 chutu 'jianchen Tu xi wen Qinwang' gu" 湖北雲夢鄭家湖墓地M274出土「賤臣繇西問秦王」觚, *Wenwu* 3 (2022): 65–66.

121. *Shiji* 6.325–26.

122. While some scholars believe that Teng was a Hann native who surrendered to Qin, this view is hardly tenable. For a discussion of this issue, see Xin Deyong 辛德勇, *Jiushi yude wenbian* 舊史輿地文編 (Shanghai: Zhongxi, 2015), 154, n. 2.

123. For a detailed summary of the case, see Lau and Staack, *Legal Practice in the Formative Stages of the Chinese Empire*, 276. Note that I do not stick to their reading of the quoted sentence.

124. The following discussion of Tui's case is indebted to You, *Zhizao "difang zhengfu,"* 207–10.

125. *LSS*, 1342–43, slip 147.

126. For an improved transcription of this case, see *Yuelushuyuan cang Qinjian (yi–san) shiwen xiudingben*, 167–69. Lau and Staack have provided a translation of the case based on an earlier transcription; see *Legal Practice in the Formative Stages of the Chinese Empire*, 303–5.

127. According to the report, Tui's case was decided and closed in 220 BCE. Also, the casefile mentioned Cangwu commandery, which was not established until 222 BCE; see *LQJJ*, vol. 1, 217, slip 8-758. Hence, the case could only have happened between 222 and 220 BCE.

128. *LSS*, 1344-46, slips 158–59.

129. *LQJJ*, vol. 1, 392.

130. The reconstruction of this slip is done by Yang Xianyun 楊先雲, "Lun 'Liye Qinjian (er)' zhuihe wu ze" 《里耶秦簡 (貳) 》綴合五則, *Chutu wenxian yanjiu* 出土文獻研究 18 (2019): 130–31.

131. *LQJJ*, vol. 2, 443.

132. *LQJJ*, vol. 2, 466.

133. *LQJJ*, vol. 1, 376.

134. *LQJJ*, vol. 1, 136.

135. *LQJJ*, vol. 1, 394, slip 8-1804; vol. 2, 356, slip 9-1754.

136. This kind of report was later called "Records of Commandery" (*junji* 郡記) or "Records of County" (*xianji* 縣記); see Lin Changzhang 林昌丈, "Han Wei Liuchao 'Jun Ji' kao lun: Cong 'Jun Shou wen shi' shuo qi" 漢魏六朝「郡記」考論: 從「郡守問士」說起, *Xiamen daxue xuebao (zhexue shehui kexue ban)* 廈門大學學報 (哲學社會科學版) 245 (2018): 136–37.

137. For the boundary and administrative geography of the Qin Dongting commandery see You, *Zhizao "difang zhengfu,"* 152–58.

138. *Shiji*, 6.314. The translation is modified from Kern, *The Stele Inscriptions of Ch'in Shih-huang*, 26.

139. Maxim Korolkov, *The Imperial Network in Ancient China: The Foundation of Sinitic Empire in Southern East Asia* (Abingdon, UK: Routledge, 2022), 104–8; Tong, "The Construction of Territories in the Qin Empire," 541–47.

140. To paraphrase a friend of mine who formerly served as a bureaucrat in the HKSAR Government, the decision-making in bureaucracy involves spending countless hours discussing nonsense and reaching the solemn conclusion that the best move is not to move.

141. Bruce L. Benson, "Understanding Bureaucratic Behavior: Implications from the Public Choice Literature," *Journal of Public Finance and Public Choice* 13, no. 2–3 (1995): 89–117.

142. Regarding examples of deceit, prevarication, and miscommunication of military organizations on the northwestern frontier of the Western Han dynasty, see Kao Chen-huan 高震寰, "Lun xibei Hanjian wenshu yu xianshi de chaju ji qi yiyi" 論西北漢簡文書與現實的差距及其意義, *Xin Shixue* 新史學 25, no. 4 (2014): 2–39. For some of the classic studies of the struggle and concealment between the emperor and local officials in late imperial China, see Pierre-Etienne Will, *Bureaucracy and Famine in Eighteenth-Century China* (Stanford: Stanford University Press, 1990), 79–96; Philip A. Kuhn, *Soulstealers: The Chinese Sorcery Scare of 1768* (Cambridge, MA: Harvard University Press, 1990), 119–20; Iwo Amelung, *Der gelbe Fluss in Shandong 1851–1911* (Wiesbaden: Harrassowitz, 2000), 227–40.

143. Yu Zhenbo 于振波, "Qin lüling zhong de 'xin qianshou' yu 'xindi li'" 秦律令中的「新黔首」與「新地吏」, *Zhongguoshi yanjiu* 3 (2009): 76. Yu also argues that the promulgation of such regulations against the officials in the new territories was due to the prevalent atrocity that administrators in the new territories ascribed to the new subjects. Ibid., 78.

144. *LSS*, 462-63, slips 55–56.

145. *LQJJ*, 89–90, tablet 8-149+8-489. For the dating of this tablet, see Lu Jialiang, "Liye Qinjian 8-149+8-489 hao du jiaodu" 里耶秦簡 8-149+8-489 號牘校讀, in *Qin Han Weijinnanbeichao shi guoji xueshu yantaohui lunwenji* 秦漢魏晉南北朝史國際學術研討會論文集, ed. Lou Jin 樓勁 and Chen Wei (Beijing: Zhongguo shehui kexue, 2018), 71.

146. Kim, "Qin Han difang sifa yunzuo yu guanzhi yanbian," 205.

147. Such a practice is seen in Qin legal stipulations dated to the Warring States and continued in the imperial Qin period; see Hulsewé, *Remnants of Ch'in Law*, 67–68, A68; *Yuelu*, vol. 4, 153–54, slips 257–61.

148. Caldwell, *Writing Chinese Laws*, 181.

149. Amelung, *Der gelbe Fluss in Shandong 1851–1911*, 228–29. Also consider the countless exaggerated, deceitful, and illogical reports regarding the grain production figures during the "Great Leap Forward" (大躍進 Da Yuejin) campaign organized by Mao Zedong, as well as the initial concealment and belated announcement of the Chernobyl nuclear disaster.

150. Mann, *The Sources of Social Power*, vol. 1, 253–60.

151. Paraphrased from Mann, *The Sources of Social Power*, vol. 1, 135.

Chapter 3

1. *Shiji*, 5.341. This traditional narrative is still accepted by some modern scholars. See, for instance, Charles Sanft, "The Qin Dynasty," in *Routledge Handbook of Early Chinese History*, ed. Paul R. Goldin (Abingdon, UK: Routledge, 2018), 157–59.

2. Tong, "Framing the Qin Collapse," 909–10.

3. For an overview of the income and economic activities of the Qiangling government, see Robin D.S. Yates, "The Economic Activities of a Qin Local Administration: Qianling County, Modern Liye, Hunan Province, 222–209 BCE," in *Between Command and Market: Economic Thought and Practice in Early China*, ed. Elisa Levi Sabattini and Christian Schwermann (Leiden: Brill, 2021), 290–304.

4. Miyake Kiyoshi, "Cong zhengfu zouxiang zhanling tongzhi: Liye Qinjian suojian liangshi zhigei yu zhutun jun" 從征服走向占領統治: 里耶秦簡所見糧食支給與駐屯軍, in *Liye Qinjian yanjiu lunwen xuanji*, 570–71.

5. *LQJJ*, vol. 1, 369, slip 8-1618; vol. 2, 58, 264, slips 9-63, 9-1121.

6. Korolkov, *The Imperial Network in Ancient China*, 134.

7. Notable works include Yates (Ye Shan), "Jiedu Liye Qi jian," 119; Zhu Jincheng 朱錦程, "Qin dui xin zhengfudi de teshu tongzhi zhengce: yi 'xindi li' de xuanyong wei li" 秦對新征服地的特殊統治政策: 以「新地吏」的選用為例, *Hunan shifan daxue shehui kexue xuebao* 湖南師範大學社會科學學報 2 (2017): 150–56; Zhang, "'Xindi li' yu 'Wei li zhi dao,'" 66–68; Kim, "Qin Han difang sifa yunzuo yu guanzhi yanbian," 201–5.

8. I am grateful to Qu Jian 瞿見 for providing me with this information.

9. For discussions on the craftsmen and soldiers' literacy, see Enno Giele (Eno Gīre エノ・ギーレ), "Kodai no shikiji nōryoku wo ikaga ni hantei suru no ka: Kandai gyōsei monjo no jirei kenkyū" 古代の識字能力を如何に判定するのか——漢代行政文書の事例研究, trans. Miyake Kiyoshi, in *Sanzennen no kanji* 三千年の漢字, ed. Takata Tokio 高田時雄 (Kyoto: Rinsen, 2009), 135; Yates, "Soldiers, Scribes, and Women," 360–64.

10. *LQJJ*, vol. 1, 282, slip 8-1137. As Leung Wai Kit 梁煒傑 has pointed out, slips 8-887, 8-1118, 8-1231, 8-1593, and 8-1704 were probably also parts of this report; see Leung, "*Liye Qinjian (yi)* 'Li que' buce fuyuan" 《里耶秦簡（壹）》《吏缺》簿冊復原, Jianbowang, April 7, 2015.

11. They are: Chang 昌 (220 BCE; *LQJJ*, vol. 2, 35–36, tablet 9-23), Yi 齝 (216 BCE; ibid., 186–87, tablet 9-713), Pu 鋪 (212 BCE; ibid., 135, tablet 12-1784a), and Yi 繹 (211 BCE; ibid., 376, tablet 9-1864).

12. *LQJJ*, vol. 2, 1–18, 492, tablets 9-1–9-12, 9-2456+9-2457.

13. For instance, Liye tablet 8-61+8-293+8-2012 records that Langye commandery was watched over by a Temporary Governor in 219 BCE. A Temporary Governor of Nan commandery in 210 BCE is also mentioned in slip 8-974. Overall, only two real Governors were documented on tablets 8-228 and 9-2076; see *LQJJ*, vol. 1, 46, 119; vol. 2, 414–15.

14. *Shiji*, 38.2370.

15. *Hanshu*, 31.1796. Note that the *Shiji*'s account does not have the character 假; see *Shiji*, 7.381.

16. Zhang Chunlong 張春龍, "Liye Qinjian zhong Qianlingxian xueguan he xiangguan jilu" 里耶秦簡中遷陵縣學官和相關記錄, *Chutu wenxian* 1 (2010): 232, tablet 14–18; Li Jingrong, "The Governance of New Territories During the Qin Unification," *T'oung Pao* 108 (2022): 16.

17. Lu, "Liye Qinjian suojian 'xiaoshi' chuyi," 99–101.

18. *Shiji*, 93.3197.

19. Takigawa Kametarō 瀧川龜太郎, *Shiki Kaichū Kōshō* 史記會注考證, punctuated and edited by Yang Haizheng 楊海崢 (Shanghai: Shanghai guji, 2015), vol. 1, 548, n. 1.

20. *The Grand Scribe's Records*, vol. 2, 6–7.

21. For this point, see also Zhu, "Qin dui xin zhengfudi de teshu tongzhi zhengce," 154–55.

22. *Yuelu*, vol. 5, 56–57, slips 53–55.

23. *Yuelu*, vol. 5, 189–90, slips 275–77.

24. *Yuelu*, vol. 5, 55, slips 49–51.

25. *Yuelu*, vol. 5, 110–11, slips 128–30.

26. *Yuelu*, vol. 6, 115–17, slips 152–53.

27. While transmitted sources do not record any promulgations of amnesties during King Zheng/the First Emperor's thirty-seven-year reign, two lawsuit cases from the unearthed Yuelu corpus indicate that the Qin ruler granted at least two amnesties. The recently discovered accession edict of the Second Emperor also reveals that he authorized a general amnesty in 210 BCE, in addition to an emergency one in 208 BCE that appears in the *Shiji*; see Lau and Staack, *Legal Practice in the Formative Stages of the Chinese Empire*, 143–44, 272–73; Barbieri-Low, *The Many Lives of the First Emperor of China*, 105–7. That said, there is no evidence that amnesties were granted regularly during the imperial Qin period.

28. *Yuelu*, vol. 7, 87–90, slips 79–87.

29. *Yuelu*, vol. 6, 173, slips 232–33. Geographically, "Jiangdong" and "Jiangnan" each referred to a specific region. In the early Chinese context, Jiangdong was usually associated with regions in Lower Yangzi such as the southern parts of present-day Auhui and Jiangsu Provinces, whereas Jiangnan covered the vast region in the south of Middle Yangzi, encompassing the southern part of Hubei Province and the whole of Hunan Province. For geographic notions of

"Jiangdong" and "Jiangnan" in the early Chinese texts, see Zhou Zhenhe, "Shi Jiangnan" 釋江南, *Sui wuya zhi lü* 隨無涯之旅 (Beijing: Sanlian, 2007), 324–26.

30. *LQJJ*, vol. 1, 108–9, tablet 8-197.

31. All tables in appendix 1 can be found in Chun Fung Tong, "Appendices for *State Power and Governance in Early Imperial China: The Collapse of the Qin Empire, 221–207 BCE*," heiDok, January 17, 2024, 1–10, https://doi.org/10.11588/heidok.00034268.

32. *LQJJ*, vol. 1, 119, slip 8-232.

33. *LQJJ*, vol. 1, 327, slip 8-1445.

34. You, *Zhizao "difang zhengfu,"* 141.

35. Yuan Yansheng 袁延勝 and Shi Junjun 時軍軍, "Zai lun Liye Qinjian zhong de 'shou' he shouguan" 再論里耶秦簡中的「守」和守官, *Gudai wenming* 古代文明 13, no. 2 (2019): 63.

36. Lu, "Liye Qinjian suojian Qin qianling xian liyuan de goucheng yu laiyuan," 210–16.

37. *Shiji*, 6.322.

38. *The Grand Scribe's Records*, vol. 1, 266.

39. *LQJJ*, vol. 2, 38, tablet 9-26. The part on which the date was inscribed is now partially broken. For a discussion of the dating of this tablet, see Zheng Wei 鄭威, "Qin Dongting jun shuxian xiao yi" 秦洞庭郡屬縣小議, *Jianghan kaogu* 5 (2019): 92.

40. Zheng, "Qin Dongting jun shuxian xiao yi," 92.

41. He Ning 何寧, *Huainanzi jishi* 淮南子集釋 (Beijing: Zhonghua, 1998), 18.1289.

42. Li, "The Governance of New Territories During the Qin Unification," 32.

43. *The Grand Scribe's Records*, vol. 2, ed. William H. Nienhauser Jr. (Bloomington: Indiana University Press, 2002), 6–8.

44. *Shiji*, 93.3197.

45. *LQJJ*, vol. 2, 218, slip 9-874+9-1723.

46. *Hanshu*, 31.1789.

47. The Qin state's predominance in economic activities is also evident in archaeological data. Wengcheong Lam observes that the Qin capital Xianyang in Guangzhong likely played a "dominant role" in the production of metal objects, and the distribution and consumption of iron and bronze products indicates that such activities were "clearly concentrated the capital area" but "not extended very far away." See Lam, *Connectivity, Imperialism, and the Han Iron Industry* (Abingdon, UK: Routledge, 2022), 194–202.

48. Korolkov, "Fiscal Transformation during the Formative Period of Ancient Chinese Empire (Late Fourth to First Century BCE)," 205–32.

49. *Liye Qinjian bowuguan cang Qinjian* 里耶秦簡博物館藏秦簡 (hereafter cited as *LQBCQ*), ed. Chutu wenxian yu zhongguo gudai wenming yanjiu xietong

chuangxin zhongxin Zhongguo renmin daxue zhongxin 出土文獻與中國古代文明研究協同創新中心中國人民大學中心 (Shanghai: Zhongxi, 2016), 142, tablet 16-5. See also Maxim Korolkov, "Between Command and Market: Credit, Labour, and Accounting in the Qin Empire (221–207 BCE)," in *Between Command and Market: Economic Thought and Practice in Early China*, ed. Elisa Levi Sabattini and Christian Schwermann (Leiden: Brill, 2021), 201–2.

50. Maxim Korolkov, *The Imperial Network in Ancient China*, 133.

51. Takatori Yuji 鷹取祐司, "Shin Kanjidai no keibatsu to shakuseiteki mibunjoretsu" 秦漢時代の刑罰と爵制的身分序列, *Ritsumeikan bungaku* 立命館文學 608 (2008): 103–10.

52. Convict laborers such as bondservants and bondwomen and robber-guards could also work as *juze shu zhai* and *xi chengdanchong*; see You Yifei, "Shuo xi chengdanchong: Qin Han xingqi zhidu xinlun" 說繫城旦舂—秦漢刑期制度新論, *Xin Shixue* 新史學 20, no. 3 (2009): 30–40.

53. Regarding the differences between the production tasks of wall-builders or grain-pounders and bondservants or bondwomen, Jia Liying 賈麗英 observes that the latter group undertook a wider range of tasks than wall-builders or grain-pounders. In particular, tasks such as transmitting administrative documents, guiding doors and gates, and running errands for officials were always assigned to bondservants and bondwomen. Jia Liying, *Chutu jiandu yu Qin Han shehui shenfen zhixu yanjiu* 出土簡牘與秦漢社會身份秩序研究 (Beijing: Zhongguo shehui kexue, 2023), 244–54.

54. LQBCQ, 130, tablet 10-1170.

55. LQJJ, vol. 2, 455–58, tablet 9-2289.

56. Tong Chun Fung, "Liye Qinjian suoshi Qindai de 'jianhu' yu 'jihu'" 里耶秦簡所示秦代的「見戶」與「積戶」, Jianbowang, February 8, 2014.

57. LQJJ, vol. 1, 257, slip 8-986.

58. Another Liye fragment also purportedly reflects this issue. It says that "the estimated number of field laborers is 158. Now 95 are used . . ." 田徒當用大男子百五十八人。·今九十五以當☒. Unfortunately, the lower end of the slip is broken so we do not know its entire contents; see LQJJ, vol. 2, 342, slip 9-1647.

59. LQBCQ, 131, slip 12-3.

60. LQBCQ, 78, tablet 7-304.

61. Korolkov, "Empire-Building and Market-Making at the Qin Frontier," 368.

62. Here I follow Hulsewé's glossary of the term *tu* 徒, reading it as "persons in a subordinate position, like labor or military conscripts, servants, convicts," and not confined to convict laborers; see Hulsewé, *Remnants of Ch'in Law*, 172, D159, n. 3.

63. For the transcription of 武 see Liu Ziwen 劉自穩, "Du Liye Qinjian zhaji" 讀里耶秦簡札記, Jianbowang, May 28, 2019.

64. LQJJ, vol. 2, 40, tablet 9-31.

65. *LQJJ*, vol. 1, 113, tablet 8-207.

66. *LQJJ*, vol. 2, 87, slip 9-205.

67. Regarding the necessary labor force for catching birds, an official letter records that in 217 BCE, the Office of Convict Labor sent two convict laborers to Erchun commune to perform bird hunting and feather collection; see *LQJJ*, vol. 1, 343, 8-1515.

68. *LQJJ*, vol. 2, 301, tablet 9-1408+9-2288.

69. *Yuelu*, vol. 4, 60–61, slips 66–67.

70. *Yuelu*, vol. 4, 69, slip 91. Slip 157 of the *Statutes and Ordinances of the Second Year* comprises a similar statute that specifies the subject "officials and commoners"; see *Gakuroku Shoin shozō kan* Shin ritsuryō (ichi) *yakuchū* 嶽麓書院所藏簡《秦律令（壹）》譯注, ed. Miyake Kiyoshi 宮宅潔 (Tokyo: Kyūko, 2023), 122.

71. Miyake, "The Military History of Qin and the Composition of Its Expeditionary Forces," 146.

72. Miyake Kiyoshi, "Shin dai yōeki, heieki seido no sai kentō" 秦代徭役・兵役制度の再檢討, *Toho gakuho* 94 (2019): 19.

73. For a summary of this case, see Lau and Staack, *Legal Practice in the Formative Stages of the Chinese Empire*, 247.

74. *Yuelu*, vol. 4, 44–45, slips 17–19.

75. For the appearance of this phrase in Shuihudi Tomb 11, see *Qin jiandu heji (Shiwen zhushi xiuding ben)*, vol. 1, 148, slip 35; 190, slips 20–21; 195, slip 32. For those in *Statutes and Ordinances of the Second Year*, see *Ernian lüling yu Zouyan shu: Zhangjiashan ersiqi hao Hanmu chutu falü wenxian shidu* 二年律令與奏讞書：張家山二四七號漢墓出土法律文獻釋讀, ed. Peng Hao 彭浩, Chen Wei 陳偉, and Kudō Motoo 工藤元男 (Shanghai: Shanghai guji, 2007), 98, slip 20; 109, slip 49; 112, slip 57; 119, slips 74–75; 121, slip 77; 161, slip 180; 192, slip 252; 196, slip 261.

76. *Yuelu*, vol. 4, 44, 60–61, slips 18, 66–67, 69; vol. 5, 39–40, 52, 70, 145–49, 195, slips 3–5, 40–41, 92, 230–37, 240–44, 291; vol. 6, 47, 48–49, 53, 64, slips 2, 6–9, 18, 50–51; vol. 7, 135, 162, slips 159, 239.

77. *Qin jiandu heji (Shiwen zhushi xiuding ben)*, vol. 2, 65, slip 124; 72, slip 137; 78, slip 148; 80, slip 151; 94, slip 201. The Longgang manuscripts constitute one wooden tablet and some 293 pieces of bamboo fragments, which were inscribed with ordinances and statutes pertaining to imperial gardens. The corpus was probably compiled and revised around the time of the Qin unification in 221BC; see ibid., 4–5.

78. Korolkov, *The Imperial Network in Ancient China*, 95–97.

79. *Qin jiandu heji (Shiwen zhushi xiuding ben)*, vol. 1, 282; Hulsewé, *Remnants of Ch'in Law*, 195, E17, in which he translates 邊縣 as "border prefecture."

80. *Yuelu*, vol. 5, 43, slips 13–14.

81. *Yuelu*, vol. 5, 43–45, slips 14–18.

82. The original editor glosses 誨 as "to tempt" or "to entice," while Chen Wei reads it as "to conspire," which is followed here.

83. The graph of this character is heavily damaged and the editor suggests reading it as 安 (*an*; peace), which is supported by Wang Bokai, "*Yuelushuyuan cang Qinjian (wu) yanjiu er ti*" 《嶽麓書院藏秦簡（伍）》研究二題, *Chutu wenxian* 15 (2019): 269–71.

84. *Yuelu*, vol. 5, 42, slip 12.

85. *LQJJ*, vol. 2, 35–36, tablet 9-23.

86. *LQJJ*, vol. 1, 217, slips 8-756–757. For an English translation of this document, see Robin D.S. Yates, "The Fate of the Defeated: Qin's Treatment of Their Enemies," *Bamboo and Silk* 5, no. 1 (2022): 17.

87. *LQJJ*, vol. 2, 302, tablet 9-1411. For a detailed discussion of the *lu* captives as evidenced by the Liye material, see Yates, "The Fate of the Defeated," 9–17.

88. *LQJJ*, vol. 1, 199, tablet 8-673+8-2002+9-1848+9-1897.

89. Lu Jialiang argues that "feather tax" refers to the tribute paid by ethnic minority groups in the region. While it is possible that part of the feather tax was contributed by ethnic minorities, the content of 8-673+8-2002+9-1848+9-1897 indicates that feathers collected by government functionaries were also deemed to be a "feather tax." See Lu, "Liye chutu Qin 'buniao qiuyu' jian chutan" 里耶出土秦「捕鳥求羽」簡初探, in *Gudai changjiang zhongyou shehui yanjiu* 古代長江中游社會研究, ed. Wei Bin 魏斌 (Shanghai: Shanghai guji, 2013), 103–4.

90. Yates, "The Qin Slips and Boards from Well No. 1, Liye, Hunan," 304.

91. Wang Zijin, "Liye Qinjian 'buyu' de xiaofei zhuti" 里耶秦簡「捕羽」的消費主題, *Hunan daxue xuebao (shehuikexue ban)* 7 (2016): 29–31.

92. *LQJJ*, vol. 1, 384, slip 8-1735. Note that the unit was missing due to a broken edge. In reference to other sources, however, the feather tax should be calculated in terms of *hou*.

93. *LQJJ*, vol. 2, 348, slip 9-1696.

94. *LQJJ*, vol. 1, 475, slip 8-2501.

95. *LQJJ*, vol. 2, 455–58, tablet 9-2289.

96. *LQJJ*, vol. 1, 355, 374, slips 8-1549, 8-1662; vol. 2, 239, slip 9-992.

97. *Huainanzi jishi*, 18.1289–90; John S. Major, Sarah Queen, Andrew Meyer, and Harold Roth, *The Huainanzi: A Guide to the Theory and Practice of Government in Early Han China* (New York: Columbia University Press, 2010), 744.

98. Korolkov, *The Imperial Network in Ancient China*, 132–33.

99. *LQJJ*, vol. 1, 418, slip 8-2014.

100. *LQJJ*, vol. 2, 495, slip 9-2472. The text reads: "陵□見在者，盡為除道運□." The editors of the *LQJJ* suspect that the first undeciphered graph is 徒 (*tu*; laborer), and the second is 食.

101. *LQJJ*, vol. 2, 38, tablet 9-26.

102. *LQJJ*, vol. 2, 122, tablet 9-436+9-464.

103. *LQJJ*, vol. 2, 251, 376, tablets 9-1079+9-1520, 9-1864; *LQBCQ*, 130, tablet 10-1170.

104. Korolkov, "Fiscal Transformation during the Formative Period of Ancient Chinese Empire (Late Fourth to First Century BCE)," 235.

105. Moonsil Lee Kim, "Discrepancy between Laws and their Implementation: An Analysis of Granaries, Statutes, and Rations during China's Qin and Han Periods," *Journal of the Economic and Social History of the Orient* 59, no. 4 (2016): 584–85. For the difficult working condition of convict laborers in the Qin and Han period, see Anthony J. Barbieri-Low, *Artisans in Early Imperial China* (Seattle: University of Washington Press, 2007), 227–41.

106. *The Grand Scribe's Records*, vol. 2, 14.

107. *LQJJ*, vol. 1, 333, tablet 8-1463.

108. As Robin Yates notes, the term 篷田 likely refers to the technique of "slash and burn" or "shifting cultivation"; see Yates, "The Fate of the Defeated," 21.

109. While editors of the *LQJJ* postulated that the graph is 感, Liu Ziwen deciphered it as 黑; see Liu, "Du Liye Qinjian zhaji."

110. *LQJJ*, vol. 2, 33–34, tablet 9-22.

111. The case was inscribed on a multi-piece manuscript. As noted by editors of the *Jiaoshi*, Liye: 9-169, 9-245, 9-238+9-211, and 9-361 should be its fragments; see *LQJJ*, vol. 2, 81.

112. Zhang, " 'Xindi li' yu 'Wei li zhi dao,' " 64–65; Kim, "Qin Han difang sifa yunzuo yu guanzhi yanbian," 204–5.

113. For the interpretation of the terminology 冗 as a kind of long-term personnel in contrast to the notion of 更, see Hirose Kunio, *Shin Kan Ritsuryō kenkyū* 秦漢律令研究 (Tokyo: Kyūko, 2010), 292–304.

114. Miyake, "Cong zhengfu zouxiang zhanling tongzhi," 584–90.

115. *LQJJ*, vol. 1, 70, tablet 8-132+8-334.

116. *LQJJ*, vol. 2, 281, slip 9-1247.

117. *LSS*, 1339.

118. Tong Chun Fung, "Shouling jian he hengshu shu: Du *Liye Qinjian* (er) zhaji liang ze" 受令簡和恒署書: 讀《里耶秦簡（貳）》札記兩則, *Jianbo* 19 (2019): 107–11.

119. Here I gloss the word 壯 as the name of Constable Zhuang. An alternative interpretation would be to understand it as an adjective such as "strong," "mature," or "able."

120. *LQJJ*, vol. 2, 260, tablet 9-1112.

121. *LQJJ*, vol. 2, 45, slip 9-32.

122. *LQJJ*, vol. 2, 377, slip 9-1866.

123. For the household numbers of the three communes of Qianling county, see Korolkov, *The Imperial Network in Ancient China*, 121–24, especially table 5.1.

124. Since dispatchment records show that documents sent from the County Commander usually arrived at the county seat within a day, the working place of the County Commander must have been near the county seat.

125. *LQJJ*, vol. 2, 155, slip 9-557. The translation is modified from Yates, "The Fate of the Defeated," 22.

126. The published material comprises three slips from this manuscript; see *LQJJ*, vol. 1, 260, 420, slips 8-1004, 8-2027; slip 8-1972+8-1688 is reconstructed by Xie Kun 謝坤 in "*Liye Qinjian (yi)* zhuihe (si)" 《里耶秦簡 (壹) 》綴合 (四), Jianbowang, November 18, 2016.

127. *LQJJ*, vol. 2, 165, 316, tablets 9-623, 9-1479; Hunan sheng wenwu kaogu yanjiusuo, "Longshan Liye Qinjian zhi 'tu bu'" 龍山里耶秦簡之「徒簿」, *Chutu wenxian yanjiu* 12 (2013): 124, tablet 10-1160. These documents evidently prove that the position of Thief Catcher was usually taken up by conscripts.

128. *Yuelu*, vol. 4, 120, slips 157–58.

129. *LSS*, 902–3, slips 412–13.

130. Hulsewé, *Remnants of Ch'in Law*, 108, C8. The only exception is a "Statute on the Appointment of Officials," which states that if a carriage driver cannot properly manage his vehicle after four years of training, his trainer must be dismissed, and he will be fined one set of armor as well as being forced repay four years statutory labor and military service. Notably, such a circumstance is not a punishment of convict-conscription; ibid., 103, C1.

131. For a detailed summary of the case, see Lau and Staack, *Legal Practice in the Formative Stages of the Chinese Empire*, 295.

132. A similar regulation can be found in a "Statute on Arrest" (Bu lü 捕律) from the *Statutes and Ordinances of the Second Year*, except that the early Western Han punishments of the timid soldiers were much lighter than that in the Yuelu version; *LSS*, 560–61, slips 142–43. One cannot help but think that these changes might be one of the measures that the Western Han administration initiated to relieve the brutality of Qin law.

133. *LSS*, 560–61, slip 141.

134. *LSS*, 470–71, slip 76.

135. *LSS*, 614–15, slip 186.

136. *LSS*, 650, slip 210.

137. *LSS*, 502–3, slips 95–96.

138. In view of the example of the crime "retreating out of cowardice" discussed earlier, these punishments might even have more severe sentencing principles and longer terms of services.

139. The jurisdiction of Jianghu commandery is believed to have overlapped highly with that of Kuaiji commandery, and scholars argue that it was the predecessor of Kuaiji; see Zhou, Li, and Zhang, *Zhongguo xingzhengquhua tongshi*, vol. 1, 41.

140. *Yuelu*, vol. 7, 61–62, slips 2–3.

141. Kiyoshi, "Cong zhengfu zouxiang zhanling tongzhi," 584.

142. For this see also Li, "The Governance of New Territories During the Qin Unification," 18.

143. *Yuelu*, vol. 4, 145–46, slips 232–36.

144. *Shiji*, 7.380.

145. You, *Zhizao "difang zhengfu,"* 180.

146. *LQJJ*, vol. 1, 63, slip 8-106.

147. The registers of convict labor record that one of the common tasks of convict laborer was "accompanying functionaries to report matters at the Governor's office" (與吏上事守府); see *LQJJ*, vol. 1, 202, 365, tablets 8-681+8-1641, 8-1586; vol. 2, 363, 466, tablets 8-2144+8-2146+9-1803, 9-2297.

148. *LQJJ*, vol. 2, 432, tablet 9-2203. Likewise, Zheng De 鄭得, a conscript in-shift coming from Chengfu 城父 county and holding the *shiwu* status, had once served as the officer-cook (*li yang* 吏養) of Qianling; see ibid., vol. 1, 231, 237, tablet 8-811+8-1572 and slip 8-850; vol. 2, 225, slip 9-918.

149. Hunan sheng wenwu kaogu yanjiusuo, "Longshan Liye Qinjian zhi 'tu bu,'" 124, tablet 10-1160.

150. *LQJJ*, vol. 2, 281, slip 9-1247. The text reveals that there were at least 200 long-term conscripts stationed in Qianling county, and each of them cultivated an average of four *mu* 畝 (1,844 square meters) of fields, so the minimum amount of field cultivation was approximately 800 *mu*.

151. *Qin jiandu heji (Shiwen zhushi xiuding ben)*, vol. 1, 155, n. 1.

152. *LQJJ*, vol. 2, 226, 363, tablets 8-781+8-1102, 8-1574+8-1787.

153. The reconstruction of tablet 8-1459+8-1293+8-1466 can be found in Yao Lei 姚磊, "Liye Qin jiandu zhuihe zhaji (yi ze)" 里耶秦簡牘綴合札記 (一則), Jianbowang, May 29, 2015. The transcription herein follows the editions of Chen Wei and He Youzu, see Chen, "'Feishu' yu 'Ruyin'" 「廢戍」與「女陰」, Jianbowang, May 30, 2015; He, "Du Liye Qinjian zhaji (si ze)" 讀里耶秦簡札記 (四則), Jianbowang, June 10, 2015.

154. For a detailed discussion, see Lu, "Liye Qinjian suojian Qin Qianling xian liyuan de goucheng yu laiyuan," 204–5.

155. *Yuelu*, vol. 4, 119, slip 154.

156. *LQJJ*, vol. 2, 331, slip 9-1581.

157. *LQJJ*, vol. 1, 80, tablet 8-140.

158. The reconstruction of tablet 8-439+8-519+8-537+8-1899 can be found in Xie Kun, "*Liye Qinjian (yi)* zhuihe (san)" 《里耶秦簡 (壹) 》綴合 (三), Jianbowang, November 17, 2016.

159. *Shiji*, 8.442.

160. *Shiji*, 91.3151.

161. Tong, "The Construction of Territories in the Qin Empire," 524–26.

162. Ōkushi Atsuhiro, "Shin dai kokka no tōitsu shihai: Shutoshite gunji teki sokumen kara" 秦代国家の統一支配: 主として軍事的側面から, in *Shiki, Kansho no saikentō to kodai shakai no chiiki teki kenkyū* 『史記』『漢書』の再検討と古代社会の地域的研究, ed. Mase Kazuyoshi 間瀬収芳 (Tokyo: Monbushō kagaku kenkyū hihojokin kenkyū seika hōkokusho, 1994), 115–22.

163. Phillip K. Thompkins, *Organizational Communication Imperatives: Lessons of the Space Program* (Los Angeles: Roxbury, 1993), 150–65; Clarissa Freitas Dias and Michael S. Vaughn, "Bureaucracy, Managerial Disorganization, and Administrative Breakdown in Criminal Justice Agencies," *Journal of Criminal Justice* 34 (2006): 545.

Chapter 4

1. This translation is modified from Alfred Forke, *Lun-hêng Part 2. Miscellaneous Essays of Wang Ch'ung* (New York: Paragon Book Gallery, 1962), 96–97.

2. Mann, *The Sources of Social Power*, vol. 1, 136.

3. For a study from a similar perspective, see Shen Gang 沈剛, "Qindai xianji dangan wenshu de chuli zhouqi: Yi Qianling xian wei zhongxin" 秦代縣級檔案文書的處理週期: 以遷陵縣為中心, *Chutu wenxian yanjiu* 15 (2016): 127–44.

4. For example, Charles Sanft argues that measures such as the unity of weights and measures, the inspection tours of the First Emperor, the enforcement of the Qin bureaucratic system and laws, and even the construction of roads and highways all became media for political communication across the realm, through which the Qin emperors successfully established communication with every member of the population; see Sanft, *Communication and Cooperation in Early Imperial China*, 33–146.

5. Harold O. Fried, C. A. Knox Lovell, and Shelton S. Schmidt, "Efficiency and Productivity," in *The Measurement of Productive Efficiency and Productivity Growth*, ed. Harold O. Fried, C. A. Knox Lovell, and Shelton S. Schmidt (Oxford: Oxford University Press, 2008), 7–8.

6. For a list of the manifold definitions of "efficiency" in contemporary public administration studies, see Mark R. Rutgers and Hendriekje van der Meer, "The Origins and Restriction of Efficiency in Public Administration: Regaining Efficiency as the Core Value of Public Administration," *Administration & Society* 42, no. 7 (2010): 755–79.

7. Rutgers and van der Meer, "The Origins and Restriction of Efficiency in Public Administration," 768–70.

8. According to Rutgers and van der Meer, this definition is derived from the classical explanation of Aristotle, who understands *efficiency* in a more substantive perspective as "active force, power, or ability; the operative agent." Rutgers and van der Meer, "The Origins and Restriction of Efficiency in Public Administration," 772.

9. Conceptually, communication involves the transmission of "information"—*data* arranged in a meaningful pattern—between the members of a given organization, as well as with people outside that organization. It is defined

as "a process in which there is some predictable relation between the message transmitted and the message received"; see Doris A. Graber, *The Power of Communication: Managing Information in Public Organizations* (Washington, DC: CQ Press, 2002), 2–3.

10. Fried, Lovell, and Schmidt, "Efficiency and Productivity," 10–11.

11. Clifford Ando, "The Ambitions of Government: Territoriality and Infrastructural Power in Ancient Rome," in *Ancient States and Infrastructural Power*, 115–48, especially 129–34.

12. For *chidao* and *zhidao*, see Wang Zijin, *Qin Han jiaotong shi gao (zengding ban)* 秦漢交通史稿 (增訂版) (Beijing: Zhongguo renmin daxue, 2013), 27–29, 32–45; Sanft, *Communication and Cooperation in Early Imperial China*, 101–21.

13. This fact was acknowledged by the ancients as well. In Wu Bei's 伍 被 memorial to the Lord of Huainan 淮南, he claimed that the Lord of Wu 吳 made ships whose "load of one ship matched that of several dozens of caravans used by central states" (一船之載當中國數十兩車); see *Shiji*, 118.3751.

14. For its transcription see *Peking daxue cang Qin jiandu*, 875–87.

15. Korolkov, "Empire-Building and Market-Making at the Qin Frontier," 467–68, tables 5.1–5.3.

16. *LSS*, 738–39, slip 266. For a more detailed discussion on the nature, function and duty of the postal system and Postmen in Qin and Western Han China, see Enno Giele (Eno Gīre エノ・ギーレ), "'Yū' seikō: Shin Kan jidai wo chūshin ni" 「郵」制攷——秦漢時代を中心に, trans. Tomiya Itaru, *Tōyōshi kenkyū* 63, no. 2 (2004): 206–39; Liu Hsin-ning 劉欣寧, "Wenshu xingzheng" 文書行政, in *Chongxie Qin Han shi: Chutu wenxian de shiye* 重寫秦漢史: 出土文獻的視野, ed. Chen Kanli (Shanghai: Shanghai guji, 2023), 95–103.

17. Huang Haobo 黃浩波, "Qindai wenshu chuandi xiangguan wenti yanjiu" 秦代文書傳遞相關問題研究 (PhD dissertation, Wuhan University, 2020), 170–78.

18. Liu, "Wenshu xingzheng," 103–5.

19. Yan Changgui 晏昌貴, "Liye Qindu 9-712+9-758 bu shi" 里耶秦牘 9-712+9-758補釋, Jianbowang, December 24, 2013.

20. Yan, "Liye Qindu 9-712+9-758 bu shi."

21. *LSS*, 1262–65.

22. *Yuelu*, vol. 4, 131, slip 192.

23. *Yuelu*, vol. 6, 57–58, slips 31–33.

24. For the transcription and English translation of this 220 BCE ordinance, see Yates, "Dated Legislation in the Late-Qin State and Early Empire," 151.

25. For a more detailed discussion regarding the principle of combined punishments, see Chen Songchang 陳松長 and Wen Junping 溫俊萍, "Lun Qin lü de zuishu chufa: yi 'Yuelushuyuan cang Qinjian' wei zhongxin" 論秦律的罪數處罰: 以「嶽麓書院藏秦簡」為中心, Jianbo yanjiu 2016 (qiudong juan) 簡帛研究 2016秋冬卷 (Guilin: Guangxi shifan daxue, 2017), 83–84.

26. A Qin mathematical manual lists that the conversion rate between a set of armor and cash was 1:1,344. Hence, six sets of armor amounted to 8,064 cash; see *Yuelushuyuan cang Qinjian (yi–san) shiwen xiudingben*, 98, slip 82.

27. According to a set of twelve debt-reckoning dossier in the Liye manuscripts (Liye: 9-1 to 9-12), the unpaid debts carried by these officials range from 384 to 11,271 cash and the mean was only 3,236.25 cash.

28. *LSS*, 740–41, slips 273–74.

29. For the transcription of this document, see *Juyan Hanjian* 居延漢簡, vol. 2, ed. Jiandu zhengli xiaozu 簡牘整理小組 (Taipei: Zhongyang yanjiuyuan lishi yuyan yanjiusuo, 2015), 139, tablet 157.14.

30. *LSS*, 738–39, slip 264.

31. *LSS*, 738–39, slip 266.

32. Yang Xianyun, "Qindai xingzhang wenshu zhidu guankui" 秦代行政文書制度管窺, in *Chutu wenxian de shijie*, 106.

33. In statistics, standard deviation is used to present the degree of variation or dispersion of a dataset. The lower the standard deviation is, the closer the dataset is to its mean. If the standard deviation of a dataset is close to its mean, it is more stable and thereby more reliable. For example, the mean and standard deviation of the retention period of the administrative documents handled by the Qianling Prefect or Vice-Prefect are 0.97 days and 2.77, respectively; after eliminating the highest and lowest values, however, they become 0.6 days and 1.14. The decrease in the standard deviation indicates that the latter is a more stabilized and reliable dataset.

34. *LQBCQ*, 136, tablets 12-1798, 12-1799.

35. All tables in appendix 2 can be found in Tong, "Appendices for *State Power and Governance in Early Imperial China*," 11–27, https://doi.org/10.11588/heidok.00034268.

36. *LQBCQ*, 144, tablet 16-52.

37. *LQJJ*, vol. 1, 1, tablet 5-1.

38. Here I follow Zhang Chi's 張馳 interpretation of the line "傳、別書," understanding it as a compound of two actions, namely, "to deliver the document" (*chuan shu* 傳書) and "to make a copy of the document" (*bie shu* 別書); see Zhang, "Du Liye Qinjian (er) 9-1861, 9-2076 xiao zha" 讀里耶秦簡 (貳) 9-1861、9-2076小札, Jianbowang, May 17, 2018.

39. He Youzu suspects the undeciphered graph is 畸 (*ji*); see his "Du Liye Qinjian zhaji (er)" 讀里耶秦簡札記 (二), Jianbowang, June 23, 2015.

40. The graph is transcribed as 奢 (*she*), which is inaccurate and thus is not adopted here.

41. *LQJJ*, vol. 1, 193, tablet 8-657.

42. *LQJJ*, vol. 1, 328, slip 8-1449+8-1484.

43. *LQJJ*, vol. 1, 343, tablet 8-1516.

44. *LQJJ*, vol. 1, 190, tablet 8-648; vol. 2, 145, 231, 197, 343, slips 9-500, 9-963, 9-748, 9-1652+9-1996.

45. Here I follow the transcriptions in *Qin jiandu heji (Shiwen zhushi xiuding ben)*, vol. 3, 8, slips 1–3.

46. *Peking daxue cang Qin jiandu*, 886, slip 118b/2-116b/2.

47. Xin Deyong, *Shishi sheng yan* 石室賸言 (Beijing: Zhonghua, 2014), 151.

48. *Yuelushuyuan cang Qinjian (yi–san) shiwen xiudingben*, 7, slips 41, 43.

49. *Peking daxue cang Qin jiandu*, 882, slip 162b/2.

50. Xin, *Shishi sheng yan*, 130.

51. *Yuelushuyuan cang Qinjian (yi–san) shiwen xiudingben*, 15, slips 1–3.

52. Yan Changgui, *Qin jiandu dili yanjiu* 秦簡牘地理研究 (Wuhan: Wuhan daxue, 2017), 282.

53. [(97 + 94.5 + 102 + 85.77) ÷ 4] = 94.82 *li*.

54. *Xuanquan Hanjian* 懸泉漢簡, vol. 2, ed. Gansu jiandu bowuguan 甘肅簡牘博物館, Gansu sheng wenwu kaogu yanjiusuo 甘肅省文物考古研究所, Shaanxi shifan daxue renwen shehui kexue gaodeng yanjiuyuan 陝西師範大學人文社會科學高等研究院, and Tsinghua daxue chutu wenxian yanjiu yu baohu zhongxin 清華大學出土文獻研究與保護中心 (Shanghai: Zhongxi, 2020), 547, slip II T0112③:21. This number is faster than the estimation of a recent study of the traveling speed of officials in the northwestern frontier, which suggests that the average speed was approximately 30 km (72.15 *li*) per day; see Takamura Takeyuki, *Kandai no chihō kanri to chiiki shakai* 漢代の地方官吏と地域社會 (Tokyo: Kyūko, 2008), 164.

55. *LQJJ*, vol. 2, 414–15, tablet 9-2076.

56. Tom Chung Yee 譚宗義, *Handai guonei lulu jiaotong kao* 漢代國內陸路交通考 (Hong Kong: Xinya yanjiusuo, 1967), 181–88; Wang, *Qin Han jiaotong shi gao (zengding ban)*, 25–26. For a reconstruction of the route from Jiangling to Deng through excavated sources, see Xin, *Shishi sheng yan*, 145–46; Yan, *Qin jiandu dili yanjiu*, 281–82. The seat of Deng county was likely in the northwest area of modern Xiangyang 襄陽 City; see *LQJJ*, vol. 2, 415, n. 4; Zhou, Li, and Zhang, *Zhongguo xingzhengquhua tongshi*, vol. 1, 424.

57. *LQJJ*, vol. 1, 217, 348, tablet 8-1523, slip 8-759.

58. *LQBCQ*, 142, tablets 16-5, 16-6; *LQJJ*, vol. 2, 447–48, tablet 9-2283.

59. For a more detailed discussion of the debt-reckoning procedures as evidenced in these documents, see Tong Chun Fung, "Qindai Qianling xian xingzheng xinxi chuandi xiaolu chutan" 秦代遷陵縣行政信息傳遞效率初探 (revised version), in *Liye Qinjian yanjiu lunwen xuanji*, 252–58.

60. Liu Ziwen points out that given that the debt-reckoning process between counties was usually time-consuming, and that the procedure would increase the workload of the crediting county, it is possible that the crediting county intentionally postponed these debt-reckoning documents so as to escape its duty; see Liu, "Liye Qinjian zhong de zhuishu xianxiang: Cong Shuihudi Qinjian yize Xingshu lü shuo qi" 里耶秦簡中的追書現象: 從睡虎地秦簡一則行書

律說起, *Chutu wenxian yanjiu* 16 (2017): 160–61. Liu's argument, nonetheless, cannot justify why the communication was centralized within 214–212 BCE, and thus, the argument is not adopted here.

61. As suggested by Fujita Katsuhisa 藤田勝久, "Liye Qinjian suojian Qindai junxian de wenshu chuandi" 里耶秦簡所見秦代郡縣的文書傳遞, *Jianbo* 8 (2013): 192.

62. *LQJJ*, vol. 2, 469, tablet 9-2314.

63. *LQJJ*, vol. 2, 378-79, tablet 9-1871+9-2469+9-2471+9-1883+9-1893.

64. *LQJJ*, vol. 1, 131, slip 8-301+8-428.

65. *Huainanzi jishi*, 18.1289–90; John S. Major et al., *The Huainanzi*, 744.

Bibliography

Transmitted Textual Sources and Their Translations

Forke, Alfred. *Lun-hêng Part 2. Miscellaneous Essays of Wang Ch'ung*. New York: Paragon Book Gallery, 1962.

Hanshu 漢書. Beijing: Zhonghua, 1962.

He Ning 何寧. *Huainanzi jishi* 淮南子集釋. Beijing: Zhonghua, 1998.

Hou Hanshu 後漢書. Beijing: Zhonghua, 1965.

Huang Hui 黃暉. *Lun Heng jiaoshi* 論衡校釋. Beijing: Zhonghua, 1990.

Major, John S., Sarah Queen, Andrew Meyer, and Harold Roth. *The Huainanzi: A Guide to the Theory and Practice of Government in Early Han China*. New York: Columbia University Press, 2010.

Pines, Yuri. *The Book of Lord Shang: Apologetics of State Power in Early China*. New York: Columbia University Press, 2017.

Shiji 史記. Revised paperback edition. Beijing: Zhonghua, 2014.

Takigawa Kametarō 瀧川龜太郎. *Shiki Kaichū Kōshō* 史記會注考證. Punctuated and edited by Yang Haizheng 楊海崢. Shanghai: Shanghai guji, 2015.

The Grand Scribe's Records. Revised vol. 1. Edited by William H. Nienhauser Jr. Bloomington: Indiana University Press, 2018.

The Grand Scribe's Records. Vol. 2. Edited by William H. Nienhauser Jr. Bloomington: Indiana University Press, 2002.

Wang Liqi 王利器. *Xinyu jiaozhu* 新語校注. Beijing: Zhonghua, 1986.

Yan Zhenyi 閻振益 and Zhong Xia 鐘夏. *Xinshu Jiaozhu* 新書校注. Beijing: Zhonghua, 2000.

Zhao Yi 趙翼. *Nianershi zhaji jiaozheng* 廿二史札記校證. Punctuated and edited by Wang Shumin 王樹民. Beijing: Zhonghua, 2013.

Zhen Dexiu 真德秀. *Daxue yanyi* 大學衍義. Punctuated and edited by Zhu Renqiu 朱人求. Shanghai: Huadong shifan daxue, 2010.

Unearthed Manuscripts and Their Translations

Barbieri-Low, Anthony J., and Robin D.S. Yates. *Law, State, and Society in Early Imperial China: A Study with Critical Edition and Translation of the Legal Texts from Zhangjiashan Tomb no. 247.* Leiden: Brill, 2015. (Abbreviated in notes as *LSS.*)

Ernian lüling yu Zouyan shu: Zhangjiashan ersiqi hao Hanmu chutu falü wenxian shidu 二年律令與奏讞書: 張家山二四七號漢墓出土法律文獻釋讀. Edited by Peng Hao 彭浩, Chen Wei 陳偉, and Kudō Motoo 工藤元男. Shanghai: Shanghai guji, 2007.

Gakuroku Shoin shozō kan Shin ritsuryō (ichi) *yakuchū* 嶽麓書院所藏簡《秦律令 (壹) 》譯注. Edited by Miyake Kiyoshi 宮宅潔. Tokyo: Kyūko, 2023.

Hulsewé, A.F.P. *Remnants of Ch'in Law: An Annotated Translation of the Ch'in Legal and Administrative Rules of the 3rd century B.C., Discovered in Yun-meng Prefecture, Hu-pei Province, in 1975.* Leiden: E.J. Brill, 1985.

Juyan Hanjian 居延漢簡, vol. 2. Edited by Jiandu zhengli xiaozu 簡牘整理小組. Taipei: Zhongyang yanjiuyuan lishi yuyan yanjiusuo, 2015.

Lau, Ulrich, and Thies Staack. *Legal Practice in the Formative Stages of the Chinese Empire: An Annotated Translation of the Exemplary Qin Criminal Cases from the Yuelu Academy Collection.* Leiden: Brill, 2016.

Liye Qinjian 里耶秦簡, vol. 1–2. Edited by Hunan sheng wenwu kaogu yanjiusuo 湖南省文物考古研究所. Beijing: Wenwu, 2012, 2018.

Liye Qin jiandu jiaoshi 里耶秦簡牘校釋, vol. 1–2. Edited by Chen Wei 陳偉. Wuhan: Wuhan daxue, 2012, 2018. (Abbreviated in notes as *LQJJ.*)

Liye Qinjian bowuguan cang Qinjian 里耶秦簡博物館藏秦簡. Edited by Chutu wenxian yu zhongguo gudai wenming yanjiu xietong chuangxin zhongxin Zhongguo renmin daxue zhongxin 出土文獻與中國古代文明研究協同創新中心中國人民大學中心. Shanghai: Zhongxi, 2016. (Abbreviated in notes as *LQBCQ.*)

Peking daxue cang Qin jiandu 北京大學藏秦簡牘. Edited by Peking daxue chutu wenxian yu gudai wenming yanjiusuo 北京大學出土文獻與古代文明研究所. Shanghai: Shanghai guji, 2023.

Qin jiandu heji (Shiwen zhushi xiuding ben) 秦簡牘合集 (釋文注釋修訂本), vol. 1–4. Edited by Chen Wei 陳偉. Wuhan: Wuhan daxue, 2016.

Xuanquan Hanjian 懸泉漢簡, vol. 2. Edited by Gansu jiandu bowuguan 甘肅簡牘博物館, Gansu sheng wenwu kaogu yanjiusuo 甘肅省文物考古研究所, Shaanxi shifan daxue renwen shehui kexue gaodeng yanjiuyuan 陝西師範大學人文社會科學高等研究院, and Tsinghua daxue chutu wenxian yanjiu yu baohu zhongxin 清華大學出土文獻研究與保護中心. Shanghai: Zhongxi, 2020.

Yuelushuyuan cang Qinjian 嶽麓書院藏秦簡, vol. 1–3. Edited by Zhu Hanmin 朱漢民 and Chen Songchang 陳松長. Shanghai: Shanghai cishu, 2011–2013. (Abbreviated in notes as *Yuelu.*)

Yuelushuyuan cang Qinjian 嶽麓書院藏秦簡, vol. 4–7. Edited by Chen Songchang 陳松長. Shanghai: Shanghai cishu, 2015, 2017, 2020, 2022. (Abbreviated in notes as *Yuelu*.)

Yuelushuyuan cang Qinjian (yi–san) shiwen xiudingben 嶽麓書院藏秦簡（壹–叁）釋文修訂本. Edited by Chen Songchang. Shanghai: Shanghai cishu, 2018.

Modern Works

Amelung, Iwo. *Der gelbe Fluss in Shandong 1851–1911*. Wiesbaden: Harrassowitz, 2000.

Ando, Clifford. "The Ambitions of Government: Territoriality and Infrastructural Power in Ancient Rome." In *Ancient States and Infrastructural Power: Europe, Asia, and America*, edited by Clifford Ando and Seth Richardson, 115–48. Philadelphia: University of Pennsylvania Press, 2017.

Aoki Shunsuke 青木俊介. "Riya Shinkan ni mieru ken no bukyoku soshiki ni tsuite" 里耶秦簡に見える県の部局組織について. *Chūgoku shutsudo shiryō kenkyū* 中國出土資料研究 9 (2005): 103–11.

Barbieri-Low, Anthony J. *Artisans in Early Imperial China*. Seattle: University of Washington Press, 2007.

Barbieri-Low, Anthony J. *The Many Lives of the First Emperor of China*. Seattle: University of Washington Press, 2022.

Benson, Bruce L. "Understanding Bureaucratic Behavior: Implications from the Public Choice Literature." *Journal of Public Finance and Public Choice* 13, no. 2–3 (1995): 89–117.

Bielenstein, Hans. *The Bureaucracy of Han Times*. Cambridge: Cambridge University Press, 1980.

Bodde, Derk. "The State and Empire of Ch'in." In *The Cambridge History of China*, vol. 1, *Ch'in and Han Empires*, edited by Denis Twitchett and Michael Loewe, 20–102. Cambridge: Cambridge University Press, 1986.

Caldwell, Ernest. *Writing Chinese Laws: The Form and Function of Legal Statutes Found in the Qin Shuihudi Corpus*. Abingdon, UK: Routledge, 2018.

Call, Charles T. "Beyond the 'Failed State': Toward Conceptual Alternatives." *European Journal of International Relations* 17, no. 2 (2010): 303–26.

Chen Hong 陳洪. *Qin wenhua zhi kaoguxue yanjiu* 秦文化之考古學研究. Beijing: Kexue, 2016.

Chen Kanli 陳侃理. "Qin Han lili yu jiceng tongzhi" 秦漢里吏與基層統治. *Lishi yanjiu* 歷史研究 1 (2022): 51–76.

Chen Kanli. "Shuihudi Qinjian 'Wei li zhi dao' ying gengming 'Yu shu': jian tan 'Yu shu' mingyi ji Qinjian zhong leisi wenxian di xingzhi" 睡虎地秦簡「為吏之道」應更名「語書」：兼談「語書」名義及秦簡中類似文獻的性質. *Chutu wenxian* 出土文獻 6 (2015): 246–57.

Chen Songchang 陳松長 and Wen Junping 溫俊萍. "Lun Qin lü de zuishu chufa: yi 'Yuelushuyuan cang Qinjian' wei zhongxin" 論秦律的罪數處罰: 以「嶽麓書院藏秦簡」為中心. *Jianbo yanjiu 2016 (qiudong juan)* 簡帛研究 2016秋冬卷, 80–85. Guilin: Guangxi shifan daxue, 2017.

Chen Suzhen 陳蘇鎮. *Chunqiu yu "Han dao": Liang Han zhengzhi yu zhengzhi wenhua yanjiu* 《春秋》與「漢道」: 兩漢政治與政治文化研究. Beijing: Zhonghua, 2011.

Chen Suzhen. *Liang Han Weijinnanbeichao shi tanyou* 兩漢魏晉南北朝史探幽. Beijing: Peking daxue, 2013.

Chen Wei 陳偉. "'Feishu' yu 'Ruyin'" 「廢戍」與「女陰」. *Jianbowang*, May 30, 2015, www.bsm.org.cn/?qinjian/6414.html.

Chen Wei. "'Wei li zhi guan ji qianshou' 1531, 0072 hao jian shi du" 《為吏治官及黔首》1531、0072號簡試讀. *Jianbowang*, January 22, 2010, www.bsm. org.cn/?qinjian/5408.html.

Chen Wei. "*Yuelushuyuan cang Qinjian (wu)*" jiaodu (xu wu). 《嶽麓書院藏秦簡〔伍〕》校讀 (續四). *Jianbowang*, March 31, 2018, www.bsm.org. cn/?qinjian/7774.html.

Chen Yingjie 陳英傑. "Shi, li, shi, shi fenhua shidai cengci kao" 史、吏、事、使分化時代層次考. *Zhongguo wenzi* 中國文字 40 (2014): 63–186.

Chittick, Andrew. "Thinking Regionally in Early Medieval Studies: A Manifesto." *Early Medieval China* 26 (2020): 3–18.

Cowgill, George L. "Onward and Upward with Collapse." In *The Collapse of Ancient States and Civilizations*, edited by Norman Yoffee and George L. Cowgill, 244–76. Tucson: University of Arizona Press, 1988.

Dias, Clarissa Freitas, and Michael S. Vaughn, "Bureaucracy, Managerial Disorganization, and Administrative Breakdown in Criminal Justice Agencies." *Journal of Criminal Justice* 34 (2006): 543–55.

Dull, Jack L. "Anti-Qin Rebels: No Peasant Leaders Here." *Modern China* 9, no. 3 (1983): 285–318.

Durrant, Stephen, Wai-yee Li, Michael Nylan, and Hans van Ess. *The Letter to Ren An and Sima Qian's Legacy*. Seattle: University of Washington Press, 2018.

Elvin, Mark. *The Pattern of the Chinese Past: A Social and Economic Interpretation*. Stanford: Stanford University Press, 1973.

Falkenhausen, Lothar von. *Chinese Society in the Age of Confucius (1000–250 BC): The Archeological Evidence*. Los Angeles: The Cotsen Institute of Archaeology Press, 2006.

Faulseit, Ronald K. "Collapse, Resilience, and Transformation in Complex Societies: Modeling Trends and Understanding Diversity." In *Beyond Collapse: Archaeological Perspectives on Resilience, Revitalization, and Transformation in Complex Societies*, edited by Ronald K. Faulseit, 3–24. Carbondale: Southern Illinois University Press, 2016.

Foster, Christopher J. "Study of the *Cang Jie pian*: Past and Present." PhD dissertation, Harvard University, 2017.

Fried, Harold O., C.A. Knox Lovell, and Shelton S. Schmidt. "Efficiency and Productivity." In *The Measurement of Productive Efficiency and Productivity Growth*, edited by Harold O. Fried, C.A. Knox Lovell, and Shelton S. Schmidt, 3–91. Oxford: Oxford University Press, 2008.

Fujita Katsuhisa 藤田勝久. "Liye Qinjian suojian Qindai junxian de wenshu chuandi" 里耶秦簡所見秦代郡縣的文書傳遞. *Jianbo* 簡帛 8 (2013): 179–94.

Giele, Enno (Eno Gīre エノ・ギーレ; Ji Annuo 紀安諾). "Handai biansai beiyong shuxie cailiao ji qi shehui shi yiyi" 漢代邊塞備用書寫材料及其社會史意義. *Jianbo* 簡帛 2 (2007): 475–500.

Giele, Enno. "Kodai no shikiji nōryoku wo ikaga ni hantei suru no ka: Kandai gyōsei monjo no jirei kenkyū" 古代の識字能力を如何に判定するのか——漢代行政文書の事例研究. Translated by Miyake Kiyoshi 宮宅潔. In *Sanzennen no kanji* 三千年の漢字, edited by Takata Tokio 高田時雄, 133–54. Kyoto: Rinsen, 2009.

Giele, Enno. "'Yū' seikō: Shin Kan jidai wo chūshin ni" 「郵」制攷——秦漢時代を中心に. Translated by Tomiya Itaru. *Tōyōshi kenkyū* 東洋史研究 63, no. 2 (2004): 203–39.

Goldin, Paul R., and Elisa Levi Sabattini. *Lu Jia's New Discourses: A Political Manifesto from the Early Han Dynasty*. Leiden: Brill, 2020.

Graber, Doris A. *The Power of Communication: Managing Information in Public Organizations*. Washington, DC: CQ Press, 2002.

Guo Hongbo 郭洪伯. "Baiguan yu zhucao: Qin Han jiceng jigou de bumen shezhi" 稗官與諸曹——秦漢基層機構的部門設置. *Jianbo yanjiu* 簡帛研究 2013, 101–27. Guilin: Guangxi shifan daxue, 2014.

Hankins, James. *Virtue Politics: Soulcraft and Statecraft in Renaissance Italy*. Cambridge, MA: Belknap Press of Harvard University Press, 2019.

Harper, Donald. "Daybooks in the Context of Manuscript Culture and Popular Culture Studies." In *Books of Fate and Popular Culture in Early China: The Daybook Manuscripts of the Warring States, Qin, and Han*, edited by Donald Harper and Marc Kalinowski, 91–137. Leiden: Brill, 2017.

He Youzu 何有祖. "Du Liye Qinjian zhaji (er)" 讀里耶秦簡札記 (二). Jianbowang, June 23, 2015, www.bsm.org.cn/?qinjian/6435.html.

He Youzu. "Du Liye Qinjian zhaji (si ze)" 讀里耶秦簡札記 (四則). Jianbowang, June 10, 2015, www.bsm.org.cn/?qinjian/6427.html.

Hirose Kunio 廣瀬薰雄. *Shin Kan Ritsuryō kenkyū* 秦漢律令研究. Tokyo: Kyūko, 2010.

Hirose Kunio. "Yiyang Tuzishan J9⑦chutu jiandu chutan" 益陽兔子山J9⑦出土簡牘初探. In *Jianbo yanjiu lunji* 簡帛研究論集, 137–55. Shanghai: Shanghai guji, 2019.

Hsing I-tien 邢義田. "Longshan Liye Qin Qianling xiancheng yizhi chutu mou xiang Nanyang li hujijian shitan" 龍山里耶秦遷陵縣城遺址出土某鄉南陽里戶籍簡試探. Jianbowang, November 6, 2007, www.bsm.org.cn/?qinjian/4954.html.

Huang Haobo 黃浩波. "Qindai wenshu chuandi xiangguan wenti yanjiu" 秦代文書傳遞相關問題研究. PhD dissertation, Wuhan University, 2020.

Huang Yijun. "Chang'an's Funerary Culture and the Core Han Culture." In *Chang'an 26 BCE: An Augustan Age in China*, edited by Michael Nylan and Griet Vankeerberghen, 153–73. Seattle: University of Washington Press, 2015.

Hubei sheng wenwu kaogu yanjiuyuan 湖北省文物考古研究院 and Yunmeng xian bowuguan 雲夢縣博物館. "Hubei Yunmeng xian Zhengjiahu mudi 2021 nian fajue jianbao" 湖北雲夢縣鄭家湖墓地2021年發掘簡報. *Kaogu* 2 (2022): 3–21.

Hunan sheng wenwu kaogu yanjiusuo 湖南省文物考古研究所. *Liye fajue baogao* 里耶發掘報告. Changsha: Yuelu, 2007.

Hunan sheng wenwu kaogu yanjiusuo. "Longshan Liye Qinjian zhi 'tu bu'" 龍山里耶秦簡之「徒簿」. *Chutu wenxian yanjiu* 出土文獻研究 12 (2013): 101–31.

Hunan sheng wenwu kaogu yanjiusuo and Yiyang shi wenwuchu 益陽市文物處. "Hunan Yiyang Tuzishan yizhi jiuhao jing fajue baogao" 湖南益陽兔子山遺址九號井發掘報告. *Hunan kaogu jikan* 湖南考古輯刊, vol. 12, 129–63. Beijing: Kexue, 2016.

Jia Liying 賈麗英. *Chutu jiandu yu Qin Han shehui shenfen zhixu yanjiu* 出土簡牘與秦漢社會身份秩序研究. Beijing: Zhongguo shehui kexue, 2023.

Kalinowski, Marc. "Hemerology and Prediction in the Daybooks: Ideas and Practices." In *Books of Fate and Popular Culture in Early China: The Daybook Manuscripts of the Warring States, Qin, and Han*, edited by Donald Harper and Marc Kalinowski, 138–206. Leiden: Brill, 2017.

Kamada Shigeo 鎌田重雄. *Shin Kan seiji seido no kenkyū* 秦漢政治制度の研究. Tokyo: Nihon gakujutsu shinkōkai, 1962.

Kamiya Masakazu 紙屋正和. "Zenkan shokō ōkoku no kansei" 前漢諸侯王国の官制. *Kyushu Daigaku Toyoshi ronshu* 九州大学東洋史論集 3 (1975): 17–35.

Kanaya Osamu 金谷治. *Shin Kan shisōshi kenkyū* 秦漢思想史研究. Tōkyō: Heirakuji, 1992.

Kao Chen-huan 高震寰. "Cong Liye Qinjian (yi) 'zuotu bu' guankui Qindai xingtu zhidu" 從《里耶秦簡（壹）》「作徒簿」管窺秦代刑徒制度. *Chutu wenxian yanjiu* 12 (2013): 132–43.

Kao Chen-huan. "Lun xibei Hanjian wenshu yu xianshi de chaju ji qi yiyi" 論西北漢簡文書與現實的差距及其意義. *Xin Shixue* 新史學 25, no. 4 (2014): 2–39.

Kern, Martin. *The Stele Inscriptions of Ch'in Shih-huang: Text and Ritual in Early Chinese Imperial Representation*. New Haven, CT: American Oriental Society, 2000.

Keum Jaewon 琴載元. "Fan Qin zhanzheng shiqi Nanjun diqu de zhengzhi dongtai yu wenhua tezheng: zailun 'wang Qin bi Chu' xingshi de juti cengmian"

反秦戰爭時期南郡地區的政治動態與文化特徵: 再論「亡秦必楚」形勢的具體
層面. *Jiandu xue yanjiu* 簡牘學研究 5 (2014): 129–40.

Keum Jaewon. "Qindai Nanjun bianhu min de Qin, Chu shenfen rentong wenti"
秦代南郡編戶民的秦、楚身份認同問題. *Jianbo yanjiu 2015 Qiudong juan* 簡
帛研究 2015 秋冬卷, 78–92. Guilin: Guangxi shifan daxue, 2015.

Kim Jonghi 金鍾希. "Qin Han difang sifa yunzuo yu guanzhi yanbian: yi guanfu
de jiquanhua xianxiang wei zhongxin" 秦漢地方司法運作與官制演變: 以官
府的集權化現象為中心. PhD dissertation, Peking University, 2021.

Kim, Moonsil Lee. "Discrepancy between Laws and their Implementation: An
Analysis of Granaries, Statutes, and Rations during China's Qin and Han
Periods." *Journal of the Economic and Social History of the Orient* 59, no.
4 (2016): 555–89.

Korolkov, Maxim. "Between Command and Market: Credit, Labour, and
Accounting in the Qin Empire (221–207 BCE)." In *Between Command
and Market: Economic Thought and Practice in Early China*, edited by Elisa
Levi Sabattini and Christian Schwermann, 162–243. Leiden: Brill, 2021.

Korolkov, Maxim. "Empire-Building and Market-Making at the Qin Frontier:
Imperial Expansion and Economic Change, 221–207 BCE." PhD dissertation, Columbia University, 2020.

Korolkov, Maxim. "Fiscal Transformation during the Formative Period of Ancient
Chinese Empire (Late Fourth to First Century BCE)." In *Ancient Taxation:
The Mechanics of Extraction in Comparative Perspective*, edited by Jonathan
Valk and Irene Soto Marín, 203–61. New York: New York University
Press, 2021.

Korolkov, Maxim. *The Imperial Network in Ancient China: The Foundation of Sinitic
Empire in Southern East Asia*. Abingdon, UK: Routledge, 2022.

Kuhn, Philip A. *Soulstealers: The Chinese Sorcery Scare of 1768*. Cambridge, MA:
Harvard University Press, 1990.

Lai Ming Chiu 黎明釗. *Fucou yu zhixu: Han diguo difang shehui yanjiu* 輻輳與秩
序: 漢帝國地方社會研究. Hong Kong: The Chinese University Press, 2013.

Lai Ming Chiu and Tong Chun Fung 唐俊峰. "Liye Qinjian suojian Qindai xian
guan, cao zuzhi de zhineng fenye yu xingzheng hudong—yi ji, ke wei
zhongxin" 里耶秦簡所見秦代縣官、曹組織的職能分野與行政互動——以計、
課為中心 (revised version). In *Liye Qinjian yanjiu lunwen xuanji* 里耶秦簡
研究論文選集, edited by Liye Qinjian bowuguan 里耶秦簡博物館, 429–56.
Shanghai: Zhongxi, 2021.

Lam Wengcheong. *Connectivity, Imperialism, and the Han Iron Industry*. Abingdon,
UK: Routledge, 2022.

Lander, Brian. *The King's Harvest: A Political Ecology of China from the First
Farmers to the First Empire*. New Haven, CT: Yale University Press, 2021.

Leung Wai Kit 梁煒傑. "*Liye Qinjian (yi)* 'Li que' buce fuyuan" 《里耶秦簡 (壹)》
《吏缺》簿冊復原. Jianbowang, April 7, 2015, www.bsm.org.cn/?qin-
jian/6354.html.

Lewis, Mark Edward. *The Early Chinese Empires: Qin and Han*. Cambridge, MA: Belknap Press of Harvard University Press, 2007.

Li Feng. *Bureaucracy and the State in Early China*. Cambridge: Cambridge University Press, 2008.

Li Feng. *Early China: A Social and Cultural History*. Cambridge: Cambridge University Press, 2013.

Li Feng. *Landscape and Power in Early China: The Crisis and Fall of the Western Zhou, 1045–771 BC*. Cambridge: Cambridge University Press, 2005.

Li Jingrong. "The Governance of New Territories During the Qin Unification." *T'oung Pao* 108 (2022): 1–35.

Li Kaiyuan 李開元. *Han diguo de jianli yu Liu Bang jituan: Jungong shouyi jieceng yanjiu (zengding ban)* 漢帝國的建立與劉邦集團: 軍功受益階層研究 (增訂版). Beijing: Sanlian, 2023.

Li Kaiyuan. *Qin beng: cong Qin Shihuang dao Liu Bang* 秦崩: 從秦始皇到劉邦. Taipei: Lianjing, 2010.

Li, Kin Sum (Sammy). "To Rule by Manufacture: Measurement Regulation and Metal Weight Production in the Qin Empire." *T'oung Pao* 103 (2017): 1–32.

Li Songru 李松儒. "Yiyang Tuzishan jiuhao jing jiandu zhong Chu Qin guodu ziti tanxi" 益陽兔子山九號井簡牘中楚秦過渡字體探析. *Zhongguo shufa* 中國書法 6 (2019): 54–56.

Li Tianhong 李天虹, Xiong Jiahui 熊佳暉, Cai Dan 蔡丹, and Luo Yunbing 羅運兵. "Hubei Yunmeng Zhengjiahu mudi M274 chutu 'jianchen Tu xi wen Qinwang' gu" 湖北雲夢鄭家湖墓地M274出土「賤臣筡西問秦王」觚. *Wenwu* 3 (2022): 64–74.

Li Yuening 李玥凝. "Qinjian 'junzi' shenfen zaitan" 秦簡「君子」身份再探. *Guwenzi yanjiu* 古文字研究 33 (2020): 407–11.

Lin Changzhang 林昌丈. "Han Wei Liuchao 'Jun Ji' kao lun: Cong 'Jun Shou wen shi' shuo qi" 漢魏六朝「郡記」考論: 從「郡守問士」說起. *Xiamen daxue xuebao (zhexue shehui kexue ban)* 廈門大學學報 (哲學社會科學版) 245 (2018): 130–39.

Ling Wenchao 凌文超. "Qindai fuji biaozhun xin kao: jian lun zizhan nian yu nianling jisuan" 秦代傅籍標準新考: 兼論自占年與年齡計算. *Wenshi* 文史 128 (2019): 5–16, 38.

Liu Hsin-ning 劉欣寧. "Wenshu xingzheng" 文書行政. In *Chongxie Qin Han shi: Chutu wenxian de shiye* 重寫秦漢史: 出土文獻的視野, edited by Chen Kanli 陳侃理, 67–158. Shanghai: Shanghai guji, 2023.

Liu Ziwen 劉自穩. "Du Liye Qinjian zhaji" 讀里耶秦簡札記. Jianbowang, May 28, 2019, www.bsm.org.cn/?qinjian/8090.html.

Liu Ziwen. "Liye Qinjian zhong de zhuishu xianxiang: Cong Shuihudi Qinjian yize Xingshu lü shuo qi" 里耶秦簡中的追書現象: 從睡虎地秦簡一則行書律說起. *Chutu wenxian yanjiu* 16 (2017): 147–164.

Loewe, Michael. *Records of Han Administration*. London: Routledge Curzon, 2002.

Lu Jialiang 魯家亮. "Liye chutu Qin 'buniao qiuyu' jian chutan" 里耶出土秦「捕鳥求羽」簡初探. In *Gudai Changjiang zhongyou shehui yanjiu* 古代長江中游社會研究, edited by Wei Bin 魏斌, 91–111. Shanghai: Shanghai guji, 2013.

Lu Jialiang. "Liye Qinjian 8-149+8-489 hao du jiaodu" 里耶秦簡8-149+8-489號牘校讀. In *Qin Han Weijinnanbeichao shi guoji xueshu yantaohui lunwenji* 秦漢魏晉南北朝史國際學術研討會論文集, edited by Lou Jin 樓勁 and Chen Wei 陳偉, 60–71. Beijing: Zhongguo shehui kexue, 2018.

Lu Jialiang. "Liye Qinjian suojian Qin qianling xian liyuan de goucheng yu laiyuan" 里耶秦簡所見秦遷陵縣吏員的構成與來源. *Chutu wenxian* 13 (2018): 201–21.

Lu Jialiang. "Liye Qinjian suojian 'xiaoshi' chuyi" 里耶秦簡所見「小史」芻議. In *Chutu wenxian de shijie: di liu jie chutu wenxian qingnian xuezhe luntan lunwenji* 出土文獻的世界：第六屆出土文獻青年學者論壇論文集, edited by Chutu wenxian yu Zhongguo gudai wenming yanjiu xietong chuangxin zhongxin Zhongguo renmin daxue fenzhongxin 出土文獻與中國古代文明研究協同創新中心中國人民大學分中心, 92–101. Shanghai: Zhongxi, 2018.

Ma Tsang Wing. "Between the State and Their Superiors: The Anxiety of Low-Ranked Scribes in the Qin and Han Bureaucracies." *Asia Major*, 3rd ser., 33 no. 2 (2020): 25–59.

Ma Tsang Wing. "Scribe, Assistant, and the Materiality of Administrative Documents in Qin–Early Han China: Excavated Evidence from Liye, Shuihudi, and Zhangjiashan." *T'oung Pao* 103, no. 4–5 (2017): 297–333.

Ma Tsang Wing. "Scribes in Early Imperial China." PhD dissertation, University of California, Santa Barbara, 2017.

Mann, Michael. "The Autonomous Power of the State: Its Origins, Mechanisms and Results." *European Journal of Sociology* 25, no. 2 (1984): 185–213.

Mann, Michael. *The Sources of Social Power*, vol. 1, *A History of Power from the Beginning to AD 1760*. Cambridge: Cambridge University Press, 2012.

Marcus, Joyce. "The Peaks and Valleys of Ancient States: An Extension of the Dynamic Model." In *Archaic States*, edited by Gary M. Feinman and Joyce Marcus, 59–94. Santa Fe: School for Advanced Research Press, 1998.

Masubuchi Tatsuo 増淵龍夫. *Shinpan Chūgoku kodai no shakai to kokka* 新版 中國古代の社會と國家. Tokyo: Iwanami, 1996.

McAnany, Patricia A., and Norman Yoffee. "Why We Question Collapse and Study Human Resilience, Ecological Vulnerability, and the Aftermath of Empire." In *Questioning Collapse: Human Resilience, Ecological Vulnerability, and the Aftermath of Empire*, edited by Patricia A. McAnany and Norman Yoffee, 1–17. Cambridge: Cambridge University Press, 2010.

Middleton, Guy D. *Understanding Collapse: Ancient History and Modern Myths*. Cambridge: Cambridge University Press, 2017.

Miyake Kiyoshi 宮宅潔. *Chūgoku kodai keiseishi no kenkyū* 中国古代刑制史の研究. Kyoto: Kyōto daigaku, 2011.

Miyake Kiyoshi. "Cong zhengfu zouxiang zhanling tongzhi: Liye Qinjian suojian liangshi zhigei yu zhutun jun" 從征服走向占領統治: 里耶秦簡所見糧食支給與駐屯軍. In *Liye Qinjian yanjiu lunwen xuanji* 里耶秦簡研究論文選集, edited by Liye Qinjian bowuguan 里耶秦簡博物館, 570–96. Shanghai: Zhongxi, 2021.

Miyake Kiyoshi. "The Military History of Qin and the Composition of Its Expeditionary Forces." Translated by Yao Zhuming. *Bamboo and Silk* 1 (2018): 121–51.

Miyake Kiyoshi. "Shin dai yōeki, heieki seido no sai kentō" 秦代徭役・兵役制度の再検討. *Toho gakuho* 94 (2019): 1–32.

Moriya Mitsuo 守屋美都雄. *Zhongguo gudai de jiazu yu guojia* 中國古代的家族與國家. Translated by Qian Hang 錢杭 and Yang Xiaofen 楊曉芬. Shanghai: Shanghai guji, 2010.

Morris, Ian. *The Measure of Civilisation: How Social Development Decides the Fate of Nations.* Princeton: Princeton University Press, 2013.

Nakayama Shigeru 仲山茂. "Shin Kan jidai no 'kan' to 'so': Ken no bukyoku soshiki" 秦漢時代の「官」と「曹」: 県の部局組織. *Tōyō gakuhō* 東洋学報 82, no. 4 (2001): 35–65.

Ōkushi Atsuhiro 大櫛敦弘. "En, Sei, Jin wa jitōshi: Shin Kan tōitsu kokka to tōhō chiiki" 燕・齊・荊は地遠し: 秦漢統一国家と東方地域. *Hainan Shigaku* 海南史學 55 (2017): 1–28.

Ōkushi Atsuhiro. "Shin dai kokka no tōitsu shihai: Shutoshite gunji teki sokumen kara" 秦代国家の統一支配: 主として軍事的側面から. In *Shiki, Kansho no saikentō to kodai shakai no chiiki teki kenkyū* 『史記』『漢書』の再検討と古代社会の地域的研究, edited by Mase Kazuyoshi 間瀬収芳, 113–31. Tokyo: Monbushō kagaku kenkyū hihojokin kenkyū seika hōkokusho, 1994.

Ou Yang 歐揚. "Yuelu Qinjian hushi fushen ling chutan" 嶽麓秦簡戶時復申令初探. Unpublished conference paper presented at "Dijiujie chutu wenxian yu falü shi yanjiu guoji xueshu yantao hui" 第九屆出土文獻與法律史研究國際學術研討會. Shanghai: East China University of Political Science and Law, October 11–13, 2019.

Peerenboom, Randall. *Law and Morality in Ancient China: The Silk Manuscripts of Huang-Lao.* Albany: State University of New York Press, 1993.

Pines, Yuri. "Chu Identity as Seen from Its Manuscripts: A Reevaluation." *Journal of Chinese History* 2 (2018): 1–26.

Pines, Yuri. *Envisioning Eternal Empire: Chinese Political Thought of the Warring States Era.* Honolulu: University of Hawaii Press, 2009.

Pines, Yuri. "The Messianic Emperor: A New Look at Qin's Place in China's History." In *Birth of an Empire: The State of Qin Revisited*, edited by Yuri Pines, Gideon Shelach, Lothar von Falkenhausen, and Robin D.S. Yates, 258–79. Berkeley: University of California Press, 2014.

Pines, Yuri. "The Question of Interpretation: Qin History in Light of New Epigraphic Sources." *Early China* 29 (2004): 1–44.

Pulleyblank, Edwin G. "The Roman Empire as Known to Han China." *Journal of the American Oriental Society* 119, no. 1 (1999): 71–79.

Renfrew, Colin. *Approaches to Social Archaeology*. Cambridge, MA: Harvard University Press, 1984.

Richardson, Seth. "Before Things Worked: A 'Low-Power' Model of Early Mesopotamia." In *Ancient States and Infrastructural Power: Europe, Asia, and America*, edited by Clifford Ando and Seth Richardson, 17–62. Philadelphia: University of Pennsylvania Press, 2017.

Richardson, Seth. "Early Mesopotamia: The Presumptive State." *Past & Present* 215 (2012): 3–49.

Richter, Matthias L. *The Embodied Text: Establishing Textual Identity in Early Chinese Manuscripts*. Leiden: Brill, 2013.

Rutgers, Mark, and Hendriekje van der Meer. "The Origins and Restriction of Efficiency in Public Administration: Regaining Efficiency as the Core Value of Public Administration." *Administration & Society* 42, no. 7 (2010): 755–79.

Sage, Steven F. *Ancient Sichuan and the Unification of China*. Albany: State University of New York Press, 1992.

Saitō Ken 齋藤賢. "Mibun koshō to shite no 'kunshi'" 身分呼稱としての「君子」. In *Gakuroku Shoin shozō kan* Shin ritsuryō (ichi) *yakuchū* 嶽麓書院所藏簡《秦律令（壹）》譯注, edited by Miyake Kiyoshi 宮宅潔, 391–403. Tokyo: Kyūko, 2023.

Sanft, Charles. *Communication and Cooperation in Early Imperial China: Publicizing the Qin Dynasty*. Albany: State University of New York Press, 2014.

Sanft, Charles. "The Qin Dynasty." In *Routledge Handbook of Early Chinese History*, edited by Paul R. Goldin, 147–59. Abingdon, UK: Routledge, 2018.

Selbitschka, Armin. "'I Write Therefore I Am': Scribes, Literacy, and Identity in Early China." *Harvard Journal of Asiatic Studies* 78, no. 2 (2018): 413–76.

Shaanxi sheng kaogu yanjiusuo 陝西省考古研究所. *Qin du Xianyang kaogu baogao* 秦都咸陽考古報告. Beijing: Kexue, 2004.

Shelach, Gideon. *The Archeology of Early China: From Prehistory to the Han Dynasty*. Cambridge: Cambridge University Press, 2015.

Shelach, Gideon. "Collapse or Transformation? Anthropological and Archaeological Perspectives on the Fall of Qin." In *Birth of an Empire: The State of Qin Revisited*, edited by Yuri Pines, Gideon Shelach, Lothar von Falkenhausen, and Robin D.S. Yates, 113–38. Berkeley: University of California Press, 2014.

Shelach, Gideon, and Yuri Pines. "Secondary State Formation and the Development of Local Identity: Change and Continuity in the State of Qin (770–221 B.C.)." In *Archaeology of Asia*, edited by Miriam T. Stark, 202–30. Malden, MA: Blackwell, 2006.

Shen Gang 沈剛. "Qindai xianji dangan wenshu de chuli zhouqi: Yi Qianling xian wei zhongxin" 秦代縣級檔案文書的處理週期: 以遷陵縣為中心. *Chutu wenxian yanjiu* 15 (2016): 127–44.

Shimokura Wataru 下倉涉. "Aru josei no kokuhatsu wo megutte: Gakurokushoin zō Shin Kan 'Shiki kō en an' ni arawaretaru dorei oyobi 'Shagin' 'Ritan'" ある女性の告発をめぐって: 嶽麓書院藏秦簡「識劫婉案」に現れたる奴隷および「舍人」「里单」. *Shirin* 史林 99, no. 1 (2016): 39–80.

Skocpol, Theda. *States and Social Revolutions: A Comparative Analysis of France, Russia, and China*. Cambridge: Cambridge University Press, 1979.

Sou, Daniel S. "Shaping Qin Local Officials: Exploring the System of Values and Responsibilities Presented in the Excavated Qin Tomb Bamboo Slips." *Monumenta Serica* 61, no. 1 (2013): 1–34.

Sun Wenbo 孫聞博. *Chubing tianxia: Qin junzhu jiquan yanjiu* 初併天下: 秦君主集權研究. Xi'an: Xibei daxue, 2021.

Tainter, Joseph. *The Collapse of Complex Societies*. Cambridge: Cambridge University Press, 1988.

Tainter, Joseph. "Why Collapse is So Difficult to Understand." In *Beyond Collapse: Archaeological Perspectives on Resilience, Revitalization, and Transformation in Complex Societies*, edited by Ronald K. Faulseit, 27–41. Carbondale: Southern Illinois University Press, 2016.

Takamura Takeyuki 高村武幸. *Kandai no chihō kanri to chiiki shakai* 漢代の地方官吏と地域社会. Tokyo: Kyūko, 2008.

Takatori Yuji 鷹取祐司. "Shin Kanjidai no keibatsu to shakuseiteki mibunjoretsu" 秦漢時代の刑罰と爵制的身分序列. *Ritsumeikan bungaku* 立命館文學 608 (2008): 98–118.

Tom Chung Yee 譚宗義. *Handai guonei lulu jiaotong kao* 漢代國内陸路交通考. Hong Kong: Xinya yanjiusuo, 1967.

Tang Xiaofeng 唐曉峰. "The Evolution of Imperial Urban Form in Western Han Chang'an." In *Chang'an 26 BCE: An Augustan Age in China*, edited by Michael Nylan and Griet Vankeerberghen, 55–74. Seattle: University of Washington Press, 2015.

Tanner, Harold M. *China: A History*. Indianapolis: Hackett, 2009.

Teng Mingyu. "From Vassal State to Empire: An Archaeological Examination of Qin Culture." Translated by Susanna Lam. In *Birth of an Empire: The State of Qin Revisited*, edited by Yuri Pines, Gideon Shelach, Lothar von Falkenhausen, and Robin D.S. Yates, 71–112. Berkeley: University of California Press, 2014.

Thompkins, Phillip K. *Organizational Communication Imperatives: Lessons of the Space Program*. Los Angeles: Roxbury, 1993.

Tian Wei 田煒. "Cong Qin 'shutong wenzi' de jiaodu kan Qin yin shidai de huafen he Qin Chu zhi ji guwen guanyin de panding" 從秦「書同文字」

的角度看秦印時代的劃分和秦楚之際古文官印的判定. In *Tian Wei yingao* 田煒印稿, 94–114. Shanghai: Zhongxi, 2018.

Tian Yuqing 田餘慶. *Qin Han Wei Jin shi tanwei* 秦漢魏晉史探微. Beijing: Zhonghua, 2011.

Tomiya Itaru 冨谷至. *Qin Han xingfa zhidu yanjiu* 秦漢刑罰制度研究. Translated by Chai Shengfang 柴生芳 and Zhu Hengye 朱恒曄. Guilin: Guangxi shifan daxue, 2006.

Tong Chun Fung 唐俊峰. "Appendices for *State Power and Governance in Early Imperial China: The Collapse of the Qin Empire, 221–207 BCE*." heiDok, January 17, 2024, https://doi.org/10.11588/heidok.00034268.

Tong Chun Fung. "The Construction of Territories in the Qin Empire." *T'oung Pao* 107 (2021): 509–54.

Tong Chun Fung. "Framing the Qin Collapse: Redaction and Authorship of the *Shiji* 史記." *Asiatische Studien/Études Asiatiques* 75, no. 4 (2021): 901–46.

Tong Chun Fung. "Liye Qinjian suoshi Qindai de 'jianhu' yu 'jihu'" 里耶秦簡所示秦代的「見戶」與「積戶」. Jianbowang, February 8, 2014, www.bsm.org.cn/?qinjian/6165.html.

Tong Chun Fung. "Qindai Qianling xian xingzheng xinxi chuandi xiaolu chutan" 秦代遷陵縣行政信息傳遞效率初探 (revised version). In *Liye Qinjian yanjiu lunwen xuanji* 里耶秦簡研究論文選集, edited by Liye Qinjian bowuguan 里耶秦簡博物館, 230–66. Shanghai: Zhongxi, 2021.

Tong Chun Fung. "The Reformation of Social Order in the Qin Empire." *Asia Major*, 3rd ser., 36 no. 1 (2023): 95–136.

Tong Chun Fung. "Shouling jian he hengshu shu: Du *Liye Qinjian (er)* zhaji liang ze" 受令簡和恒署書: 讀《里耶秦簡（貳）》札記兩則. *Jianbo* 簡帛 19 (2019): 107–23.

Tse, Wicky W.K. *The Collapse of China's Later Han Dynasty, 25–220 CE*. Abingdon, UK: Routledge, 2018.

Tu Cheng-sheng 杜正勝. *Bianhu qimin: Chuantong zhengzhi shehui jiegou zhi xingshi* 編戶齊民: 傳統政治社會結構之形式. Taipei: Lianjing, 1990.

Vogelsang, Kai. *Geschichte als Problem: Entstehung, Formen und Funktionen von Geschichtsschreibung im Alten China*. Wiesbaden: Harrassowitz, 2007.

Wang Bokai 王博凱. "*Yuelushuyuan cang Qi jian (wu)* yanjiu er ti" 《嶽麓書院藏秦簡（伍）》研究二題. *Chutu wenxian* 15 (2019): 264–72.

Wang Zijin 王子今. "Liye Qinjian 'buyu' de xiaofei zhuti" 里耶秦簡「捕羽」的消費主題. *Hunan daxue xuebao (shehuikexue ban)* 7 (2016): 27–31.

Wang Zijin. *Qin Han jiaotong shi gao (zengding ban)* 秦漢交通史稿（增訂版）. Beijing: Zhongguo renmin daxue, 2013.

Wang Zuoxi 王琢璽. "Zhoudai Jianghan diqu chengyi dili yanjiu" 周代江漢地區城邑地理研究. PhD dissertation, Wuhan University, 2019.

Watanabe Hideyuki 渡邊英幸. "Shin no jiko ishiki to tasha ninshiki" 秦の自己意識と他者認識. In *Shin teikoku no tanjō: kodai-shi kenkyū no kurosurōdo* 秦帝国の誕生: 古代史研究のクロスロード, edited by Momiyama Akira 籾山明 and Rōtāru fon Farukenhauzen ロータール・フォン・ファルケンハウゼン (Lothar von Falkenhausen), 1–47. Tokyo: Rokuichi, 2020.

Weingarten, Oliver. "Delinquent Fathers and Philology: *Lun Yu* 13.18 and Related Texts." *Early China* 37 (2014): 221–58.

Will, Pierre-Etienne. *Bureaucracy and Famine in Eighteenth-Century China.* Stanford: Stanford University Press, 1990.

Wu Fangji 吳方基. *Xinchu Qinjian yu Qindai xianji zhengwu yunxing jizhi yanjiu* 新出秦簡與秦代縣級政務運行機制研究. Beijing: Zhonghua, 2021.

Xie Kun 謝坤. "*Liye Qinjian (yi)* zhuihe (si)" 《里耶秦簡 (壹)》綴合 (四). Jianbowang, November 18, 2016, www.bsm.org.cn/?qinjian/7415.html.

Xie Kun. "*Liye Qinjian (yi)* zhuihe (san)" 《里耶秦簡 (壹)》綴合 (三). Jianbowang, November 17, 2016, www.bsm.org.cn/?qinjian/7413.html.

Xin Deyong 辛德勇. *Jiushi yude wenbian* 舊史輿地文編. Shanghai: Zhongxi, 2015.

Xin Deyong. *Shishi sheng yan* 石室賸言. Beijing: Zhonghua, 2014.

Xu Shihong 徐世虹. "Qin Han jiandu zhong de buxiao zui susong" 秦漢簡牘中的不孝罪訴訟. *Huadong zhengfa xueyuan xuebao* 華東政法學院學報 46 (2006): 124–29.

Yan Buke 閻步克. *Cong jue benwei dao guan benwei: Qin Han guanliao pinwei jiegou yanjiu (zengding ben)* 從爵本位到官本位: 秦漢官僚品位結構研究 (增訂本). Beijing: Shenghuo, dushu, xinzhi sanlian, 2017.

Yan Changgui 晏昌貴. "Liye Qindu 9-712+9-758 bu shi" 里耶秦牘9-712+9-758補釋. Jianbowang, December 24, 2013, www.bsm.org.cn/?qinjian/6147.html.

Yan Changgui. *Qin jiandu dili yanjiu* 秦簡牘地理研究. Wuhan: Wuhan daxue, 2017.

Yang Chengliang 陽承良. "Yiyang Tuzishan yizhi chutu daxing kongxinzhuan xiangguan wenti chuyi" 益陽兔子山遺址出土大型空心磚相關問題芻議. *Hunan sheng bowuguan guankan* 湖南省博物館館刊, vol. 14, 349–52. Changsha: Yuelu, 2018.

Yang Kuan 楊寬. *Zhanguo shi* 戰國史. Shanghai: Shanghai renmin, 2003.

Yang Xianyun 楊先雲. "*Liye Qinjian (er)* zhuihe wu ze" 《里耶秦簡 (貳)》綴合五則. *Chutu wenxian yanjiu* 18 (2019): 129–38.

Yang Xianyun. "Qindai xingzhang wenshu zhidu guankui" 秦代行政文書制度管窺. In *Chutu wenxian de shijie: di liu jie chutu wenxian qingnian xuezhe luntan lunwenji* 出土文獻的世界: 第六屆出土文獻青年學者論壇論文集, edited by Chutu wenxian yu Zhongguo gudai wenming yanjiu xietong chuangxin zhongxin Zhongguo renmin daxue fenzhongxin 出土文獻與中國古代文明研究協同創新中心中國人民大學分中心, 102–10. Shanghai: Zhongxi, 2018.

Yao Lei 姚磊. "Liye Qin jiandu zhuihe zhaji (yi ze)" 里耶秦簡牘綴合札記 (一則). Jianbowang, May 29, 2015, www.bsm.org.cn/?qinjian/6413.html.

Yates, Robin D.S. (Ye Shan 葉山). "Cosmos, Central Authority, and Communities in the Early Chinese Empire." In *Empires: Perspectives from Archaeology and History*, edited by Susan E. Alcock, Terence N. D'Altroy, Kathleen D. Morrison, and Carla M. Sinopoli, 351–68. Cambridge: Cambridge University Press, 2002.

Yates, Robin D.S. "Dated Legislation in the Late-Qin State and Early Empire." *Asia Major*, 3rd ser., 35 no. 1 (2022): 121–63.

Yates, Robin D.S. "The Economic Activities of a Qin Local Administration: Qianling County, Modern Liye, Hunan Province, 222–209 BCE." In *Between Command and Market: Economic Thought and Practice in Early China*, edited by Elisa Levi Sabattini and Christian Schwermann, 244–317. Leiden: Brill, 2021.

Yates, Robin D.S. "The Empire of the Scribes." In *Birth of an Empire: The State of Qin Revisited*, edited by Yuri Pines, Gideon Shelach, Lothar von Falkenhausen, and Robin D.S. Yates, 141–53. Berkeley: University of California Press, 2014.

Yates, Robin D.S. "The Fate of the Defeated: Qin's Treatment of Their Enemies." *Bamboo and Silk* 5, no. 1 (2022): 1–72.

Yates, Robin D.S. "Jiedu Liye Qinjian: Qindai difang xingzheng zhidu" 解讀里耶秦簡: 秦代地方行政制度. *Jianbo* 8 (2013): 89–137.

Yates, Robin D.S. "The Qin Slips and Boards from Well No. 1, Liye, Hunan: A Brief Introduction to the Qin Qianling County Archives." *Early China* vol. 35 (2013): 291–329.

Yates, Robin D.S. "Reflections on the Foundation of the Chinese Empire in the Light of Newly Discovered Legal and Related Manuscripts." In *Dongya kaoguxue de zaisi: Zhang Guangzhi xiansheng shishi shi zhounian jinian lunwenji* 東亞考古學的再思: 張光直先生逝世十週年紀念論文集, edited by Chen Kwang-tsuu 陳光祖, 473–97. Taipei: Academia Sinica, 2013.

Yates, Robin D.S. "Soldiers, Scribes, and Women: Literacy among the Lower Orders in Early China." In *Writing and Literacy in Early China*, edited by Li Feng and David Prager Branner, 339–69. Seattle: University of Washington Press, 2012.

Yates, Robin D.S. "State Control of Bureaucrats under the Qin: Techniques and Procedures." *Early China* 20 (1995): 331–65.

Yoffee, Norman. "Orienting Collapse." In *The Collapse of Ancient States and Civilizations*, edited by Norman Yoffee and George L. Cowgill, 1–19. Tucson: University of Arizona Press, 1988.

Yoffee, Norman. *Myths of the Archaic State: Evolution of the Earliest Cities, States and Civilizations*. Cambridge: Cambridge University Press, 2005.

You Yifei 游逸飛. "Shuo xi chengdanchong: Qin Han xingqi zhidu xinlun" 說繫城旦舂—秦漢刑期制度新論." *Xin Shixue* 新史學 20, no. 3 (2009): 1–52.

You Yifei. *Zhizao "difang zhengfu": Zhanguo zhi Hanchu junzhi xin kao* 製造「地方政府」: 戰國至漢初郡制新考. Taipei: Guoli taiwan daxue, 2021.

Yu Zhenbo 于振波. "Qin lüling zhong de 'xin qianshou' yu 'xindi li'" 秦律令中的「新黔首」與「新地吏」. *Zhongguoshi yanjiu* 中國史研究 3 (2009): 69–78.

Yuan Yansheng 袁延勝 and Shi Junjun 時軍軍. "Zai lun Liye Qinjian zhong de 'shou' he shouguan" 再論里耶秦簡中的「守」和守官. *Gudai wenming* 古代文明 13, no. 2 (2019): 57–64.

Yun Jae Seug 尹在碩. "Qin Han lü zhong de buxiao zui susong yu hanyi" 秦漢律中的不孝罪訴訟與含義. In *Qin Han shi luncong* 秦漢史論叢, vol. 11, edited by Zhongguo Qin Han shi yanjiuhui 中國秦漢史研究會, 316–336. Changchun: Jilin wenshi, 2008.

Zhang Chi 張馳. "Du Liye Qinjian (er) 9-1861, 9-2076 xiao zha" 讀里耶秦簡 (貳) 9-1861、9-2076小札. Jianbowang, May 17, 2018, www.bsm.org.cn/?qinjian/7842.html.

Zhang Chunlong 張春龍. "Liye Qinjian zhong Qianlingxian xueguan he xiangguan jilu" 里耶秦簡中遷陵縣學官和相關記錄. *Chutu wenxian* 出土文獻 1 (2010): 232–34.

Zhang Jinguang 張金光. *Qin zhi yanjiu* 秦制研究. Shanghai: Shanghai guji, 2004.

Zhang Menghan 張夢晗. "'Xindi li' yu 'Wei li zhi dao': yi chutu Qinjian wei zhongxin de kaocha" 「新地吏」與「為吏之道」: 以出土秦簡為中心的考察. *Zhongguo shi yanjiu* 中國史研究 3 (2017): 61–70.

Zhang Rongqian 張榮強. *Han Tang zhangji zhidu yanjiu* 漢唐籍帳制度研究. Beijing: Shangwu, 2010.

Zhao, Dingxin. *The Confucian-Legalist State: A New Theory of Chinese History*. Oxford: Oxford University Press, 2015.

Zhao Yan 趙岩. "Qin lingzuo kao" 秦令佐考. *Ludong daxue xuebao (zhexue shehuikexue ban)* 魯東大學學報 (哲學社會科學版) 31, no. 1 (2014): 66–70.

Zheng Wei 鄭威. "Liye bufen she Chu jiandu jiexi" 里耶部分涉楚簡牘解析. In *Chu wenhua yanjiu lunji* 楚文化研究論集, vol. 11, edited by Chu wenhua yanjiuhui 楚文化研究會, 344–51. Shanghai: Shanghai guji, 2015.

Zheng Wei. "Qin Dongting jun shuxian xiao yi" 秦洞庭郡屬縣小議. *Jianghan kaogu* 5 (2019): 89–94.

Zhong Wei 鐘煒. "Liye Qinjian suojian xian yi kao" 里耶秦簡所見縣邑考. *Henan kejidaxue xuebao* 河南科技大學學報 2 (2007): 18–21.

Zhongguo shehui kexue yuan Kaogu yanjiusuo 中國社會科學院考古研究所, editors. *Zhongguo kaoguxue: Qin Han juan* 中國考古學: 秦漢卷. Beijing: Zhongguo shehui kexue, 2010.

Zhou Zhenhe 周振鶴. "Shi Jiangnan" 釋江南. *Sui wuya zhi lü* 隨無涯之旅, 324–34. Beijing: Sanlian, 2007.

Zhou Zhenhe, Li Xiaojie 李曉傑, and Zhang Li 張莉. *Zhongguo xingzhengquhua tongshi: Qinhan juan* 中國行政區劃通史: 秦漢卷. 2nd ed. Shanghai: Fudan daxue, 2017.

Zhu Jincheng 朱錦程. "Qin dui xin zhengfudi de teshu tongzhi zhengce: yi 'xindi li' de xuanyong wei li" 秦對新征服地的特殊統治政策: 以「新地吏」的選用 為例. *Hunan shifan daxue shehui kexue xuebao* 湖南師範大學社會科學學報 2 (2017): 150–56.

Index

Note: Page numbers in *italics* indicate figures,
bold indicate tables in the text,
and references following "n" refer to notes.

Accessory Scribe (Zu Shi), 40, 50, 60; Lawsuit Reinvestigation (Fuyu Zu Shi), 67–68. *See also* Scribe
acting officials, 84–86
administrative documents, 33, 43, 88, 119–20; Chu, 48, 49, 51–53, *52*; forgery of, 66; Qin (*see* Liye manuscripts). *See also* communication
ancient Rome: citizenship, 36, 50; literacy and universal ruling class, 36, 160; road system and infrastructural power, 122; Second Punic War, 76; territorial expansion, 76
Ando, Clifford, 22
Anlu county, 43, 65, *145*
amnesty (*she*), 83, 103, 189n27
anti-Qin insurgencies/rebellion, 6–7, 49, 55, 61, 65, 111; elites of eliminated polities, 158; indigenous officials, 53; local governments and, 115–16, 117, 156, 162; security gap and, 163; vigilantes and militias, 158, 163
Antragsdelikt, 58

Assistant (Zuo), 38, 39, 45–50, 53, 79, 81, 82, 112–13; Commander, 180n45; Commune, 93; Junior, 46; administrator communities, 50; age restriction on, 46; indigenous population in new territories as, 47; influx of, 47; literacy through practical experiences, 45; marginalization, 45; in Qianling county, 47–48
Assistant Director (Ling Zuo), 47–48, 180n50
August Thearch (Huangdi), 3, 11

Ba (non-Qin group), 3
Ba commandery: offices of salt in, 98
Baigongcheng, **143**
Battle of Changping, 3, 29, 96
Battle of Julu, 7; massacre of Qin soldiers after, 54
Beidi commandery, 128
black-headed ones (*qianshou*), 44, 57, 58, 68–69, 179n31. *See also* new subjects; officials
bo game, 109
Bo march, 139, *139*

complex societies, collapse of: law of diminishing marginal returns, 25–27; Marcus' dynamic model, 25; Tainter's theory, 25–27

Confucian-Legalist state, 21

conscripts: debt-reckoning process of, 151, 200n59–60; dissipation of military power, 114–16; exile, 88, 111, 114, 154; expelled, 112, 113; increasing numbers of, 109–10; in-shift, 106, 112, 196n148; intricate conscription system, 106; levying, 105–6; logistical efficiency, 110–11; long-term, 106, 112; military duties, 106; as officials' servants, 112; old territories, 106; penal, 112; shortage of, 13, 24, 78, 105–17; as substitutes for other human resources, 112

Constable (Jiao Zhang/Ting Zhang), 80, 82, 89, 106, 115, 194n119. *See also* Zhuang, Constable of Qianling county

constantly notated document (*hengshu shu*), 150

convict laborers: austere working conditions, 91; categories, 90; demand for, 90; as disposable goods, 91; distribution of, 99; feather collection, 101–2; fiscal model and, 89–90; logistical efficiency, 99–100; maintenance cost, 103; manual production activities, 90; penal system on, 90; quality, 93–94; "Registers of Convict Laborers" (*zuotu bu*), 90, 91, 101–2; reforms and measures, 94–98; routine administrative tasks, 90; shortage of, 89–105; turnover rate, 91; unsustainability, 103–5

cooks (*yang*), 90, 112, 114, 196n8

counties (*xian*), 4, 21, 65, 67, 69, 78, 88, 100; communication (*see* communication); community leaders and, 60; debt-reckoning process, 200n60; government, 4, 86; peripheral, 47; walls, 116. *See also* commanderies; *specific county*

County Commander (Xian Wei), 4, 93, 106, 107, 108–9, 115, 133, 136, *137*, 139, 194n124

County Prefect (Xian Ling), 4, 57, 60, 64–65, 67, 82–83, 92, 99, 113, 131–38, *134*, *135*, 139, 152

County Vice-Prefect (Xian Cheng), 4, 57, 64–65, 81, 84, 86, 86–87, 99, 101, 107, 132–38, *134*, *135*, 139, 150, 152

cowardice (*weiruan*), 67, 195n138

Cowgill, George, 7, 16, 17–18

cultural diversity, 34

cultural identity, 9, 12, 37–38, 54–55

cultural integration, 11

cultural others ("barbarians"), 68, 72, 108

Dangyang commune, *145*, 146

daoxue, 15, 172n3

Daze commune, 111

De, Judicial Scribe of Qianling county, 112

Deng county, *145*, 147, 148, 200n56

Dingyin county, 82

Diviner (Bu), 38

distorting the facts (*wangshi*), 63, 185n109

distorting the law (*wangfa*), 63

Dongting commandery, 70, 78; administrative communication (*see* communication); conscripts, 111; convict laborer placement, 98, 99, 104–5; military campaigns logistics, 102–3; shortage of official, 81, 84,

www.ingramcontent.com/pod-product-compliance
Lightning Source LLC
Chambersburg PA
CBHW020346270326
41926CB00007B/334

9781438499383